The Life of Jesus in the Writings of Origen of Alexandria

Origen of Alexandria stands at the headwaters of the entire history of Gospel reading. In this study of the earliest extant Gospel commentaries, Samuel B. Johnson explores questions, often associated with modern Gospel criticism, that were already formative of the first moments of the Christian interpretative tradition. Origen's approach to the Gospels in fact arose from straightforward historical and literary critical judgments: the Gospel narratives interweave things that happened with things that did not. Origen discerned that the Gospels depict events in Jesus's life not merely as matters of historical fact but also figuratively. He did not just interpret the Gospels allegorically. Johnson demonstrates that Origen believed the Gospel writers themselves were figurative readers of the life of Jesus. Origen thus found no contradiction between discerning the truth of the Christian Gospels and facing the critical challenges of their literary form and formation. Johnson's study shows how they constitute a single, unified vision.

Samuel B. Johnson is Assistant Professor of Biblical Studies at Mount St. Mary's Seminary & School of Theology.

The Life of Jesus in the Writings of Origen of Alexandria

SAMUEL B. JOHNSON
Mount St. Mary's Seminary & School of Theology

CAMBRIDGE
UNIVERSITY PRESS

CAMBRIDGE
UNIVERSITY PRESS

Shaftesbury Road, Cambridge CB2 8EA, United Kingdom

One Liberty Plaza, 20th Floor, New York, NY 10006, USA

477 Williamstown Road, Port Melbourne, VIC 3207, Australia

314–321, 3rd Floor, Plot 3, Splendor Forum, Jasola District Centre, New Delhi – 110025, India

103 Penang Road, #05–06/07, Visioncrest Commercial, Singapore 238467

Cambridge University Press is part of Cambridge University Press & Assessment, a department of the University of Cambridge.

We share the University's mission to contribute to society through the pursuit of education, learning and research at the highest international levels of excellence.

www.cambridge.org
Information on this title: www.cambridge.org/9781009465601

DOI: 10.1017/9781009465571

When citing this work, please include a reference to the DOI 10.1017/9781009465571

First published 2025

A catalogue record for this publication is available from the British Library.

A Cataloging-in-Publication data record for this book is available from the Library of Congress

ISBN 978-1-009-46560-1 Hardback

For Jess

"I will open my mouth in parables…"

Contents

Acknowledgments

Every so often, the fragment of an idea – really an impression halfway between a thought and a daydream – stirs me to wonder whether in some more angelic age one might be granted to "sequence" one's intellectual genome; to uncover, that is, the vast reaches of one's spiritual ancestry, strand by strand, and thereby to know fully the family of minds and hearts that have made one's own. These acknowledgments remain but a shadowy mirror of that truer genealogy.

To my first teachers – my mother, Jayne, and my late father, Martin – I owe the "love of learning and the desire for God." One could not ask for dearer schoolmates than my first: Amy, Isaac, and Esther. Thereafter Hillsdale College became, and still remains, for me a ceaselessly resounding summons to "cast out into the deep"; Justin Jackson and Stephen Smith, especially, along with the Classics department (Joseph Garnjobst and Eric Hutchinson merit special mention), taught me how to weave the nets that have made all subsequent catches possible.

The University of Notre Dame's Department of Theology drew the whole arc of my prior formation up into itself and gave it new life – or really, gave me a new life. The surpassing generosity of donors (Richard and Peggy Notebaert), staff (Cheron Price and Sherry Nadai), and librarians (Alan Krieger) granted me perfect freedom to sit at the feet of a faculty without equal. The inestimably rich seven years I passed in this paradise flowered forth in company with those "seeking understanding," many of whose insights remain woven into the following pages: Kirsten Anderson, Jeremiah Coogan, Colum Dever, Robert Edwards, Travis Lacy, Christopher Mooney, Paul Wheatley, and Matthew Vale.

In this present season, I have found myself buoyed and buttressed on all sides: from my students and colleagues at Mount St. Mary's Seminary & School of Theology; to my in-laws, Edward and Denise Kneller; to all those who have labored to see it find its home at Cambridge University Press (Beatrice Rehl and the anonymous reviewers especially) – so many hands have framed the most peaceful sanctuary for this project's completion.

This book, which began its life as my PhD dissertation, found its fuel and fire within vast "storerooms of things new and old": Khaled Anatolios, Nathan Eubank, David Lincicum, and Cyril O'Regan – my committee, whose work and teaching are themselves demonstrations of spirit and power. And John Meier, of blessed memory, became its most gracious paraclete along the way. Above all, there is not a line of this work that has not been touched by the presence of my doctoral advisor, John Cavadini: "under his shadow has it lived…"

Finally, my children Ephraim, Levi, Amos, and Hazel have often – even now, as I write these words – so tenderly called me out of this work, out of myself, and thus toward its truer end. If anything of value lies buried in the following pages, it proceeds first and forever from my wife Jessica's self-giving. To her this book owes its life; to her I owe my life; and to her both are lovingly dedicated.

Abbreviations

All abbreviations follow the *SBL Handbook of Style*, Second Edition (2014).

1 Apol.	Justin Martyr, *First Apology* (*Apologia i*)
All.	Heraclitus, *Homeric Problems* (*Quaestiones homericae*)
Ant.	Josephus, *Jewish Antiquities* (*Antiquitates judaicae*)
Ant. rom.	Dionysius of Halicarnassus, *Roman Antiquities* (*Antiquitates romanae*)
Apol. Hier.	Rufinus of Aquileia, *Apology against Jerome* (*Apologia adversus Hieronymus*)
Cels.	Origen, *Against Celsus* (*Contra Celsum*)
Comm. Cant.	Origen, *Commentary on the Song of Songs* (*Commentarius in Canticum*)
Comm. Jo.	Origen, *Commentary on the Gospel of John* (*Commentarii in evangelium Joannis*)
Comm. Matt.	Origen, *Commentary on the Gospel of Matthew* (*Commentarium in evangelium Matthaei*)
Comm. Rom.	Origen, *Commentary on Romans* (*Commentarii in Romanos*)
Comm. ser. Matt.	Origen, *Commentariorum series in evangelium Matthaei*
Decal.	Philo, *On the Decalogue* (*De decalogo*)
Dial.	Origen, *Dialogue with Heraclides* (*Diologus cum Heraclide*)
FC	Fathers of the Church
Fr. Eph.	Origen, *Fragments from the Commentary on the Epistle to the Ephesians* (*Fragmenta ex commentariis in epistulam ad Ephesios*)

Fr. Luc.	Origen, *Fragments from the Commentary on Luke* (*Fragmenta in Lucam*)
Fr. Matt.	Origen, *Fragments from the Commentary on Matthew* (*Fragmenta ex commentariis in evangelium Matthaei*)
Fr. Prov.	Origen, *Fragments from the Commentary on Proverbs* (*Fragmenta ex commentariis in Proverbia*)
GCS	Die griechischen christlichen Schriftsteller
Geogr.	Strabo, *Geography* (*Geographica*)
Gig.	Philo, *On Giants* (*De gigantibus*)
Herm. Sim.	Shepherd of Hermas, Similitude(s)
Hist. eccl.	Eusebius, *Ecclesiastical History* (*Historia ecclesiastica*)
Hom. Cant.	Origen, *Homilies on the Song of Songs* (*Homiliae in Canticum*)
Hom. Ezech.	Origen, *Homilies on Ezekiel* (*Homiliae in Ezechielem*)
Hom. Isa.	Origen, *Homilies on Isaiah* (*Homiliae in Isaiam*)
Hom. Jer.	Origen, *Homilies on Jeremiah* (*Homiliae in Jeremiam*)
Hom. Jes. Nav.	Origen, *Homilies on Joshua* (*In Jesu Nave homiliae xxvi*)
Hom. Judic.	Origen, *Homilies on Judges* (*Homiliae in Judices*)
Hom. Lev.	Origen, *Homilies on Leviticus* (*Homiliae in Leviticum*)
Hom. Luc.	Origen, *Homilies on Luke* (*Homiliae in Lucam*)
Hom. Ps.	Origen, *Homilies on the Psalms* (*Homiliae in Psalmos*)
LCL	Loeb Classical Library
Life	Josephus, *The Life of Josephus*
LSJ	H. G. Liddell, R. Scott, H. S. Jones. *A Greek-English Lexicon*. 9th ed. with revised supplement. Oxford: Clarendon, 1996.
LXX	*Septuaginta. Id est Vetus Testamentum graece iuxta LXX interpretes*. Edited by Alfred Rahlfs and Robert Hanhart. Stuttgart: Deutsche Bibelgesellschaft, 2006.
Math.	Sextus Empiricus, *Against the Mathematicians* (*Adversus mathematicos*)
Or.	Origen, *On Prayer* (*De oratione*; *Peri proseuchēs*)
PG	Patrologia Graeca (= *Patrologiae Cursus Completus: Series Graeca*). Edited by J.-P. Migne. 162 vols. Paris, 1857–1886.
Philoc.	Origen, *Philocalia*
Princ.	Origen, *On First Principles* (*De principiis*; *Peri archōn*)
SC	Sources chrétiennes. Paris: Cerf, 1943–
Troj.	Dio Chrysostom, *Trojan Discourse (Trojana; Or. 11)*

Prologue

The Scandal of the Gospels

There has never been a time when the life of Jesus has not presented some occasion for scandal. Although the primordial scandal of the Christian Gospel unfolded around the figure of a crucified Messiah,[1] this book takes as its principal subject a derivative scandal: the scandal of the Christian *Gospels*; namely, the impediments – even offenses – to literary, historical, and logical sense that only seem to multiply in proportion to one's intimacy with the narratives of the four Evangelists. The suggestion of such things will itself be scandalous to some.

Yet from its earliest days, Christian tradition has set the life of Jesus before the eyes of its beholders as a "sign of contradiction," and such scandals, like the central figure of the Christian Gospel, have similarly precipitated the "falling and rising of many."[2] One cannot forget, after all, that scandals presented themselves to the early Christian imagination as occasions for passage – passage from *human things* to *divine*, from the *wisdom of the world* to the *wisdom of God*.[3] At the same time, the scandals occupying this study have also provoked passage in the opposite direction, as readers of every age have given reason to find in the narratives of Jesus's life not demonstrations of "spirit and power" so much as demonstrations of the material powers of religious discourse alone. This book also concerns such passages.

More precisely, this book is about the dawn of critical reading of the Gospels in the writings of Origen of Alexandria (c. 185–254 CE). Among his many considerable achievements, Origen holds the distinction of

[1] See 1 Cor 1:23 and Gal 5:11; cf. Mark 14:27. [2] Luke 2:34.
[3] Cf. Matt 16:23 and 1 Cor 1:20–21.

having produced our earliest extant commentaries on the Gospels.[4] This fact alone entitles these works to a great deal more attention than they have received. Even more to Origen's merit, "first" does not mean "primitive," nor, in his case, is "premodern" convertible with "precritical."

Curiously, Origen did not find any contradiction between discerning the truth of the Christian Gospel and facing the critical challenges of the Christian Gospels. It seems rather that his sense of the former developed directly out of his sense of the latter. In fact, for Origen, those who have discovered no impediments in their reading of the events recorded in the four Gospels will have made less progress in their understanding of the life of Jesus than those who have. So this study will account for both – Origen's sense of the truth of the Gospel and his engagement with the critical challenges of the Gospels – as a single unified vision.

In what, exactly, does the truth of the Christian Gospel consist? And how does its truth correspond to the veracity of the Gospel narratives themselves, especially in their relation to history? What even are the Gospels, after all, in literary terms? And how does one's answer to this question come to bear on the preceding questions? In short, how is the life of Jesus to be read? And, finally, how understood? Such questions animated the whole course of Origen's lifelong study of the Gospels. And it is the burden of this book to unfold for the reader his answers – or really, his readings – in their substance, development, and ultimately, logic.

[4] See R. E. Heine, "Origen's Gospel Commentaries" (2022), 211–12. Origen also remains our sole source for fragments from one of the few known Gospel commentaries prior to his own: Heracleon's on John. In the preface to his Latin translation of Origen's homilies on Luke, Jerome notes that Origen also wrote a commentary on Luke – all of which has been lost but for selected fragments – in addition to thirty-two books on John (roughly nine extant in Greek, with fragments) and twenty-five books on Matthew (eight extant in Greek, with fragments; an anonymous Latin translation also preserves the portion covering Matt 16:13–27:66).

PART I

FIRST PRINCIPLES: WHAT IS A GOSPEL, ACCORDING TO ORIGEN?

1

What Is a Gospel?

Reintroducing Origen

"What is more necessary than the critical examination of a Gospel?"[1]

In 1835, the appearance of David F. Strauss's *The Life of Jesus Critically Examined* signaled a new epoch in the study of Christian origins. Strauss's novel application of the concept of myth to the Gospels in order to explain the formation of their narratives has since been judged to mark the "before" and "after" of contemporary Gospel criticism, and the *Life of Jesus*'s broader religious and cultural impact finds peers only in the likes of Luther's Ninety-Five Theses and Darwin's *Origin of Species.*[2] Passing generations of scholarship have only proved the perduring

[1] Origen, *Comm. Jo.* 1.2.12.

[2] According to Albert Schweitzer, the critical study of the life of Jesus "falls, immediately, into two periods, that before Strauss and that after Strauss" (*The Quest of the Historical Jesus* [1906], 11). C. C. McCown, *The Search for the Real Jesus: A Century of Historical Study* (1940): Strauss's *Life of Jesus* "created a sensation all over Europe and America" (p. 5), an "epoch-making work" that "not only called forth in the theological field a movement which [is] still in progress" but "also exercised a decisive influence upon philosophy and the general state of culture," with effects "as deep and permanent as they were spectacular" (p. 17). H. Harris, *David Friedrich Strauss and His Theology* (1973), ix: "The rise of historical criticism owes more to Strauss than to any other theologian"; ibid., 41: "The book produced a reaction, unseen since the days of the Reformation." W. Baird, *History of New Testament Research, Vol. 1: From Deism to Tübingen* (1992), 246: "This book was the most revolutionary religious document written since Luther's Ninety-Five Theses." F. C. Beiser, *David Friedrich Strauß, Father of Unbelief: An Intellectual Biography* (2020), 6: "If we ask ourselves which books of the nineteenth century had the greatest effect on the decline of religion, we would have to put first and foremost, even before Darwin's *Origin of Species*, David Friedrich Strauß's *Das Leben Jesu.*"

strength of Strauss's fundamental proposal: namely, that "the Christian religion, like all others, has its myths";[3] and that the myth of the Gospels consists in those narratives "relating directly or indirectly to Jesus, which may be considered not as the expression of a fact but as the product of an idea of his earliest followers."[4] The Gospels, in short, present an idea of Jesus "invested with imagery."[5]

More than an ex nihilo fabrication, Strauss introduced his concept of the "evangelical mythus" with an imposing reconstruction of the history of Gospel interpretation leading up to his work. Here, a lone figure rises from antiquity so as to "almost transcend the limits" of premodernity and "verge towards" Strauss's own mythical view: Origen of Alexandria.[6] By including him at the headwaters of *The Life of Jesus Critically Examined*, Strauss recognized the considerable challenge Origen's work on the Gospels poses to a total identification of the premodern with the precritical. Origen resists straightforward taxonomy. And his presence within Strauss's genealogy of the critical examination of the life of Jesus should stir contemporary readers from slipping into their own forms of genealogical presumption regarding when, exactly, reading of the Gospels first became critical or what the term "critical" even means.[7]

[3] David F. Strauss, *Das Leben Jesu kritisch bearbeitet* (1835), §14 (a section added in the second edition, 1837); English quotations are based on George Eliot's translation of the fourth edition (1846). See U. Köpf, "Ferdinand Christian Baur and David Friedrich Strauss" (2017), 11: "The consistent application of the concept of myth to the history of Jesus … was the independent achievement of Strauss." Cf. G. Theissen and A. Merz, *The Historical Jesus: A Comprehensive Guide* (1998), 3: "Scholarship can never go back behind [*The Life of Jesus*'s] basic thesis of the mythical transformation of the Jesus tradition." Cf. F. Bermejo Rubio, "The Fiction of the 'Three Quests': An Argument for Dismantling a Dubious Historiographical Paradigm" (2009), 217–23.

[4] Strauss, *Life of Jesus*, §15 (a section added to the third edition, 1838).

[5] Strauss, *Life of Jesus*, §14.

[6] Strauss, *Life of Jesus*, §4. A pair of brief sections on ancient approaches to Greek myth and allegorical reading of the Old Testament precede, but Strauss cites Origen alone vis-à-vis the Gospels.

[7] Such as those that begin with H. S. Reimarus, the English deists, or the Enlightenment in general. On the bewildering history of the term "critical," see B. Bravo, "*Critice* in the Sixteenth and Seventeenth Centuries and the Rise of the Notion of Historical Criticism" (2006), 135–95. On the place of the "critical" in early Christian reading practices beyond Origen, cf. L. Ayres, "Irenaeus vs. the Valentinians: Toward a Rethinking of Patristic Exegetical Origins" (2015); R. M. Berchman, "In the Shadow of Origen: Porphyry and the Patristic Origins of New Testament Criticism" (1995); R. M. Grant, *Heresy and Criticism: The Search for Authenticity in Early Christian Literature* (1993).

1.1 GENEALOGIES OF JESUS

It has become something of a truism that readers in antiquity never find themselves more alienated from the critical standards of their contemporary counterparts than in their predilections for what has become known (often with suspicion) as allegorical reading. This book, along with Strauss, contends the opposite. In fact, it is precisely on this point – viz., the proximity of the critical and allegorical view of the Gospels – that Strauss hangs Origen's transcendence of his own age, where many might imagine the interpretive approaches of modernity and antiquity stand at the furthest remove.[8]

There is good reason, then, to countenance Origen as a kind of critical reader of the Gospels. But what kind? Strauss's presentation underscores the difficulty of fashioning a portrait adequate to such a unique figure. On the one hand, no other reader of the Gospels prior to the seventeenth century even merits Strauss's mention. On the other hand, one cannot mistake inclusion for unqualified approval. Though readers should be wary of receiving Strauss's presentation of Origen uncritically, his concluding judgments of Origen, once generalized and restyled as questions, retain their force.[9] Did theological presuppositions and ecclesial commitments ultimately dull Origen's critical capacities vis-à-vis the life of Jesus?[10] Did Origen find himself "constrained" to adopt an allegorical approach to the Gospel narratives solely because of "contradictions which had arisen between them and his own mind," that is, because there was much in "the New Testament writings which so little accorded with his *philosophical* notions"?[11] Since Strauss himself answers these questions with an unequivocal "yes," Origen's value for him amounts to no more (and no less) than a stage sublated into the realization of the ideal of

[8] Cf. Strauss, *Life of Jesus*, §12 (see Chapter 3); cf. F. Watson, "Toward a Literal Reading of the Gospels" (1998). A path thus opens up for addressing B. Neuschäfer's closing question in *Origenes als Philologe* (1987) about how the competing portraits of Origen the literary critic vs. Origen the allegorist can be reconciled (p. 292). Cf. P. W. Martens, *Origen and Scripture: The Contours of the Exegetical Life* (2012), 63 n. 137; cf. R. M. Grant, *The Earliest Lives of Jesus* (1961), 46. See H. Strutwolf, "Kelsos und Origenes: Die Anfänge der Schriftkritik" (2022), 350.

[9] For my treatment of a few of Strauss's more pointed criticisms, see Sections 3.1 and 4.6.

[10] Strauss, *Life of Jesus*, §4. In other words, is critical examination of the Gospels so inimical to Christian faith and tradition that their integration can never exceed the strictures of a zero-sum game? Cf. B. F. Meyer on the ostensible "incompatibility between intellectual honesty and traditional Christian belief" in contemporary Gospel criticism (*The Aims of Jesus* [2002], 15).

[11] Strauss, *Life of Jesus*, §4 (emphasis added).

the "more modern mythical view." Yet Strauss's judgment of Origen's place in the history of "critical examination of the life of Jesus" is as brief as it is striking, and a genealogy of his *evangelical mythus* is not the only way to tell the story.

Strauss sets the question but does not settle it. He is right to offer Origen a place within the history of critical reading of the Gospels – even a venerable one, as its very founder. However, his presentation is also paradigmatic of perennial doubts regarding Origen's interpretive capacities. Strauss's qualified approbation has not lacked accompaniment from the voices of more recent generations of Gospel scholarship, as Origen continues to accrue (at least measured) endorsements into the present day.[12] The sentiment that Origen "anticipated modern criticism," however, has not yet arisen from a thoroughgoing inquiry into Origen's own account, on his own terms, of the historical and literary challenges occasioned by the narratives of the life of Jesus. So, the judgment remains premature. Strauss and his heirs place the burden upon this study to retrieve Origen's own first principles of Gospel reading. *What Is a Gospel, according to Origen?*

1.2 WHAT IS A GOSPEL? SUBJECT AND PURPOSE

"Gospel." What does the word mean? And why is it applied, especially, to four books of the New Testament – that "according to Matthew," "according to Mark," "according to Luke," and "according to John"? Following the New Testament tradition's own breadth of usage, Origen

12 Brevard Childs lauded "the exegetical and theological potential offered by Origen of seeing in the Gospels a literary genre different from that of historical reporting" (*The New Testament as Canon: An Introduction* [1984], 146). Francis Watson has presented Origen as the first to recognize that the "apparent contradictions" between the four Gospels "compel the reader to seek the truth on a different plane to that of sheer factuality" (*Gospel Writing: A Canonical Perspective* [2013], 14); see also his *The Fourfold Gospel: A Theological Reading of the New Testament Portraits of Jesus* (2016). Dale Allison, also, has written that no biblical scholar prior to the modern era was more "clear-eyed" than Origen, "who in the third century anticipated modern criticism" (*The Historical Christ and the Theological Jesus* [2009]), 2; cf. Allison, *Constructing Jesus: Memory, Imagination, and History* (2010), 444–46. See also A. Y. Collins, "Historical Jesus: Then and Now" (2008), 9: "The 'modern' problem of the historical Jesus was already raised, to some degree, by [...] Origen. He described the Gospels as 'histories' but also stated that they narrate certain events that could not have happened."

understands the term in several ways.[13] But for present purposes, one meaning takes precedence: *narratives of the life of Jesus*. Although this preliminary definition might seem self-evident, it is not nearly so trivial as it might first appear.[14] So for the sake of a brief introduction to the topic at hand, it is necessary to recapitulate how Origen comes to this conclusion and why it is essential to do so.

In its barest lexical sense, "Gospel" (εὐαγγέλιον) means a "discourse that bears tidings of something which, due to some benefit it confers, will likely gladden the hearer when (s)he receives what is announced."[15] In simpler terms, this definition amounts to a more precise articulation of the common gloss of "Gospel" as "good news" (εὐ-αγγέλιον). In more analytical terms, one could call this the *final cause* of a "Gospel"; the function or purpose of this kind of discourse is to relate tidings of joy and well-being to its hearers. The Christian Gospel, in particular, consists in relating the "saving advent" of Christ.[16]

However, this definition does not suffice either for the strict purposes of this study or for Origen's own introduction of the topic, insofar as it also applies to "those writings not entitled 'Gospels'."[17] In Origen's view, the Acts of the Apostles, the various epistles, and John's Apocalypse – even the Law and the Prophets and thus the whole of Christian scripture – proclaim the coming of the Lord.[18] Defining the term "Gospel" by purpose or function is necessary, therefore, but not sufficient.

So Origen proceeds to provide another way of clarifying what is meant, strictly speaking, by the word "Gospel": by contents or subject matter (its *material* cause or principle, as it were). "In the precise sense of the expression," everything written in the rest of the New Testament (and Old, by extension) "will not be 'Gospel' when compared to the narrative

[13] Origen devotes the majority of the *Commentary on John*'s magisterial preface to an examination of the "what the term 'Gospel' means, and why these books have this title" (*Comm. Jo.* 1.5.27; cf. 1.15.88). Original language citations of Origen are drawn from the latest critical editions noted in the Bibliography. Though I have retranslated every passage, I did so with extensive reference to existing translations (see Bibliography), to which my own remain indebted. Translations of scripture have drawn from the NRSV and NETS, with frequent adjustments.

[14] On the emerging application of the term εὐαγγέλιον to written texts (and not just to the Christian proclamation itself) in the generations prior to Origen, see J. Kelhoffer, "'How Soon a Book' Revisited: ΕΥΑΓΓΕΛΙΟΝ as a Reference to 'Gospel' Materials in the First Half of the Second Century" (2004); A. Y. Reed, "Εὐαγγέλιον: Orality, Textuality, and the Christian Truth in Irenaeus' *Adversus Haereses*" (2002); F. Watson, *What Is a Gospel?* (2022), 4–12.

[15] *Comm. Jo.* 1.5.27 (cf. *Fr. Matt.* 1). [16] *Comm. Jo.* 1.5.28. [17] *Comm. Jo.* 1.6.32.

[18] See *Comm. Jo.* 1.6–7 (cf. 1.3.17).

of the deeds, sufferings, and words of Jesus."[19] Similarly, though Origen acknowledges that the New Testament knows a more general meaning of the term "evangelist," he suggests that the title belongs, principally, to those who narrated (διηγέομαι) the various events of Jesus's life as their principal subject matter.[20]

In summary, a sort of hierarchy of lexical precision forms as Origen's introduction of the term unfolds: the Old Testament writings may be called "Gospel" inasmuch as they share in the glad tidings that belong, in a more direct sense, to the New Testament writings as a whole.[21] Yet even the New Testament writings as a whole are called "Gospel" only insofar as they proclaim the coming of this Christ, which is detailed most completely in those writings entitled "Gospel," as Origen says, in the strict sense – those, that is, whose constitutive material is the narrative(s) of the life of Jesus.[22]

Therefore, the designation "Gospel," according to Origen's most precise usage, does not simply adhere to any writing that bears these "glad tidings." This broader definition can be said to belong to the whole of Christian scripture, relatively speaking, since Christ's advent has "made all things, as it were, Gospel."[23] Nor is a Gospel just any form of "kerygmatic discourse" meant to produce and further establish certain beliefs about Jesus, for so do all the apostolic writings.[24] Rather, in the case of the Christian Gospel, the term, properly speaking, designates a proclamation of something beneficial, something that would bring joy to

[19] *Comm. Jo.* 1.3.20. The term διήγησις ("narrative"; also "explication" or "exposition") corresponds to the self-designation found in the Lukan preface: "Inasmuch as many have undertaken to draw up a narrative [διήγησιν] of the things which have come to pass among us..." (Luke 1:1). For clarity's sake and for reasons that will become increasingly apparent as the argument progresses, I will generally translate διήγησις as "narrative" and ἱστορία as "historical narrative" throughout.

[20] *Comm. Jo.* 1.3.18.

[21] *Comm. Jo.* 1.6.36: The term "Gospel," here meant in a more particular way (ἐξαιρέτως), is "proper to the New Testament, though it is laid up in all the scriptures."

[22] Cf. *Comm. Jo.* 1.3.20.

[23] *Comm. Jo.* 1.6.33. In this passage (and those surrounding), one need only note the various qualifications Origen employs, like πως εἰπεῖν and ὡσεί, to recognize that he is using the term "Gospel" relatively (which is not to say "falsely") vis-à-vis any writing other than the four canonical Gospels.

[24] See *Comm. Jo.* 1.3.18, which discusses how the New Testament's designation of some as "evangelists" in a broader sense (cf. 1 Cor 12:28, Eph 4:11, and 2 Tim 4:5) means that the title does not belong "exclusively" to those who narrated Jesus's life: "since an 'evangelist' is characterized also by 'kerygmatic discourse' [ἐν προτρεπτικῷ λόγῳ] ... we shall not hesitate to say that the things written by the apostles are, in a certain way, 'Gospel.'"

any who receive it, *precisely under the form of a narrative* – and specifically, under the form of narratives of "Jesus's deeds, sufferings, and words."[25]

Though the preceding paragraphs may seem to make something of an obvious point, the lyrical power of Origen's vision of a deliverer whose coming has made "all things Gospel" has charmed a number of contemporary readers into depreciating his intricately developed sense of the nature of the Gospel narratives. Take, for example, the following: "Origen wishes to see all of the New Testament books in fact as a single genre, that of Gospel."[26] It is difficult to overstate how misleading statements like this can be. Left unquestioned, they flatten the true dimensions of Origen's historical- and literary-critical engagement with the Evangelists' narratives and dispose future readers to overlook how his critical insights form the very fountainhead of his theological vision.

Such imprecisions have motivated my recovery of Origen's causal categories to impose a little more order on the subject.[27] It is true, as we have already seen, that all the New Testament writings share in a single evangelical purpose (i.e., *final cause*): to proclaim the coming of the Christ and all that his advent means. But it should be obvious that Origen does *not* mean all of these texts can therefore be reduced to a single genre. Origen is well aware that to say, for instance, the Pauline epistles and John's Gospel belong to the same genre is to empty the word of virtually

[25] *Comm. Jo.* 1.3.20.

[26] See K. J. Torjesen, *Hermeneutical Procedure and Theological Method in Origen's Exegesis* (1986), 128–29, which overemphasizes the kerygmatic dimensions of Origen's definition at the expense of the narrative dimensions. See similarly J. Behr, *John the Theologian and His Paschal Gospel: A Prologue to Theology* (2019), 112. Cf. Watson, *What Is a Gospel?* 12 and 22.

[27] These categories were standard fare in the prolegomena to commentaries in Origen's broader intellectual milieu. In the *Metaphysics*, Aristotle famously states that one cannot know a thing until one knows its causes; the ancient commentary tradition (on Aristotle, Plato, Homer, and others) followed a similar pattern of discerning a work's "causes" for the purposes of introducing a text (prior to interpreting it). There are clear markers that Origen appropriated this emerging tradition in his own commentary prefaces, and, in a way, Part I of this book corresponds to a similar schema: Chapter 1 (on the Gospels' subject and purpose) takes up questions often associated with a work's material and final "causes"; Chapter 2 (on their literary form) takes up questions often associated with a work's formal "causes"; Chapter 3 (on their literary formation) takes up questions often associated with a work's instrumental "causes." See R. E. Heine, "The Introduction to Origen's Commentary on John Compared with the Introductions to the Ancient Philosophical Commentaries on Aristotle" (1996). See also Heine, "The Prologues of Origen's Pauline Commentaries and the *Schemata Isagogica* of Ancient Commentary Literature" (2001).

any meaning. Similarly, one can say that the New Testament as a whole shares a universal subject (i.e., *material cause*), for in the end the apostles all "proclaim Jesus."[28] But any account of Origen's sense of the ultimate unity of the New Testament writings must avoid subjecting his equally clear sense of their differences to erasure. Depreciating the supreme capital Origen invests in a critical approach to the Gospel narratives – *as* narratives – risks misconstruing his entire profile as an interpreter of the Gospels.

1.3 THIS STUDY: SUBJECT AND PURPOSE

Taking "narratives of Jesus's life" as shorthand for what Origen specifies as "Gospel" in the strict sense also serves to specify the boundaries of this study. Without attempting to unravel Origen's enigmatic statement that Christ's coming "has made all things Gospel" here, I can for now at least happily confirm that this book is not about "all things." The delicacy of the primary task before us similarly disallows lengthy diversions into how he comes to consider the whole of the Old Testament writings as "Gospel" too. Even Origen's understanding of the Christian Gospel in general, proclaimed variously by Peter, Paul, and other apostles ("evangelists" in the broader sense) throughout the New Testament writings, falls outside the strict scope of this inquiry.[29] Rather, I will maintain a sharp focus on the prime matter, so to speak, of the four canonical Gospels, to which Origen himself believes the title "Gospel" most properly belongs: narratives of the life of Jesus.[30]

Should the material borders of my own inquiry appear overly restrictive, I have only done so in view of this project's far weightier formal concerns. Every difficulty – and thus every reward – attendant to this study lies for the most part in the way of coming to terms with Origen's understanding of the literary form of the Gospels. What sort of thing are the narratives of the life of Jesus, literarily speaking? (History? Biography? Fiction? Myth?) And what bearing does their narrative form

[28] *Comm. Jo.* 1.8.47. See Torjesen, *Hermeneutical Procedure*, 129 (emphasis added): "Here is the underlying unity between the Gospels and the epistles: *Both have the same subject matter.*"

[29] On the preaching and writings of Paul and Peter as "Gospel," see *Comm. Jo.* 1.4.25–26; cf. *Comm. Jo.* 1.3.18.

[30] Cf. *Comm. Jo.* 1.4.21, which speaks of the four Gospels "as if they were the elemental principles [στοιχείων] of the faith of the church."

have on the form of interpretation proper to them? Whatever "scandals" critical examination of the Gospels – individually and as a fourfold – may occasion for any reader (ancient or modern), they tend to arise in the course of addressing these questions. The scandals associated with Origen's approach to the Gospels certainly do.

Thus the overarching question of this book: *how does Origen account for the literary form of the Gospels?* As the ensuing chapters of Part I detail what kind of thing the Gospels are for Origen, they will lay the groundwork for discriminating what kind of reader of the Gospels Origen is. The order of argument, bound to Origen's own, cannot be reversed. The immediate task, then, is to attend to his first principles for approaching the historical and literary challenges occasioned by critical examination of the narratives of Jesus's life (Chapter 2). Yet even more than his view of the Gospel narratives' literary *form*, Origen's sense of their literary *formation* directly inspires how he comes to read and understand them (Chapter 3). So coming to terms with how Origen accounts for the Gospel writers' literary activity is essential for any account of Origen's own reading practices and, finally, the interpretations themselves (see Chapters 4–7 in Part II).

Educated readers of every age know that identifying literary form or genre is requisite for setting about interpreting any piece of writing. Origen is no exception. And if his interpretive judgments have occasionally struck modern ears as rather strange, they at least reflect the rather strange difficulty of the task – a difficulty underscored by the fact that fundamental questions regarding the Gospels' genre, historicity, literary form, literary formation, etc., remain rather astonishingly unsettled to the present day.[31] Be that as it may, Origen knew well that what one believes *the* Gospel is follows closely upon what one believes *a* Gospel is. The present inquiry therefore elevates itself beyond critical concerns alone. For folded into the very heart of the question of literary form lies the question that directs this study as a whole: *what, for Origen, does the life of Jesus, as narrated in the Gospels, mean?*

1.4 CLARIFYING ORIGEN BY ORIGEN

As a matter of emphasis, this book will proceed primarily by way of writing a history of interpretation; that is, my object is to present Origen's

[31] See Chapters 2 and 3. Cf. R. M. Calhoun, D. P. Moessner, and T. Nicklas (eds.), *Modern and Ancient Literary Criticism of the Gospels: Continuing the Debate on Gospel Genre(s)* (2020); Watson, *What Is a Gospel?*

reading of the Gospels on his own terms, following his own arguments, and according to his own purposes. Such an enterprise simultaneously involves (invoking R. G. Collingwood) a reenactment of Origen's own thought processes and judgments, a "re-thinking for ourselves the thought of our author."[32] Toward this end, I will set about the present endeavor for the most part by way of "clarifying Origen by Origen"[33]: first establishing his first principles of Gospel reading (Part I) and then employing them to illuminate particular interpretations (Part II), while conversely, looking back from particular interpretations in order to illustrate the coherence of his judgments about the nature of the Gospels.[34]

This means, on the one hand, that evaluations of Origen's oeuvre by contemporary standards of Gospel interpretation must suffer some subordination. By using the language of "criticism," I imply no a priori definition of what constitutes "critical reading"; I mean only to approximate the network of interpretive questions involved in Origen's own unrelenting call for critical examination (ἐξέτασις) of the Gospels.[35] Nor, on the other hand, do I intend to instrumentalize these commentaries as sources for reconstructing early Christian beliefs about the nature and person of Christ. Christological definition and speculation, though by no means absent from Origen's commentaries, remain ancillary to his principal project: critical, interpretive, and finally contemplative engagement with the Gospel narratives themselves. I arrange the aims of this book accordingly.

Nevertheless, all of this is a point of order, not exclusion. When properly bridled to the primary object, measured comparisons with later standards of coherence – whether critical or theological – become indispensable for clarifying Origen's own perspicacity. In fact, this study

[32] R. G. Collingwood, *The Idea of History* (1946), 215 and 283.

[33] Playing on the phrase "clarifying scripture by scripture," a principle of central importance to Origen (and the broader ancient literary milieu: "clarifying Homer by Homer"); see Martens, *Origen and Scripture*, 61.

[34] Cf. Origen's own stated approach for *On First Principles* (which I intend to emulate here vis-à-vis his view of the Gospels): out of its fundamental elements and by way of exemplary illustrations reconstructing a single coherent body of thought (*Princ.* pr.10).

[35] On the various shades of ἐξέτασις (and a related term, βάσανος), see J. A. Harrill, "'Exegetical Torture' in Early Christian Biblical Interpretation: The Case of Origen of Alexandria" (2017); cf. J. Walker, *Rhetoric and Poetics in Antiquity* (2000), 32, 134, 176–77. As Martens has pointed out (*Origen and Scripture*, 79–80), Origen's sense of λογική also involved what we might now designate under the discipline of linguistics (particularly its philological components); cf. *Comm. Cant.* pr.3: λογική consists in discerning the "proper and improper meanings of words and expressions, genres and forms, and to teach the tropes of each and every kind of expression."

would be ill-served not to draw from the modern disciplines of New Testament studies and early Christian theology precisely as auxiliary voices, however, habituated their contemporary divergence into autonomous and often mutually exclusionary discourses. Origen, at least, knew no such discord; so a proper portrait of his approach to the Gospels must undertake, in some form, a reintegration of these disciplines in order to reproduce its subject faithfully.

1.5 SPOKEN IN FIGURES

I believe Origen's work on the Gospels rises to such heights of critical clarity that he ought (at the very least) to be mentioned in the same breath as Hermann Reimarus or David Strauss in landmark histories of life of Jesus research. Yet accounts of Origen's interpretive sensibilities have varied so wildly since late antiquity that contemporary readers may find it difficult to think of his figurative construal of the Gospels as anything other than an exotic import from Northern Egypt – for some a charming novelty and even lustrous development in early Christianity's "historically-effected consciousness"[36]; for others an ill-advised "Hellenization" and even insidiously "gnostic" subversion of the Evangelists' true voice(s); but for most, in the end, a thing unquestionably alien to the Eastern Mediterranean soil of the New Testament.[37] Whatever the verdict, Origen is the innovator.

Throughout this book, however, I will endeavor to demonstrate that the most serious impediments to rendering Origen's understanding of the Gospels intelligible arise not because his thought is alien to the clear-eyed study of the New Testament, but because his language has become alien to us. With specific regard to the Gospels, I will argue that Origen understands his position – viz., that the narratives of Jesus's life were composed, principally, in order to signify something – to amount to a rather straightforward critical judgment. In brief, my overarching intent is to demystify what Origen means by a "figurative" or even "allegorical" approach to the Gospels and to show that, fundamentally, his language

[36] Cf. H.-G. Gadamer, *Truth and Method* (2004), 278–397.

[37] See R. P. C. Hanson, *Allegory and Event: A Study of the Sources and Significance of Origen's Interpretation of Scripture* (1959), 25: Alexandrian allegory "is almost entirely foreign to Palestinian exegesis." For a friendlier reader who nonetheless sees a "gnosticizing" tendency in Origen's Gospel commentaries, see J. Daniélou, *Origen* (1955), 91–97.

means nothing more (and nothing less) than to say that the life of Jesus narrated in the Gospels is not passed down to its readers as a matter of unambiguous facticity. The Evangelists, just as the one whose life they share, *have spoken these things* to us *in figures*.[38]

[38] John 16:25. Cf. R. Zimmermann, "Imagery in John: Opening Up Paths into the Tangled Thicket of John's Figurative World" (2006), esp. 10–15.

2

Literary Form

Impediments and Impossibilities

"Does this scandalize you?"[1]

What is a Gospel, according to Origen? Chapter 1 laid the requisite groundwork with a pair of definitions that, in themselves, should not be matters of much dispute: firstly, that the primary purpose or function of a "Gospel" is proclamation, and secondly, that the Christian Gospel's primary subject is the life of Jesus, his "deeds, sufferings, and words." But the most pivotal – and tortuous – question now beckons: what is a Gospel, in terms of its literary form or genre?[2]

Chapter 1 began to address the question of the Gospels' literary form by showing that, for Origen, the designation "Gospel" does not refer, strictly speaking, to just any form of early Christian proclamation but specifically narratives (διηγήσεις) of the life of Jesus. But again, this is hardly controversial. Now it is necessary to account for Origen's understanding of the nature of Gospel narrative itself. If, in the strictest sense, the title "Gospel" designates not just any discourse announcing the coming of Christ but rather one that does so under the form of narratives of his life, what kind of narratives are they? What sort of thing are the Gospels, literarily speaking?

[1] John 6:61.

[2] The ambiguity of the term "form" works in Origen's favor here. He does use the term εἶδος when discussing the nature of Gospel narrative (see, e.g., *Princ.* 4.3.1); however, he never attempts a lengthy definition of γένος ("genre" or *Gattung*) in the abstract. For now, readers may understand the term to refer broadly to the cluster of literary characteristics that Origen believes will naturally appear to any careful reader of the Gospels – just like the form of a statue (its *formal* cause, as it were) can be distinguished from its material without having to decide precisely what "genre" of statuary it might belong to.

2.1 GOSPEL GENRE: A PROVOCATION

The following passage from *Against Celsus* (a late work, c. 248 CE) offers a particularly concise and programmatic introduction to Origen's view of the major difficulties attendant to discerning the nature of the Gospel narratives:

> The truth of the records of what happened to Jesus cannot be fully seen in their mere letter and historical narrative; for each of them shows themselves, to those who approach the writing more attentively, to be a sign of something as well.[3]

Since this passage – its terms of engagement and the complex of questions it raises – readily serves as a lodestar of this study, virtually every word merits closer attention.

Origen does not prevaricate: he is after the "truth of what is recorded to have happened to Jesus." But in what sense are the Gospel narratives true, in Origen's view? Especially if not (just) literally or historically true, as he implies? What, exactly, is the nature of these "records" (τὰ ἀναγεγραμμένα)? Origen does not detail here the ways in which he does and does not consider the Gospels to be literally or historically true. He does, however, intimate the view that the records of Jesus's life set down by the Evangelists harbor dimensions irreducible to their most immediate or obvious sense. Attentive readers, Origen suggests, will inevitably find themselves confronted by narratives of an inescapably symbolic quality. The whole question then, it appears, turns on what he means by *sign of something*. And it is not entirely clear.

So the passage does not yet offer a solution, but rather a provocation toward a solution. For the purposes of this chapter, its immediate value consists in the direct literary claim it makes on the Gospels. According to Origen, any consideration of these narratives will remain incomplete as long as one assumes that their truth is reducible to the "bare letter" of a "historical narrative" – as if, that is, the narratives are so undeveloped that the meaning of "what is recorded to have happened" should be obvious to anyone.[4] Origen does not categorically deny a literal and historical dimension underlying these records; he simply questions the

[3] *Cels.* 2.69.

[4] *Cels.* 2.69. Cf. F. M. Young on ἡ λέξις as a technical term in ancient Greco-Roman education (here with reference to Quintilian) in *Biblical Exegesis and the Formation of Christian Culture* (1997), 78: "Reading a classic in school meant analysing its sentences into parts of speech ... noting linguistic usage and style, discussing different meanings of words, elucidating figures of speech or ornamental devices. This is what was meant by attending to *ta rheta*, the things stated, the letter of the text, and understanding *pros lexin*, according

sufficiency of these categories to account for the nature of the Gospel narratives in their *entirety* (πᾶσα).[5] There may be literal, historical truth here, but there is *also* (καί) something more going on.

Those who are conversant with the Gospels in a "more perceptive" way may come to sense that these narratives exceed the boundaries of a mere chronicle or transcript of facts.[6] Or, in Origen's own terms, it would seem that these records of the life of Jesus show, or really, *demonstrate* themselves (ἀποδείκνυται) to have been invested with certain figurative qualities – whatever it is they might signify (σύμβολόν τινος).[7] However one construes what these texts were made to signify (note the sublimely demure τι), it is not something extrinsic to the composition of the Gospel narratives themselves. In fact, Origen seems to indicate that the things recorded to have "literally" and "historically" happened in the Gospel narratives are set before us precisely *as* signs. And, as the reader comes to realize this through observant engagement with the text itself, the truth of the Gospels can finally be considered, even contemplated (θεωρία).[8]

to the word, the letter, the reading." Cf. J. A. McGuckin, "Origen as Literary Critic in the Alexandrian Tradition" (2001). On ἱστορία, see Section 2.2.

5 *Cels.* 2.69. Here I am thinking especially of any reader not yet dispossessed of that scholarly simulacrum that has haunted such an unfortunate number of readers from late antiquity to the present day – the "Origen against history." For my treatment of this (mis)construal, see Chapter 4.

6 *Cels.* 2.69. The word συνετώτερον echoes, perhaps, language drawn from Isa 6:9–10 in Matt 13:10–23 (and parallels) about those who hear but do not "perceive."

7 *Cels.* 2.69. The English words "symbol," "sign," and even "figure" may say more than Origen means here; σύμβολόν τινος can be taken as simply as "emblematic of" or "indicative of" something. Origen employs a range of related terms (σημεῖον, χαρακτήρ, τύπος, εἰκών, etc.) without any more substantive differences among them than various English terms that similarly evoke a sense of imagery, figuration, or symbolism (on the interchangeability of σύμβολον and σημεῖον, for instance, cf. *Comm. Jo.* 10.24.138, *Comm. Jo.* 13.64.452, and *Comm. Matt.* 11.17; Origen also uses the phrase σημεῖον τίνος in *Comm. Matt.* 12.3 without any apparent difference in meaning than that of σύμβολόν τινος in *Cels.* 2.69). See also *Comm. Jo.* 13.64.450: "signs" are what we call "things that are indicative of something else beyond what occurred." On Origen's "exegetical lexicon" (with copious references to his broader corpus), see P. W. Martens, "Revisiting the Allegory/Typology Distinction: The Case of Origen" (2008), esp. 296–306, which demonstrates the "general principle" that "while Origen draws upon a rich vocabulary to describe his exegetical practice, most of these terms fall into two categories": literal and nonliteral (p. 298). Cf. R. Gögler, *Zur Theologie des Biblischen Wortes bei Origenes* (1963), 357–64. Cf. H. de Lubac, *History and Spirit: The Understanding of Scripture according to Origen* (2007), 141–43. On the link between symbol/sign and allegory/figure language in *Cels.* 2.69 specifically, see Martens, *Origen and Scripture*, 298–99.

8 *Cels.* 2.69.

In other words, for Origen, *the Gospels present the life of Jesus in historical narratives of a principally figurative nature.*[9] But what motivated him to come to this conclusion? It is best, firstly, to try to take him at his word. In a manner firmly contrary to David Strauss's concluding judgment of Origen in *The Life of Jesus Critically Examined*, the vision of the Gospels submitted here is neither spontaneously generated out of philosophical presuppositions nor artificially limited by ecclesial commitments.[10] Origen, at least, does not imply anything of the sort. No, the Evangelists' records *demonstrate themselves* to be as he has said, at least to those who "approach the writing more perceptively."[11] So we remain securely within the orbit of the question of literary form.

A satisfactory portrait of how Origen arrives at the judgment that the Gospel narratives are principally figurative in nature can only emerge through firsthand engagement with his Gospel readings (representative examples of which will occupy Part II). For now, it is enough to allow the crucial concepts and criteria to emerge – Origen's "first principles" of Gospel narrative. The thesis Origen offers in answer to Celsus's cultured critiques of the Gospels carries us to the threshold of an answer. Crossing the threshold, however, requires a preliminary passage over Origen's earlier and more comprehensive account of the historical and literary difficulties intrinsic to Gospel narrative, along with the basic principles

9 For clarity's sake (and following Origen), I will proceed with "figurative" as the primary designation for distilling the whole complex of terms that variously express the judgment that a given text harbors dimensions that exceed pure literalism or naked transparency to fact. It has a less vexed scholarly history than "allegorical" and remains less rhetorically fraught than "mythical" or "fictional" (both then and now – "figurative" is, after all, applicable to myth and fiction as well, without presuming a stance on facticity or verity). I hope, however, that a correlative effect of this study is to return "allegory" to a simplicity nearer to Origen's sense of the term: "to speak (or write) figuratively." Etymologically speaking (and in Origen's usage), "allegorical" and "figurative" mean the same thing: to "say something in another way" (ἄλλος – ἀγορεύω; τρόπος – λέγω). Cf. Heraclitus (an Alexandrian grammarian active toward the end of the first century CE), *Homeric Problems* 5.1–2: "the very word exhibits its own meaning," for language that "says something one way [ἄλλα ἀγορεύων], while signifying something other than what it says, is given the name 'allegory' [ἀλληγορία] precisely for this reason." Cf. Tryphon (an Alexandrian contemporary of Heraclitus), *De tropis* 1.2: "Allegory" is a way of speaking that "indicates one thing, strictly speaking, but presents it with something else in mind." On Origen's own developing preference for "figure/figurative" language, cf. Heine, *Matthew*, I:18. I might add that the qualification "principally" (as opposed to, say, "exclusively" or "exhaustively") is Origen's own; see, for example, *Princ.* 4.2.9 (τοῦ προηγουμένου σκοποῦ), *Cels.* 4.49 (κατὰ τὸν προηγούμενον νοῦν), and *Comm. ser. Matt.* 77 (*tamen principaliter Evangelistarum propositum fuit respiciens ad mysteria*).

10 Cf. Strauss, *Life of Jesus*, §4 (see Section 4.6).

11 *Cels.* 2.69.

he develops to navigate them. And so we turn from *Against Celsus*, Caesarea, and the close of Origen's career back to *On First Principles* (c. 229–30 CE), Alexandria, and its beginnings.

2.2 THE FORM OF HISTORY

Chapter 1 introduced Origen's basic identification of the Gospels as narratives of the "deeds, sufferings, and words of Jesus."[12] The preceding quotation from *Against Celsus* allows us to specify the kind of narrative found in the Gospels one degree further: a form of "historical narrative," yes, but one arranged so as to signify something. The question that naturally follows, however, cuts much more swiftly and deeply to the marrow of Origen's own profile as a critical reader of the Gospels: in what way does he understand the Gospel narratives to be "historical"? Since every aspect of this study – or any study of the life of Jesus, really – pivots on this question, this section will produce an elementary grammar for the qualities that, according to Origen, constitute "historical narrative" in the Gospels.

In the section of *On First Principles* devoted to "How Divine Scripture is to be Read and Understood," Origen develops two foundational principles regarding the nature of Gospel narrative.[13] First and foremost, Origen aligns the Gospel narratives' literary form with that of the histories of Israel. They are, in general, the "same form of literature."[14] Secondly, the Gospels' likeness to Jewish biblical narrative means, in Origen's view, that the narratives of Jesus's life similarly do not possess a perfectly straightforward relationship to facticity. In view of how fundamental these two principles become for every archetypal interpretation examined in the coming chapters, it is crucial to observe how Origen first advances them.

As he sets about introducing his approach to the Christian scriptures as a whole, Origen argues that historical narratives throughout the canonical writings – in the Law, the Prophets, the Gospels, etc. – generally include material that inhibits readers from reducing their narratives to mere chronicles of fact. These narratives are not, in other words, plainly "coherent and polished" histories; for, he writes, they have been arranged

12 *Comm. Jo.* 1.3.20.

13 *Princ.* 4.2.1–4.3.15; on ἀνάγνωσις (here "reading") as a technical term for the preliminary steps of textual interpretation, see Young, *Biblical Exegesis*, 73 and 84.

14 *Princ.* 4.3.1: τοῦ αὐτοῦ εἴδους τῶν λόγων.

in such a way (by the divine word no less!) that none lack an interspersing of "certain stumbling blocks [σκάνδαλα], as it were, and impediments and impossibilities in their midst," which prevent readers from being "thrown off by the enticing simplicity of their style" and from assuming that "nothing besides the obvious could be meant" by them.[15] Thus, without evincing any naivety about the immense diversity of the canonical writings, Origen identifies for his readers a literary quality that amounts to something of a universal characteristic of biblical narrative: a complicated relationship to facticity.[16]

Origen's repeated insistence – here and throughout his Gospel commentaries – on a certain likeness of form between the Gospel narratives and the stories of Israel invites readers to reapply his broader claims about the biblical histories in general directly to Gospel narrative specifically. For "not only did the spirit arrange" the writings "prior to [Christ's] coming" in this way; it "has done something similar with the Gospels as well."[17] That is, Origen explains, like the histories of Israel, "neither is the historical narrative" of the Gospels "completely unmixed [ἄκρατον], there being things interwoven that did not physically happen."[18]

Here, as the argument's trajectory begins to emerge, readers must exercise care. Origen does not betray a totalizing rhetoric. Thus far, the

[15] *Princ.* 4.2.9 (drawing from Rom 9:32–33 and 1 Pet 2:8, citing a version of Isa 8:14). For similar language, see the fragment from *Hom. Jer.* 39 (preserved in *Philoc.* 10.1). Such passages pose a considerable challenge to the notion that "for early Christians, virtually nothing the evangelists related about Jesus was considered to be overly fantastical or impossible" (M. D. Litwa, *How the Gospels Became History: Jesus and Mediterranean Myths* [2019], 4). On the unrefined style of Christian scripture in general, see the fragments from *Comm. Jo.* Book 4 preserved in *Philoc.* 4 (cf. *Fr. Matt.* 301.1); cf. *Comm. Jo.* 13.54.367 on John's "lack of skill in language." See also *Cels.* 6.1–5 and 7.58–61 (fittingly collected in *Philoc.* 15).

[16] Origen believes other forms of ancient *historiae* share a similar quality (see Section 2.4). A critical sensitivity to the various ways biblical narrative resists literal reading is already evident in Philo; see, for example, *Conf.* 14 (where language of stumbling blocks also appears) and, more broadly, M. R. Niehoff, *Jewish Exegesis and Homeric Scholarship in Alexandria* (2011), 77–94 and 133–51. Cf. R. Bloch, "Philo's Struggle with Jewish Myth" (2019). Cf. A. van den Hoek, "Philo and Origen: A Descriptive Catalogue of their Relationship" (2000).

[17] *Princ.* 4.2.9: "seeing as it happens to be the same spirit and from the one God." On matters of authorship (human and divine), see Chapter 3. Cf. *Comm. Cant.* 3.12.

[18] *Princ.* 4.2.9: προσυφασμένων κατὰ τὸ σωματικὸν ἐχόντων μὴ γεγενημένων. "Nor," he goes on, do the "commandments therein entirely exhibit what is reasonable [τὸ εὔλογον]." Cf. *Comm. Matt.* 10.1. Origen is fond of προσυφαίνω and συνυφαίνω (from ὑφαίνω, to *weave, ply the loom*) for describing the "mixed" character of biblical narrative (used twice in *Princ.* 4.2.9 alone). Cf. Theon on the weaving together (συμπλέκω) of different forms of narrative in *Progymnasmata* 74–75.

most one can say about what the Gospels are, literarily speaking, is that they are *not* reducible to a single, homogenous thing. Origen is, in fact, taking a firm stance against oversimplified accounts – in this particular case, warning readers that the Gospels, in the end, will not respond well to those who completely literalize every saying or presume every narrative depicts events in a way plainly transparent to "what happened." In sum, regarding the form of the narratives of Jesus's life found in the Gospels, the first thing Origen lets us say is that they are *mixed*.[19]

Before detailing the several angles from which Origen arrives at this view (and his reasons for considering it essentially indisputable), we should disentangle the second – and more scandalous – of the two fundamental principles outlined here a bit further: namely, that the Gospel narratives are "interwoven" with "things that didn't happen."[20] Firstly, the reader must not confuse *historia* (ἱστορία) and "history." Like many of his learned contemporaries, Origen employs *historia* above all as a literary designation, not an immediate judgment about the historicity or facticity of what is narrated (though by no means exclusive of such).[21]

19 On this point, Origen anticipates one of the few positions that just about any contemporary New Testament scholar would affirm. The seemingly interminable debates over Gospel genre habitually orbit around the question of how one ought to construe the Gospels' complicated relationship to facticity, but all agree (excepting the most rigid fundamentalists) that the Gospels *have* a complicated relationship to facticity, to say the least. The very diversity of proposed solutions to the question only foregrounds the fundamental agreement – that the literary form or genre of the Gospels is otherwise than mere history alone – even if consensus on specifics remains elusive. For bibliography, cf. n. 31 in Chapter 1 and n. 39 in Section 2.4.

20 *Princ.* 4.2.9. On the irrationality (τί ἂν εἴη ἀλογώτερον τοῦ;), implausibility (ἀπιθανωτάτη), or impossibility (ἀδύνατον) of taking a number of Jesus's commands literally, cf. *Princ.* 4.3.3 and *Comm. Matt.* 15.1–5, 15, as well as *Hom. Lev.* 7.5.4–5 (cf. De Lubac, *History and Spirit*, 226).

21 Broadly speaking, in the second and third centuries, ἱστορία designated a form of writing that took as its subject a particular time or place, or a certain person or people, which the author arranged in an orderly manner (meaning chronological or sequential at least in appearance, in either continuous or episodic fashion); cf. Sextus Empiricus (c. 160–c. 210 CE), *Adv. Math.* 257, as well as 249–50, citing Tauriscus. The material recorded in such narratives may be "historical" in a popular contemporary sense (having to do with matters of fact); it may not. A ἱστορία could play host to a number of literary forms: the inclusion of fictional or mythical sources, the alteration of factual ones, and even whole-cloth invention on the part of the author could all comprise a ἱστορία. Even a collection of myths could be called ἱστορία, and the term ἱστορικός could mean "mythographer" (see S. M. Trzaskoma, "Mythography" [2017] and S. R. Asirvatham, "Historiography" [2017]; cf. R. Nünlist, *The Ancient Critic at Work: Terms and Concepts of Literary Criticism in the Greek Scholia* [2009], 259 n. 10). Cf. Young, *Biblical Exegesis*, 79–80. Cf. B. Studer, "Der Begriff der Geschichte im Schrifttum des Origenes von Alexandrien" (2003).

That is, when Origen calls a narrative *historical*, he does not thereby presume, by definition, that everything in it "happened" (γενόμενον), even if this is the way a *historia* naturally styles itself. He only means that the author has arranged the material in a "historical manner," that is, "in the form of a historical narrative."[22] A *historia* records events "*as (if) they* happened" (ὡς γεγονότα), a formulation exquisitely phrased to capture the precise range of the term: a *historia*, in this strictly literary sense, narrates something either *as it happened* or *as if it happened*, sometimes intermingling both in the same narrative.[23]

Within the fabric of the life of Jesus, therefore, Origen distinguishes several threads generally characteristic of biblical narrative as a whole: Broadly speaking, the Gospel narratives "weave together" things that *did* happen historically with things that *didn't* happen.[24] The latter category can be further subdivided into (1) things that *couldn't* have happened and (2) things that *could've* happened but *didn't*.[25] That is, just like the stories that appear throughout the scriptures of Israel, the narratives of the "deeds, sufferings, and words of Jesus"[26] share the distinct characteristic of having woven together "things that happened" with things that either *didn't* or *couldn't* have happened – in other words, an interspersing of

[22] *Cels.* 5.29 (ἐν ἱστορίας τρόπῳ) and 5.31 (ἐν ἱστορίας σχήματι). For the phrase ἐν ἱστορίας σχήματι, see Dionysius of Halicarnassus (c. 60 BCE–c. 7 CE), *Ant. rom.* 1.41.1, on stories that narrate the deeds of Heracles in the form of history (τῶν ἐν ἱστορίας σχήματι τὰς πράξεις αὐτοῦ διηγησαμένων). Similarly, Strabo (c. 64 BCE–c. 24 CE), in *Geogr.* 1.2.35, criticizes prose writers who "compose stories on many subjects in the form of history [ἐν ἱστορίας σχήματι], even if they do not expressly acknowledge that they are dealing in myths [τὴν μυθοφραφίαν]. For it is self-evident that they are weaving in myths [μύθους παραπλέκουσιν] intentionally, not through ignorance of the facts [τῶν ὄντων], but intentional invention of the impossible [πλάσει τῶν ἀδυνάτων], to gratify [χάριν] the taste for the marvelous and the entertaining" (trans. H. L. Jones, LCL [1917], 156–59). At the risk of an overly tidy typology, Origen's sense of ἱστορία is more "Herodotean" than "Thucydidean"; see Litwa, *How the Gospels Became History*, 11–12 (citing Diodorus of Sicily, Dionysius of Halicarnassus, Strabo, and Josephus): "When writers included fantastical elements, they wrote what ancient authors referred to as 'mythical' or 'mythologized histories.' This tradition of historiography ... was associated with Herodotus and was widespread both before and after the Gospels were written"; though "mythic historiography might have been rejected by historians wishing to pose as strict (in the Thucydidean tradition)," it was "still a widespread form of historiography." Origen still ultimately rejects "myth"-language for reasons that will be discussed below. Cf. Strauss, *Life of Jesus*, §8.

[23] *Princ.* 4.3.1: ἀναγεγραμμένα μὲν ὡς γεγονότα, οὐ γεγενημένα δὲ κατὰ τὴν λέξιν.

[24] *Princ.* 4.2.9: γενόμενα κατὰ τὴν ἱστορίαν and τὸ μὴ γενόμενον, respectively.

[25] *Princ.* 4.2.9: μηδὲ δυνατὸν γενέσθαι and δυνατὸν μὲν γενέσθαι, οὐ μὴν γεγενημένον, respectively.

[26] *Comm. Jo.* 1.3.20.

"impediments" and "impossibilities" for a transparently historical understanding.

To summarize these two fundamental principles for approaching the Gospels: the kind of narratives that Origen imagines the Evangelists compose is directly comparable to the kind of narratives one finds scattered throughout the canonical writings, and especially the histories of Israel. One may make a great deal of progress in coming to terms with Origen's view of Gospel narrative simply by establishing his sense of this shared literary heritage. One could even say that the two principles advanced in this section are really two aspects of one principle: Origen locates the Gospels' *literary* similarity to Jewish biblical narrative precisely in the way the *historical* interests of both share a similarly complex relationship to facticity.

2.3 NOT THAT SIMPLE: FACTICITY FURTHER QUALIFIED

Crucial questions naturally follow: what kind of judgment ought readers employ to say something narrated in the Gospels didn't or even couldn't have happened? And how, in general, does Origen himself decide a particular Gospel narrative – or certain aspects thereof – didn't literally happen? I have highlighted the language of "complexity" not only because it is Origen's (οὐδὲ ἄκρατον) but also for the sake of preserving the subtlety of his position. Origen believes the Gospels interweave things that did and didn't happen. That much is true. But it must also be added that he finds the categories of "factual/historical" and "not factual/unhistorical" insufficient for capturing the full dimensions of the Gospels' literary character.

The most immediate impediment to a historicized reduction of the Gospels is, of course, contradictions among the four canonical Gospels – particularly, when some discord or disagreement emerges between parallel events (παραπλήσια) recorded in more than one Gospel.[27] As a matter of general principle, Origen maintains that historical disagreement is a fundamental and indisputable fact of experience when attentively comparing the four Gospels.[28] "On the basis of

[27] Origen uses a variety of terms to express this dynamic (ἀσυμφωνία, διαφωνία, διάφορον, διακοπή), which will appear repeatedly throughout the texts covered in Chapter 6 especially.

[28] See *Comm. Jo.* 10.3.14. Origen notes issues between the parallel accounts of John the Baptist's imprisonment (*Comm. Jo.* 10.3.10–14), the Temple demonstration (*Comm. Jo.*

numerous passages," he writes, anyone who "critically examines the Gospels regarding their lack of harmony, historically speaking," cannot help but suffer a bit of vertigo; in view of which, one can either "shrink from confirming the Gospels to be true and side with one of them at random (not daring to reject the faith completely)" or, "accepting that there are four, [say] that their truth is not in their corporeal features."[29]

Origen, then, does presuppose something of his readers: they are those who accept the Gospels to be true (ὡς ἀληθῶς) in *some* way. Such readers, however, must then acknowledge that they are left with two options. Either they must choose one of the Gospels to be the "right" or "historical" one (reducing "truth" to matters of facticity), a choice that Origen holds, presciently, cannot in the end be anything but random.[30] Or, admitting "the four," they must come to understand that what is true about the Gospels does not lie, principally, in their "corporeal characteristics."

Now most contemporary readers must, in all honesty, grant that categories of this sort – "corporeal," often in contrast to "spiritual" or "intelligible" – cannot shake a certain antiquated air. Such terms find little currency in modern criticism at least. Nevertheless, I maintain that one need not resolve Origen's more speculative deliberations on the nature of corporeality as a theological or philosophical datum in order to grasp his fundamental point about the nature of Gospel narrative here. Readers will in fact find that Origen far more frequently employs these categories

10.20.119–22.130), and the anointing of Jesus (*Comm. ser. Matt.* 77), to name only the most obvious examples of things that "could've happened but didn't." For example, John the Baptist *could have* been imprisoned at any stage of Jesus's ministry, but it *doesn't* happen at the same time in the Synoptics and John. Jesus *could have* been anointed as narrated in any of the four Gospels, but the timing, location, characters involved, and nature of the anointing lead one to conclude that it *didn't* happen in exactly the way each Evangelist presents it (see Section 6.2). Jesus *may have* performed some dramatic action in the temple, but John and "the Three" disagree over its relation to his final ascent to Jerusalem (see Section 6.3).

[29] *Comm. Jo.* 10.3.14: ἐν τοῖς σωματικοῖς χαρακτῆρσιν.

[30] To this day, it is impossible to say whether any one of the Gospels is more "accurate" than another. At least since W. Wrede's *The Messianic Secret* (*Das Messiasgeheimnis in den Evangelien* [1901]), Markan priority cannot be taken to mean that Mark is any more historically transparent than the other Synoptics (cf. Papias as quoted by Eusebius, *Hist. eccl.* 3.39.15–16). And though in certain respects major tracts of John appear less transparent to history than the Synoptics, the fourth Gospel still may be more precise than the others in certain chronological and cultural matters; see J. P. Meier, *A Marginal Jew: Rethinking the Historical Jesus, Vol. 1: The Roots of the Problem and the Person* (1991), 45, as well as the series edited by P. N. Anderson, F. Just, and T. Thatcher, *John, Jesus, and History*, Vols. 1–3 (2007, 2009, 2016).

for relentlessly historical- and literary-critical purposes. What Origen predominantly means by such qualifications (κατὰ τὸ σωματικόν, κατὰ τὸ σῶμα) is, with respect to the subject at hand, quite straightforward. It furnishes him with a more precise way of expressing the nature of a narrative beyond categories of brute facticity. When he judges that some narrative – or some aspect of a narrative – in the Gospels didn't happen "bodily," he is often only suggesting that what is narrated would not have been physically or empirically observable, or at least not in the exact way the narrative represents it.[31]

Origen deploys the distinction in several ways according to what individual cases demand, ranging anywhere from: *this may have happened in an empirically observable way but certain details have been altered* (location, timeframe, figures involved, and specifics of actions or words),[32] to: *this likely didn't happen in any empirical way, but represents some truth of Jesus's (or his followers') interior vision or subjective experience* (by nature "immaterial," which is to say, "intelligible" or "spiritual" phenomena),[33] and even: *this expresses some idea or understanding developed by the Evangelists, perhaps in view of something that happened (or as an account or interpretation thereof)*.[34] The qualification adds a further degree of subtlety to claiming something "didn't happen." That is, to say something "didn't *physically* happen" is not the same as saying "it didn't happen *at all*" or even "it didn't happen *historically*," but rather that it simply didn't happen in the most surface-level (πρόχειρος; ἐπιπόλαιος) sense of the narrative.[35]

As a general principle, therefore, the qualification "corporeally" allows Origen to admit the presence of historical or literal implausibilities and

[31] Evidence for this claim will appear throughout Part II. For more theological or philosophical construals of Origen's use of "body"-language vis-à-vis scripture (often centering around *Princ.* 4.2.4 and *Hom. Lev.* 5.1), see A. van den Hoek, "The Concept of σῶμα τῶν γραφῶν in Alexandrian Theology" (1989); K. J. Torjesen, "'Body,' 'Soul,' and 'Spirit' in Origen's Theory of Exegesis" (1985), esp. 20–21 (cf. Torjesen, *Hermeneutical Procedure*, 39–43); J. D. Dawson, "Plato's Soul and the Body of the Text in Philo and Origen" (2003). I am most sympathetic to G. E. Sterling's account (though applied primarily to Philo) in "The Body as Metaphor: The Structure of a Human and the Meaning of Scripture" (2019).

[32] See Sections 6.1–6.3 on the healing of the blind, anointing, and Temple demonstration.

[33] See Sections 4.3, 5.2, 7.2, 7.3, and 7.5 on Jesus's baptism, Zechariah's vision in the Temple, and the Son of Man sayings, respectively.

[34] See Sections 3.3, 3.4, 4.5, 5.1, 5.3, 5.4, 6.5, and 7.4 (all addressing the Evangelists' vision[s] of the life of Jesus and its impact on their literary activity).

[35] Cf. Martens, *Origen and Scripture*, 66. Something experienced subjectively or interiorly can be "historical" without being "bodily," strictly speaking.

impossibilities without requiring him to judge a narrative to be "false" de facto.[36] But readers must resist oversimplifying the approach by presuming that Origen judges that a narrative didn't or couldn't have happened only because it is contradicted by a similar narrative in another canonical Gospel.[37] When Origen insists that the nature of the Gospel narratives themselves "demonstrate" that there is more going on there than straightforward history (at least to those who approach them "more perceptively"), his reasons for doing so just as frequently involve judgments arising from the individual passages themselves.[38]

2.4 PURPOSE OF THE FORM: COMPARATIVE LITERATURE

The preceding sections occasion one last crucial question: does the "mixed" character of Gospel narrative admit of any other comparisons? Origen has already identified the nearest likeness: the kind of historical narratives found throughout the scriptures of Israel. As a matter of direct literary precedent, the comparison is coherent – even likely – enough.[39] But what about the world of literature outside of the Christian Bible?

[36] *Comm. Jo.* 10.3.14: ἀληθὲς αὐτῶν οὐκ ἐν τοῖς σωματικοῖς χαρακτῆρσιν. In *Against Celsus*, Origen develops an apologia for Christian scripture on the grounds that many ancient pieces of literature are held to be true without being historically or literally true all the way down (cf. *Cels.* 4.38–39 and 6.42–43).

[37] Cf. C. J. Berglund, "Understanding Origen: The Genre(s) of the Gospels in Light of Ancient Greek Philology and Modern Genre Theory" (2016), at 213: "It is precisely the juxtaposition of four canonical narratives that prompts him to prefer a theological interpretation, and forces him to adopt a complex view of the nature of the Gospels." Cf. Watson, *Gospel Writing*, 14 and 548–52.

[38] Cf. *Cels.* 2.69. See Chapters 4 and 5 especially.

[39] Origen's position approximates that of a number of more recent scholars who have called for a reconsideration of Jewish biblical narrative as the most direct and constitutive literary precedent for the Gospels, finding themselves equally unconvinced by, on the one hand, taking the Gospels to be utterly *sui generis* (a view typically associated with R. Bultmann and form criticism more broadly) or, on the other hand, reducing the question of Gospel genre mostly to Greco-Roman parallels (cf. R. Burridge, *What Are the Gospels? A Comparison with Graeco-Roman Biography* [1992], esp. 26–54). See, for instance, A. Y. Collins' review of Burridge, where she argues that his comparison to Greco-Roman *bioi* tends to "mask the similarities between the Gospels and Jewish historical and apocalyptic works" ([1995], 246; see similarly her *Is Mark's Gospel a Life of Jesus?* [1990] and *Mark: A Commentary* [2006], 15–43). On the so-called "Primary History" (Genesis through Kings) providing the most likely candidates for inspiring the Gospels' literary form, see R. E. Brown, "Jesus and Elisha" (1971), and D. Allison, *Constructing Jesus*, 443. In a complementary vein, see M. E. Vines, *The Problem of Markan Genre: The Gospel of Mark and the Jewish Novel* (2002), esp. 144.

Origen does not take the Gospels to be *sui generis* vis-à-vis the rest of the scriptures; does he consider this biblical form of historical writing to be utterly without analogy to other literary forms in antiquity?

Simply put: no. But not for the reasons one might suspect. Note that the categories developed in the preceding section function negatively; that is, Origen speaks of those aspects of Gospel narrative that lead one to judge that certain things *didn't* happen. On the question of *positive* criteria of historicity, Origen proves more reserved. On occasions when he finds himself obliged to defend the facticity of a particular event, more often than not he argues only for its plausibility against philosophical presuppositions alien to the world of the New Testament (and the early Jewish milieu from which it sprang).[40] But he never develops a taste for anything analogous to criteria of authenticity, and in the face of clear contradictions, he never ventures to name the more authentic version of an event.[41] "Attempting to substantiate almost any historical narrative as fact, even if it is true, and to produce complete certainty about it, is one of the most difficult tasks and, in some cases, is impossible."[42]

Thus, in comparing the narratives of Jesus's life with "just about any *historia*," Origen does not turn to Thucydides, Herodotus, or any other

40 Much of which occurs in *Against Celsus*, where he frequently works to displace presuppositions of an (Epicurean) atomist or reductive materialist variety (see Chapter 4).

41 See especially his treatment of the events surrounding Jesus's (final) ascent to Jerusalem in *Comm. Jo.* 10 and *Comm. Matt.* 16 and of the various anointing narratives in *Comm. ser. Matt.* 77 (covered in Chapter 6). Origen also rarely comments on literary dependence, though he does appear to hold to Matthean priority; cf. *Comm. Matt.* 11.5 (comparing Matt 14:22 [τοὺς μαθητάς: "*the* disciples"] with Mark 6:45 [τοὺς μαθητὰς αὐτοῦ: "*his* disciples"): "Mark has made a small alteration [ὀλίγον ἐναλλάξας] in recording his text," with his "slight adjustment [τῆς ὀλίγης παραλλαγῆς]" indicating "something more definite by the addition of the pronoun"; cf. *Or.* 26.1: "Luke, after 'your kingdom come,' omits ['your will be done on earth as in heaven'] and puts next, 'give us our daily bread.'" Cf. *Fr. Luc.* 125 and 173–74. Cf. Eusebius, *Hist. eccl.* 6.25.2–7.

42 *Cels.* 1.42. Cf. H. Chadwick (trans.), *Contra Celsum* (1953), 40 n. 1: "Direct apprehension, καταληπτικὴ φαντασία, is a fundamental idea in Stoic epistemology; it is an impression on the mind of such a kind that no doubt can be entertained as to its truth." Cf. Allison, *The Historical Christ and the Theological Jesus*, 57. See also Martens, *Origen and Scripture*, 49–50: "At a basic level, historical analysis (ἱστορικόν) began with the issue of facticity: did passages narrate what actually transpired? Ancient literary scholars assessed this sort of probability by applying the methods of refutation (ἀνασκευή) and confirmation (κατασκευή)." Cf. R. M. Grant, *The Earliest Lives of Jesus*, 40. Cf. Sextus Empiricus's complaint in *Adv. Math.* 266–68 on the difficulty of imposing any order upon (μέθοδος), or establishing criteria for (κρίσις), inquiries into what is true or false in a historical narrative.

text that has come to be known as Greco-Roman biography, but rather invites his readers to

> suppose, for example, that someone argues the Trojan War never happened, mostly because some impossible thing has been mixed into its story – whether about a certain Achilles having had Thetis (a sea-goddess) as his mother and Peleus (a man) as his father, or about Sarpedon being a son of Zeus, or Ascalaphus and Ialmenus of Ares, or Aeneas of Aphrodite.[43]

In order to mount his *apologia* for how one ought to approach the kinds of narratives one finds in the Gospels, Origen turns first to the literary classics of Greco-Roman antiquity. One cannot help but be struck by how vast the categorical horizon of *historia* stretches before contemporary English readers who would never dream of applying the word "history" to the *Iliad*. We are reminded, again, that the strictest sense of the term here means only a chronologically ordered narrative (at least in appearance), which can play host equally to passages of factual and non-factual origins – a "story." But even in cases as extreme as Homeric epic, does the mixed character of their narratives de facto negate the possibility of any historical referent or factual substrate at all? Even if everyone seems to agree there must have been *some* war in Ilium that then became "interwoven with fictional elements," how, Origen asks, would one definitively "establish such a thing?"[44] What about the case of classical tragedy, where one might meet an occasional Sphinx, but just as often encounters nothing particularly incredible whatsoever – how could one demonstrate such stories do or don't originate in very real referents?[45]

The force of Origen's rhetorical questions drives the reader elsewhere. What reader of classical epic and tragedy would expend his or her interpretive energies attempting to demonstrate the empirical facticity of

[43] *Cels.* 1.42. Origen raises the stakes by invoking figures mythologized by divine births. Cf. Dio Chrysostom, *Troj.* and Strabo, *Geogr.* 1.2.7–10 (as noted by Chadwick, *Contra Celsum*, 40 n. 2). Origen's language here (τὸ ἀδύνατον προσπεπλέχθαι λόγον) is also reminiscent of Strabo on Homer in *Geogr.* 1.1.10 (μυθώδη τινὰ προσπέπλεκται τοῖς λεγομένοις). Cf. R. Hunter, "Homer in Origen, *Against Celsus*" (2021).

[44] *Cels.* 1.42: πῶς ἂν κατασκευάσαιμεν τὸ τοιοῦτον.

[45] *Cels.* 1.42: "Suppose also that someone does not believe the story about Oedipus and Jocasta, and Eteocles and Polyneices, the sons of them both, because the story of the half-maiden Sphinx has been intermixed with it [προσπεπλέχθαι τῷ λόγῳ]. How could we make a demonstrative argument [ἀποδείξαιμεν] about something like this? So also in the case of the Epigoni, even if there is no such thing mixed up with the story [ἐπιπεπλεγμένον ᾖ τῷ λόγῳ], or in that of the return of the Heraclidae, or innumerable other instances."

this or that part of their narratives with perfect certitude?[46] Such an endeavor, Origen argues, would miss the whole point of the work. Rather, "any who approach these stories [ταῖς ἱστορίαις] generously, who want to keep themselves from being misled" when reading them, will, after "seeking out the intention of those who fashion [stories] of this sort," have to judge "what things they will receive" as having been expressed in a figurative way (τροπολογήσει), and "what they will discount as having been set down only for the sake of entertaining people."[47]

Has a particular work of fiction (πλάσμα) been written simply to entertain, or has the author made use of the story to disclose what could not be expressed otherwise? Was the *Iliad* written solely so that it might establish the Trojan War as a matter of indisputable fact for its readers? Or, Origen asks, was it written to depict some truth of the world and the human condition – that is, written "figuratively"? What are the great epics and tragedies of antiquity if not, in the broadest sense, "figurative"?[48] The task Homer (or Aeschylus, or Sophocles, or Euripides) sets before his readers is not to decide whether they will accept what has been written as a demonstrable fact of history. No, these works demand their readers to judge (κρινεῖ) whether or not they will receive (συγκαταθήσεται) what has been depicted as true.[49]

"We have said this," Origen concludes,

> in anticipation of the whole question of the story [ἱστορίαν] about Jesus in the Gospels; we do not call those who are ready and willing to naïve and irrational belief, but wish to show that those who approach [the Gospels] need an open mind, a great deal of critical study [πολλῆς ἐξετάσεως], and, if I may put it this way, a means of entry into the intention of the writers in order to discover the thought process with which each [narrative] was recorded.[50]

Origen lets the comparison stand before his readers as an invitation, one which, as Robert Lamberton puts it, "turns on the quality of εὐγνωμοσύνη" – a generosity or openness of mind – "that is also an openness to the text and a willingness to acknowledge levels of meaning within it, and at the same time to withdraw belief from that which is

[46] *Cels.* 1.42: κατασκευάζειν ὡς γεγενημένην καὶ καταληπτικὴν ποιῆσαι περὶ αὐτῆς φαντασίαν.

[47] *Cels.* 1.42: διὰ τὴν χάριν. [48] Cf. E. Auerbach, "Figura" (1984), 11–28.

[49] Note how far we are from speculating about the legitimacy of "allegorical" reading of Homer; this is not about whether or not every detail of Homeric epic of Attic tragedy can be decoded (as if it were J. Bunyan's *The Pilgrim's Progress* or G. Orwell's *Animal Farm*), but about the simple fact that literature is often written with an eye toward depicting ("figuratively") some idea, or, in a more ancient idiom, some "incorporeal" – that is to say, intelligible or spiritual – truth.

[50] *Cels.* 1.42.

entirely unacceptable without rejecting the rest."[51] This generosity, however, does not find its term merely in the mind of the reader.[52] Rather, in the case of classical myth and tragedy, by "searching out the intention of those who have fashioned fictions of this sort," and in the case of the Gospels, by discovering some "means of entry into the intention of the writers," one may then develop a notion of the thought process or meaning (διανοία) underlying these stories.[53] Once the basic form of a narrative has been determined, the reader must diligently venture an account of why it might have been composed this way.

In conclusion, Origen does not construct the comparison in order to deny the Gospels any historical substrate or to dismiss the significance of the historicity of events underlying the Gospel narratives. Reader beware – any attempt to over-read the comparison in this way misses the clear intent of the entire passage, which is precisely to deflect readers from such prejudgments, to redirect them from tempting the labyrinthine paths of historical demonstrability and so reducing matters of interpretation to proofs of facticity. Origen is simply making an appeal for the Gospels to be read like works of literature. This, in the first instance, is what he means by taking Gospel narrative to be principally figurative: they are not set down to provide their readers with the means to prove the indisputable facticity of events from the life of Jesus, nor are they set down merely to entertain; rather, like many works of literature, the Gospels were composed, above and before all, to signify something more than the barest and most superficial sense conveyed by the narrative.[54]

2.5 DISTINCTION WITHOUT A DIFFERENCE? NAMING THE FORM

What then is the reader to do with the undeniable similarity between Origen's descriptions of the "mixed" character of epic or tragic narrative

[51] R. Lamberton, *Homer the Theologian: Neoplatonist Allegorical Reading and the Growth of the Epic Tradition* (1986), 82.

[52] One of the gravest errors one can make vis-à-vis Origen on the Gospels is to align his approach so closely with reader-response styles of interpretation that one ignores the claims he is making on the intrinsic form of the writings themselves (see Chapter 3).

[53] The subtle difference in terminology cannot be accidental (τὸ βούλημα τῶν ἀναπλασαμένων τὰ τοιαδί vs. τὸ βούλημα τῶν γραψάντων); Origen appears, quite consciously, to choose *not* to refer to the Gospel narratives as πλάσμα nor to the activity of the Evangelists as ἀναπλάσσω here (and throughout his corpus), for reasons that will be discussed in the next section and at much more length in Chapter 4.

[54] *Cels.* 2.69; cf. *Cels.* 2.38.

in *Against Celsus* and of biblical narrative in *On First Principles*?[55] However closely Origen's language approximates, and perhaps even appropriates, the literary terminology of his intellectual *milieu*, one must mark his unremitting refusal to apply the categories of *fiction* (πλάσμα) and *myth* (μῦθος) to the Gospels.[56] Is this a distinction without a difference? Should we conclude that, actually, Origen does (in spirit, if not in letter) agree with Strauss that "the Christian religion, like all others, has its myths"?[57]

It is true, Origen cautions, that there is no set pattern or ratio of the various threads (happened vs. didn't) in the narrative fabric of the biblical writings as a whole. On some occasions, only a "few passages are interpolated that are not physically true," while at other times, there are "a greater number."[58] But then, turning to the Gospels

[55] Cf. *Cels.* 1.42 and *Princ.* 4.2.9.

[56] Origen's rather oblique phrasing throughout *Princ.* 4 is striking, given that the categories of *myth* and *fiction*, along with their relationship to *historia*, received similar (if not perfectly consistent) definitions in literary circles with which he could not have been entirely unfamiliar. See, for example, Sextus Empiricus, *Adv. Math.* 1.263–64 on the diverse forms of *historia* (τῶν ἱστοριῶν διαφορᾶς): "Of the kinds of historical writing [τῶν ἱστορουμένων] one part is history [ἱστορία], another myth [μῦθος], another fiction [πλάσμα]: of these *history* presents certain things which are true [ἀληθῶν] and have happened [γεγονότων]" (Sextus gives the poisoning of Alexander the Great as an example); "*fiction* presents things that didn't happen [μὴ γενομένων] but are told in a way that resembles things that happen [ὁμοίως τοῖς γενομένοις]" (e.g., imagined situations in comedies); and "*myth* presents things which have never happened and are false [ἀγενήτων καὶ ψευδῶν]" (e.g., Pegasus springing from the slit throat of Medusa or Odysseus being turned into a horse). Cf. *Adv. Math.* 1.251–53 on Asclepiades of Myrlea (second to first century BCE), who also "subdivides the historical [τὸ ἱστορικόν] into three; for he says that 'of history one division is true, one false, one as if true [ὡς ἀληθῆ]: the *factual* [τὴν πρακτικήν] is true, that of *fictions* and *myths* is false, and that *as if true* takes such forms as comedy and mimes.' And of true history, again, there are three parts: one sort is that about the characters [τὰ πρόσωπα] of gods and heroes and illustrious men, another about places and times, the third about deeds." Cf. Theon's *Progymnasmata* 72 (first century CE), where *myth* is defined as a "false discourse giving an image of the truth [λόγος ψευδὴς εἰκονίζων ἀλήθειαν]" and *narrative* (διήγημα) as a "discourse descriptive of things that have happened or as if they had happened [γεγονότων ἢ ὡς γεγονότων]" (cf. *Princ.* 4.3.1: ὡς γεγονότα). For an overview of possible Greco-Roman precedents and parallels for Origen's approach, see Grant, *The Earliest Lives of Jesus*, 38–49 and 65–66 (along with a glossary at 119–23). Cf. Young, *Biblical Exegesis*, 76–96.

[57] Strauss, *Life of Jesus*, §14 (see Section 1.1).

[58] *Princ.* 4.2.9. This may be why Origen later allows myth-language vis-à-vis certain parts of the Pentateuch in *Cels.* 5.42, but never does so vis-à-vis the Gospels: "These truths were proclaimed in a rather mythical way [μυθικώτερον] still ... but now to those who seek for the meaning [τὸν λόγον] and wish to advance in it, what hitherto were myths [οἱ τέως

specifically, he again warns against totalizing misappropriations of his position:

> But that no one may suppose we assert, with respect to it *all*, that *not one* of the narratives actually happened because *some* didn't, and that *none* of the commands are to be observed as stated, because some are irrational or impossible when taken literally, or that what is written about the savior wasn't observably true, or that *no* teaching about the law or commandment of his is to be kept, it must be said that it is perfectly clear to us that *certain parts* of the historical narrative are true... For there is considerably more of what is historically true than what is woven out of pure spirit.[59]

Origen forecloses all quick exits. The Gospels resist facile reduction – to unqualified "histories" of fact, yes, but also to undifferentiated "fiction" or "myth." This, I maintain, is not a distinction without a difference (*pace* Robert Grant), if only because Origen affirms that passages originating in historical events substantially outweigh those that don't, at least to a degree that direct identification with Greco-Roman myth or fiction would prove quite misleading on purely literary terms.[60] Along with many still opposed to the much-maligned mythicist view, Origen does not believe the characters or events of the Gospels were invented by the Evangelists whole cloth: "woven of pure spirit."[61]

μῦθοι], if I may say it this way, have been transformed [μετεμορφοῦντο] into the truth that had been hidden within them."

59 *Princ.* 4.3.4. This passage challenges R. Grant's claim that, for Origen, there is "no middle ground between history and fiction or myth. To lay more stress on the creativity of the Evangelists as historians would have meant that he could not pass so easily from literal truth or untruth to allegory" (*Earliest Lives of Jesus*, 56). See Chapter 3 on the question of the Evangelists' creativity.

60 Grant rightly notes that Origen appears to have recognized an unavoidably prejudicial freight to "myth" and "fiction" language. But even if Origen's definitions of biblically derived categories like "parable" and "enigma" share a striking resemblance to the usage of "fiction" and "myth" in other literary circles, these terms do not exhaust the subtleties of his understanding of the Gospels' literary form in its entirety (cf. *Earliest Lives of Jesus*, 66). See *Fr. Prov.* 1.6 on "parable": "a parable is a discourse about something that did not literally happen but could have happened, which, in a figurative way, becomes indicative [τροπικῶς δηλωτικός] of something by way of translating [ἐκ μεταλήψεως] what was spoken in the parable"; and on "enigma": "an enigma is a description of something that did not happen – nor could have – as if it happened [ὡς γεγονότων], meant to signify something inexpressible [ἀπόρρητόν τι] in a cryptic way." *Fr. Prov.* 1.6 also notes how "parables" (so defined) can clarify "enigmas, such as: 'A man went out to sow his field...' For this did not literally happen, but rather refers to something else." On "parable," see also *Comm. Cant.* pr.3, *Comm. Matt.* 10.4, and *Comm. Matt.* 14.12.

61 One can only speculate how Origen might have compared the Gospels to other Greco-Roman "lives" (*bioi*) that interweave fictive elements – which is not to say he would find such a comparison "wrong," only that he finds other comparisons more serviceable. The

On this question, therefore, one finds that the analogy with classical epic and tragedy never amounts to more than that; similitude finally gives way to dissimilitude. Origen is, after all, quite comfortable using "memory"-related language to describe the Gospels, with terms that hardly find fitting application to the writings of Homer or the tragedians.[62] Yet, as Chapter 3 will show, Origen's sense of how the Evangelists variously "memorialize" this life resists reduction to facile notions of photographic memory. The Gospels may draw from memories of historical events in a way that cannot be said of classical epic or tragedy.[63] Nevertheless, passages that don't (or couldn't) transparently correspond to "what happened" remain a formal feature, even a constitutive one, of the four Evangelists' "commentaries" on the life of Jesus. The preceding, in sum, is another way of saying the Gospels interweave things that happened with things that didn't. And the cumulative effect of this "mixed" form, Origen concludes, drives the reader to understand them as "otherwise" than mere history alone.[64]

point is, for Origen, completely identifying the literary presentation of the figures of Jesus or John the Baptist with that of Heracles or Odysseus would be misleading if only because the latter are literary inventions to a degree that finally amounts to a difference of kind.

62 Terms like ὑπομνήματα (*commentarii* in Latin, along with ἀπομνημονεύματα), which is notoriously difficult to translate – often rendered "memoirs," but also with the sense of "memoranda," that is, something written *from* memory perhaps, but also *for* remembrance, and therefore also a standard term for "commentary" (Origen refers to Heracleon's writings on John as ὑπομνήματα in *Comm. Jo.* 6.15.92; cf. C. J. Berglund, *Origen's References to Heracleon* [2020], 53–76). For a broader discussion of the term vis-à-vis the Gospels, see C. Keith, *The Gospels as Manuscript: An Early History of the Jesus Tradition as Material Artifact* (2020), 49–60. Cf. Clement of Alexandria, as quoted in Eusebius, *Hist. eccl.* 2.15.1–2. On the Gospels as ἀπομνημονεύματα in Origen, see Grant, *The Earliest Lives of Jesus*, 119–20. Cf. Justin Martyr *1 Apol.* 66.3 and 67.3; cf. Papias, as quoted in Eusebius, *Hist. eccl.* 3.39.15–16.

63 See *Cels.* 2.13: "For surely they will not say that Jesus's own pupils and hearers handed on the Gospels' teaching without writing it down [χωρὶς γραφῆς], and that they left *their* disciples without their memoirs [or *commentaries*] about Jesus in writing [χωρὶς τῶν περὶ Ἰησοῦ ἐν γράμμασιν ὑπομνημάτων]." Compare *Cels.* 7.54 on Heracles: "Since [Celsus] refers us to Heracles, let him show us records of his words [ἀπομνημονεύματα λόγων αὐτοῦ]." See also *Comm. Jo.* 20.1.1: "We pray that the Gospel may be revealed in what we examine [ἐξεταζόμενα], and that we may neglect nothing ... in the writings that serve as memoirs [ὑπομνηματικοῖς γράμμασιν; or *commentaries*]... May God, therefore, send the word itself to us, revealing itself, that we may become beholders of its depths." One beholds the word's "depths" in the depths of the Evangelists' memory. See also *Comm. Jo.* 10.3.10 on whether or not events in the Gospels were "successfully memorialized [ἀπομνημονευθέντων]" (treated in Section 6.3; cf. *Comm. Jo.* 6.34.171 and *Comm. Matt.* 16.12).

64 Cf. *Comm. Jo.* 10.4.18–20: τὸ ὡς κατὰ τὴν ἱστορίαν ἑτέρως γενόμενον.

So one can make too much of the analogy. One can also make too little of it. Again, as a matter of general principle, Origen allows a basic likeness of form between classical myth and the kind of historical narrative we find in the Gospels: at least, that is, in the interweaving of what did and did not happen, or of what could and could not have happened, for the sake of depicting some truth in figures. There is thus also a likeness in interpretive approach, in Origen's view, since such mixed narratives, if they are meant to do more than merely inform or entertain, invite the reader to determine what of them is to be understood figuratively and why. But they also differ essentially, both in *genera* and in *species*: generally, in that Origen understands much of what is narrated in the Gospels to have some kind of origins in historical events; specifically, in that these narratives subsist in the deeds, sufferings, and words of Jesus and, inseparably, the vast matrix of Jewish scriptural expectations and images out of which his life and teachings were woven.

2.6 FACTS AND FIGURES

One should not mistake the preceding for a fully developed line of argument. We have not yet allowed Origen to advance much beyond the sphere of stipulation, since, on his own terms, rigorous demonstration of the "first principles" introduced here won't be possible until Part II. Only when one approaches the various records of the "deeds, sufferings, and words" of Jesus directly can they "show themselves" to be the kind of literature Origen has proposed.[65] There are no shortcuts.

> For the meticulous reader will be pulled in multiple directions regarding particular points, being unable to show without a great deal of interrogation whether the supposed historical narrative happened literally or not... Therefore one who approaches [these texts] in a rigorous way must ... diligently interrogate where it is true in a literal sense and where it is impossible.[66]

As Origen impresses the difficulty of such an "interrogation" upon his readers,[67] the *impediments* and *impossibilities* standing in the way of a strictly literal or historical reading of the Gospels become a summons to return to the narratives themselves with an "open mind" and a "great

[65] Cf. *Cels.* 2.69. [66] *Princ.* 4.3.5.

[67] Terminology (βάσανος/βασανίζειν) that literally means (to prove by) *touchstone* but also has connotations of *torture* (and inquiry thereby). See A. J. Harrill, "'Exegetical Torture' in Early Christian Biblical Interpretation."

deal of critical study."[68] So too, the rest of this book is a kind of interrogation of Origen *as* the very kind of critical reader he believes the Gospels call for.

In any case, Origen's general principles of "what a Gospel is" in terms of subject matter and literary form can now be reduced to summary. The four canonical Gospels share the following qualities: they all narrate the deeds, sufferings, and words of Jesus in the form of history; these historical narratives are of a mixed character, interweaving things that happened with things that didn't, with an eye toward presenting the events recorded to have happened to Jesus figuratively. Whatever it is the various narratives might have been meant to signify, they are written to signify *something*. And thus, the cumulative effect of such narratives can be said to be *principally* figurative. Origen takes all of this to be obvious enough to the careful reader that the judgment amounts to something of a self-evident historical- and literary-critical fact.[69]

In light of the preceding, future chapters will take "life of Jesus" as shorthand for what Origen thinks the universal subject matter of the Gospels is and "figurative" as shorthand for what he understands their fundamental literary quality to be – a kind of literature, that is, that interweaves what did, didn't, and couldn't have happened in order to relate something more than mere historical facticity, to depict something in figures, to signify something, even something spiritual (meaning, for now, "not a matter of empirical observation alone"). Therefore: if, for Origen, one can neither call the Gospels "mythical narratives" (given the limits of the analogy to precedents in Greco-Roman antiquity) nor "historical narratives" alone (especially in view of how "historicity" and "facticity" have become identified in contemporary English usage), then let us call them "figurative narratives." That is, in short: the Gospel narratives range from *histories in a figurative mode* to *figures in a historical mode*.

[68] Cf. *Cels.* 1.42. [69] Cf. *Princ.* 4.3.1.

3

Literary Formation

Seeing in the Spirit

"What else can we suppose except that they were written to be read figuratively?"[1]

Origen's own order of argument obliges us to prescind from turning to his readings for one more chapter. The logic of his account does not jump from a judgment about the literary qualities of the Gospel narratives to a judgment about the manner of interpretation proper to them: *"the Gospels cannot be taken literally, through and through; therefore, we should read them as follows…"* One more critical premise intervenes. Prior to interpreting particular passages, Origen asks his reader to consider not only "what does the form itself mean?" but also "whence this form?"

In this chapter, therefore, we turn from the question of the Gospels' literary *form* to that of their literary *formation.* How does Origen account for the principally figurative nature of Gospel narrative? What, if anything, can the form of the literary artifact tell us of its formation, and perhaps, what the authors themselves looked to present in their writings? And what then is ultimately responsible for Origen's figurative sense of the Gospels?

3.1 MYTH AND ALLEGORY: TURNING TO THE AUTHORS

On this series of questions, we find ourselves with an interlocutor of considerable caliber. It is precisely on the matter of literary formation that I insist on David Strauss's exceptional insight into Origen's view of the Gospels. According to Strauss, no preceding understanding of the

[1] *Cels.* 4.49; cf. Martens, *Origen and Scripture*, 81–87.

Gospels shared closer proximity to the emerging "mythical point of view" than "ancient allegorical interpretation"[2] – an astonishing claim left largely unexamined since his *Life of Jesus* was first published. Strauss's comparison of the mythical and allegorical views nevertheless remains, in the history of scholarship on early criticism of the Gospels, almost scandalously in need of further cross-examination.

Despite their distinct differences on certain fundamental premises, from the vantage of this study, no contemporary reader cuts closer to the heart of Origen's sense of the figurative nature of the Gospels than Strauss.

> For while both the natural explanations of the Rationalists and the mocking of the Deists belong to that form of opinion which, while sacrificing all divine meaning in the sacred record, still clings to its historical character [*historische Form*]; *the mythical agrees with the allegorical in sacrificing the historical reality of the narratives in order to preserve in them an absolute inherent truth.*[3]

It remains to be seen whether, in practice, Origen "sacrifices the historical reality" of the Gospel narratives in the same way Strauss does. Nevertheless, Strauss and Origen share a common adversary: those who "sacrifice all divine meaning" out of a misguided obligation to a superficial sense of the Gospels' historicity (or lack thereof), which presumes that to stray from a perfect transparency to what literally happened is to be "false."[4] In this, they discover an unexpected kinship. For, to continue the thought in Origen's voice, if the Gospel narratives were "in their entirety plainly coherent and polished history," one might "doubt that anything besides the obvious could be meant" by them; the presence of impediments and impossibilities to a purely historical reading, however, prevents readers from being "thrown off by the enticing simplicity of their style" to such a degree that they, never "stirred from the letter," would "learn nothing more divine."[5]

A fortiori, note where Strauss locates the basis (*Grund*) underlying both the mythical and the allegorical views, which

> equally allow that the author relates that which is seemingly historical [*scheinbar Geschichtliches*], but they suppose him, under the influence of a higher inspiration

[2] Strauss, *Life of Jesus*, §12. [3] Strauss, *Life of Jesus*, §12 (emphasis added).

[4] See Theissen/Merz, *Historical Jesus*, 4: "In contrast to Reimarus, Strauss no longer explains the unhistorical by deliberate deception but by an unconscious process of mythical imagination." Cf. Harris, *David Friedrich Strauss and His Theology*, 43. Cf. Litwa, *How the Gospels Became History*, 1. Cf. *Cels.* 3.39.

[5] *Princ.* 4.2.9 (cited in Section 2.2).

(known or unknown to himself), to have made use of this historical semblance merely as the shell of an idea, a religious representation.[6]

Strauss understands that both the mythical and allegorical views, in the first instance, originate in a particular view of the authors. It is the Gospel writer, according to Strauss, who writes in the form of historical narrative, yes, but "makes use of the historical" for the sake of some "religious representation."[7]

Crucial differences remain, but they are equally instructive. It simply isn't precise to say that Origen considered historical narrative in the Gospels, as a rule, to be *merely* the "shell of an idea." Yet those familiar with more extreme caricatures of Origen should be struck by Strauss's "shell" language, even if the similarity in locution cannot be anything but accidental. Both Richard Hanson and Daniel Boyarin, for instance, have accused Origen of making the letter of the narratives a mere "shell" for his own religious philosophy.[8] In Strauss's case, though, he isn't talking about interpreters, and he isn't using the word pejoratively. He is making a direct claim about the authors. The "mythical view" belonged, first of all, to the Evangelists. So before one censures Origen's writings for making the "historical semblance" of the life of Jesus narrated in the Gospels the vessel of his own conceptions, Strauss obliges the reader to ask whether (Origen recognizes that) the Evangelists did so first.

Therefore, any post-Straussian bid to explain Origen on the Gospels must come to terms with whether, and in what sense, the mythical and allegorical views ground their accounts of the literary formation of the Gospel narratives in the same logic. Does the allegorical view differ

[6] Strauss, *Life of Jesus*, §12, with a footnote referencing Origen, *Comm. Jo.* 6.2 and 10.4, concerning the question of how "conscious" the shaping of this material was on the part of the author (cf. Strauss, *Streitschriften III* [1837], 167–69). For an illuminating example of this principle applied to a particular pericope, see Strauss's concluding paragraph on the Transfiguration in *Life of Jesus*, §107.

[7] Note the subtle rephrasing from the first and second edition of *Das Leben Jesu* ("als bloße Hülle einer übergeschichtlichen Wahrheit oder Meinung": *a supra-historical truth or belief*) to the third and fourth ("als bloße Hülle eines Ideellen, einer religiösen Vorstellung").

[8] See Hanson, *Allegory and Event*, 25: "Behind Alexandrian allegory lies the assumption that the allegorical sense is the deeper, more important one, to which the literal is only the shell or outer part." Cf. D. Boyarin, *Intertextuality and the Reading of Midrash* (1990), 109; and D. Boyarin, "Philo, Origen, and the Rabbis on Divine Speech and Interpretation" (2007), 128. In response, see J. D. Dawson, *Christian Figural Reading*, 51: "Although Origen draws on the Pauline language of inner and outer, Boyarin ... amplifies the implied inferiority of what is 'outer' with his own word, 'shell'" (cf. p. 59). Cf. D. Turner, "Allegory in Christian Late Antiquity" (2010), 77.

essentially from saying that the Gospel writers themselves began the process of mythologizing the life of Jesus under the influence of some "higher inspiration"? Strauss thinks so, but for one discrete reason:

> The *only essential distinction* therefore between these two modes of explanation is, that according to the allegorical this higher inspiration [*Geist*] is the immediate divine agency; according to the mythical, it is the spirit of a people or a community... Thus the allegorical view attributes the narrative to a supernatural source, whilst the mythical view ascribes it to that *natural* process by which legends are originated and developed.[9]

Strauss locates the heart of the difference but misdiagnoses it. He, like Origen, grounds his view of Gospel writing in some "higher inspiration" – that is, in spirit (*Geist*). But the process of literary formation cannot be attributed to any source other than the human spirit, ostensibly because the "absolute cause" never "disturbs the chain of secondary causes by single arbitrary acts of interposition."[10] Strauss's uncharacteristically crude construal of nature and supernature, symptomatic as it is of some of his era's more underdeveloped philosophies of history, finds the same myopia extend into his philosophy of artistic inspiration or literary consciousness.[11] Be that as it may, this "essential distinction" between the two modes of explanation stands before the reader as a stipulation, not a demonstration. Does it hold before the direct witness of Origen's writings? Does he attribute the formation of the Gospel narratives to a supernatural source in such a way as to dissolve the natural processes of literary formation?

It is difficult to overestimate these questions' repercussions for the whole subject of this book. Only after describing the allegorical and mythical views' agreement on the subject of literary form but disagreement on the question of literary formation does Strauss allow himself to express (what he perceives to be) the necessary consequences of this "essential distinction" for one's interpretive approach:

> To which it should be added, that the allegorical interpreter ... may with the most unrestrained arbitrariness separate from the history every thought he deems to be worthy of God, as constituting its inherent meaning; while the mythical interpreter, on the contrary, in searching out the ideas which are embodied in the

[9] Strauss, *Life of Jesus*, §12 (emphasis added). Cf. R. F. Walsh, *The Origins of Early Christian Literature: Contextualizing the New Testament within Greco-Roman Literary Culture* (2021), 50–104.

[10] Cf. Strauss, *Life of Jesus*, §16.

[11] See Section 4.6 for a fuller treatment of this topic.

narrative, is controlled by regard to conformity with the spirit and modes of representation of the people and of the age.[12]

Thus we uncover an archetypal expression of the great Origenian accusation, repeated or implied under innumerable forms throughout the centuries: namely, that Origen's theological or philosophical commitments ultimately corrupt the interpretive potential of his otherwise considerable critical capacities.[13] Insofar as the allegorical mode of explanation stipulates that the Evangelist writes under the aegis of some unmediated divine agency (so Strauss's logic unfolds), then one is left, finally, with the reader alone.[14] Accepting that the Gospels originate from a "supernatural source" licenses interpreters to make their every thought the "inherent meaning" of these narratives, as long as they (or their tradition) consider it "worthy of God."[15]

The allegorical view, according to Strauss, is right about the nature of Gospel writing (making use of history for the sake of an idea), but wrong about its source – a presumption with ruinous interpretive effects. Readers who perceive the Gospels' literary form correctly but misapprehend its basis will find their interpretive judgments consigned to the "most unrestrained arbitrariness." To attribute the Gospels' literary formation to "arbitrary acts of [supernatural] interposition" is to invite equally arbitrary acts of interpretation. If one does not accept the stipulation that these texts were inspired by an "immediate divine agency," Strauss says, then one is left with nothing more than the self-reflected spirit of the interpreter. Long before liberal Protestantism, the allegorists gazed into the deep well of the Gospel tradition and saw only the reflection of their own speculations.[16]

[12] Strauss, *Life of Jesus*, §12. Cf. Watson, "Toward a Literal Reading of the Gospels," 213. In this section, Strauss sometimes parenthetically pairs the allegorical view with the "moral": that is, the Kantian, in whose *Religion within the Boundaries of Mere Reason* (1793) the allegorical view was "all at once called up from its grave and revived" (*Life of Jesus*, §7).

[13] Cf. Strauss, *Life of Jesus*, §4.

[14] Cf. Strauss, *Life of Jesus*, §12.

[15] Strauss's language makes it difficult to imagine that he did not write this passage with something like *On First Principles* Book 4 (here 4.2.9) in view, which he had already cited in §4.

[16] For this famous image, see G. Tyrrell, *Christianity at the Crossroads* (1909), 49: "The Christ that [Adolf] Harnack sees, looking back through nineteen centuries of Catholic darkness, is only the reflection of a liberal Protestant face, seen at the bottom of a deep well." On the ways this phrase has since been used and abused, see J. C. Poirier, "Seeing What Is There in Spite of Ourselves: George Tyrrell, John Dominic Crossan, and Robert Frost on Faces in Deep Wells" (2006). Cf. Schweitzer, *Quest*, 6: "But it was not only each

Strauss's order of argument reflects Origen's (and this book's): form, to formation, to interpretation. His conclusions do not. But his presentation provides a particularly articulate type of a whole history of misreading. Subsequent generations of more direct and sustained studies of Origen's "allegorism" have generally vindicated Strauss's diagnosis, consciously or not. While scholarly judgments have generated a spectrum of evaluative rulings ranging from cautious yet laudatory retrievals to excoriating interdictions, there is a tendency for all parties to agree that the allegorical view presumes a transaction between the interpreter and the divine spirit alone.[17] This, of course, leaves Origen exposed. The question of literary form, therefore, does not resolve itself until it comes to a point in the question of literary formation. Origen's entire approach hangs in the balance.

Strauss's presentation of the topic provides a first and necessary step for dissuading readers from traveling a particularly well-worn dead end: locating Origen's figurative impulse solely in his own genius, rather than in the form of the narratives themselves.[18] Even if he ends up condemning

epoch that found its reflection in Jesus; each individual created Jesus in accordance with his own character. There is no historical task which so reveals a man's true self as the writing of a Life of Jesus." For a more frequently taken way to answer this accusation from an Origenian perspective, see H. Crouzel, *Origen* (1989), 83.

[17] Even those sympathetic to Origen's approach tend to argue for its coherence on reader-response, reception-historical, or theological grounds alone (for representative examples, cf. J. A. McGuckin, "Structural Design and Apologetic Intent in Origen's *Commentary on John*" [1995], esp. 442, and P. Kolbet, "Rethinking the Rationales for Origen's Use of Allegory" [2013]). See F. M. Young, *Biblical Exegesis*, 36: "Ancient literary criticism did not grasp the notion of an anachronistic reading, because it was essentially about reader reception and response" (cf. F. M. Young, "John and the Synoptics: An Historical Problem or a Theological Opportunity?" [2018]).

[18] So the "hellenizing," "platonizing" Origen "against history." I need not rehearse the frequently cited critiques here; a fine summary can be found in H. De Lubac, *History and Spirit*, 15–50. The modern prophets of this school remain E. De Faye and R. P. C. Hanson. De Faye considered Origen to be "really a religious philosopher far more than an interpreter of the Scriptures" who "imagines he is explaining Scriptures, whereas he is really exploiting them on behalf of his own dogmatic teaching" (*Origen and His Work* [1926], 38, 46; cf. E. A. Dively Lauro, *The Soul and Spirit of Scripture within Origen's Exegesis* [2005], 15–16). Hanson, similarly, concludes that on "countless occasions" Origen is guilty of "reading into the mind of the biblical author thoughts which are really his own" (*Allegory and Event*, 363). Following De Lubac, the most forceful counterpoint is P. W. Martens, "Origen against History? Reconsidering the Critique of Allegory" (2012). The accusation stretches back into the generations directly following Origen (and even his own); see De Lubac, *History and Spirit*, 23–33; see also Martens, "Origen Against History?" 652, n. 23 for a summary of Pamphilus of Caesarea's *Apology for Origen* (written c. 307–10 CE; see esp. §§87 and 122–26). Note also Diodore of Tarsus's (died c. 390 CE) perfectly distilled caricature of "allegory" in the

the Origenian approach with the same verdict ("unrestrained arbitrariness"), by disclosing the nearness of the mythical and allegorical views on the form of the Gospels (narratives that interweave things that didn't literally happen for the sake of depicting a spiritual truth or religious idea), Strauss opens a path forward by inviting the question of whether his particular construal of the allegorical view's way of explaining their formation ("immediate divine agency") adequately represents Origen's own position. Does Origen's sense of inspiration exclude ascribing the higher idea or religious representation – to which the Evangelists apparently conformed their narratives – "to that *natural* process by which legends are originated and developed" in "the spirit of a people or a community"? If not, the sentence of "unrestrained arbitrariness" may not be so inevitable, nor the ever-so-subtle disagreement between the mythical and allegorical views found where Strauss locates it.

3.2 THE SPIRIT OF THE EVANGELISTS: GOSPEL FORMATION IN THEORY

So then, by his own account, how does Origen explain the literary formation of the Gospels? And, thus, upon what does he base his figurative view? Like Strauss, Origen's order of argument moves fluidly from considering the critical difficulties occasioned by the literary form of the Gospels to addressing questions of formation that naturally follow. In Book 10 of his *Commentary on John*, Origen writes that if one neither shrinks from considering the Gospels to be true (in some sense) nor wishes to choose one over the others, then a careful examination of numerous passages – especially those narrating parallel events in contradictory ways – compels one to say that what is true about them must subsist in something other than strict historical facticity alone.[19] In other words, if one is willing to give the Gospels the benefit of the doubt by proposing

prologue to his *Commentary on the Psalms*, where the term simply denotes whatever erases the underlying sense of a text (followed by Theodore of Mopsuestia [c. 350–428 CE] in his *Commentary on Galatians* 4:24a and treatise *Against the Allegorists*; cf. D. T. Runia, *Philo in Early Christian Literature: A Survey* [1993], 265–69). Cf. J. Behr, *The Case Against Diodore and Theodore: Texts and their Contexts* (2011), 35–47. Even before Origen, it seems Celsus anticipated the substance of these criticisms (cf. *Cels.* 4.48–49, 51). For a variation on the theme in a contemporary key, see Dawson's response to both E. Auerbach and D. Boyarin's critiques of Origen in *Christian Figural Reading and the Fashioning of Identity*.

[19] See *Comm. Jo.* 10.3.14 (cited in Section 2.3).

that their departures from plain historicity result neither from passive mistakes nor active deception, then one must say that they arise in the course of endeavoring to depict something figuratively.[20] This quite natural critical judgment (unfolding with a certain syllogistic force) drives Origen, in the very next sentence, to look for an explanation in an equally natural source: the Evangelists' own purposes. The whole unified vision, I suggest, is expressed summarily in Origen's conviction that *the Evangelists were themselves figurative readers of the life of Jesus.*[21]

Origen proceeds to develop a thought experiment about four hypothetical authors "in order to grasp some notion of what the Evangelists were up to with respect to such matters" – namely, questions of how or why the Gospels took the form(s) they did.[22] Like his treatment of literary form in *On First Principles*, Origen sets about the thorny task of outlining what appears to be basic to all four writers. So the thought experiment is important (and labyrinthine) enough to cite and comment on at some length:

> Say that there are certain people who see in the spirit; and say that God reveals himself to them – becoming manifest in select seasons of their progress through the words he addresses to the holy and that mode of presence by which he draws near to them.[23]

It is not an overstatement to say that Origen's entire understanding of the Gospels emanates from this single insight: the Evangelists *see in the spirit* (βλέπουσι τῷ πνεύματι). Therefore, readers must be aware that matters as basic as capitalization can immediately flatten Origen's subtlety of expression here. In view of Strauss and the kind of misreading he typifies, I have decided to forgo capitalizing "spirit" not so as to suppress any reference to divine inspiration, but rather for fear of excluding Origen's rich sense of the human spirit, including its capacities for participating in divine spirit without any interruption of its natural activity. If anything, I think it is best to preserve what is likelier an intentional ambiguity. "The spirit itself testifies with our spirit."[24]

[20] Cf. *Comm. Jo.* 6.34.171; Origen does allow for mistakes (mostly text-critical) in the process of transmission (cf. *Comm. Matt.* 15.14, *Comm. Jo.* 6.40.204–6.41.211, *Hom. Ps.* 77 1.1, and *Comm. ser. Matt.* 117).

[21] On the Gospel writers as "readers," cf. M. Pierce, A. Byers, and S. Gathercole (eds.), *Gospel Reading and Reception in Early Christian Literature* (2022), i and throughout. Cf. S. Butler, *The Matter of the Page: Essays in Search of Ancient and Medieval Authors* (2011), 11. Cf. *Hom. Ps.* 15 2.1.

[22] *Comm. Jo.* 10.4.15.

[23] *Comm. Jo.* 10.4.15. I have followed Cécile Blanc's translation here (SC 157).

[24] Rom 8:16. For Origen's view of the "different meanings behind the designation 'spirit'" across the biblical writings, see *Comm. Rom.* 7.1.1–4. On the likelihood of a double

Origen elsewhere differentiates his sense of inspiration from other ancient models of poetic or oracular inspiration precisely by insisting on the preservation of the human spirit's natural integrity. In direct contrast to the manic ecstasies of Delphic priestesses, for example, Origen holds that the Jewish prophetic tradition rather bears witness to a kind of inspiration that was understood to intensify – and not suspend – each author's mental and spiritual capacities.[25] Origen's thought experiment in the *Commentary on John* operates according to a similar logic.[26] Through the life of Jesus, a certain vision of God – his words and presence with his people – began to lay itself before each of the Evangelists. Insofar as each Evangelist, in turn, lays this life before their readers as belonging to the words and presence of God (however various the ways and degrees[27]), they subordinated whatever was true about this life as a

entendre here, see *Comm. Rom.* 7.6.6: "There [Paul] calls his own spirit the holy spirit's grace that is given by God to humankind"; and *Comm. Jo.* 6.11.68: "If the God of the universe, having made himself belong [οἰκειωθείς] to those who are holy, becomes 'their' God … how much more will it be possible for the holy spirit, having made itself belong to the prophets, to be called *their* spirit, that the spirit might thus be said to be the 'spirit of Elisha' and the 'spirit of Isaiah'?" See similarly *Comm. Matt.* 13.2 (citing Rom 8:16, along with 1 Cor 2:11 just after) on "whether the 'spirit of Elijah' is the same thing as the 'spirit of God in Elijah' or if these are different from one another… For the apostle shows clearly that even though the spirit of God is in us, it is other than the spirit of each person which is in him where he says, 'The spirit itself testifies with our spirit.'"

25 In a kind of consummate prolepsis of the Thomistic principle "Grace does not destroy but rather perfects nature" (*Summa Theologiae* I, Q.I, A.8 ad 2), see Origen's comparison of the Jewish prophets with the priestesses at Delphi in *Cels.* 7.1–10. In *Cels.* 7.3, for example, Origen insists that "it is not the work of a divine spirit to lead [a person] into a state of ecstasy and frenzy so that [one] loses possession of [one's] consciousness. The person inspired by the divine spirit ought to … possess the clearest vision at the very time when the deity is in communion with him"; cf. *Cels.* 7.4: "Because of the touch, so to speak, of what is called the holy spirit upon their soul [the Jewish prophets] became clearer of mind and more radiant of soul… If the Pythian priestess is out of her senses and has no control of her faculties when she prophesies, what sort of spirit must we think it which poured darkness upon her mind and rational thinking?" Cf. also *Cels.* 7.7 and *Comm. Rom.* 7.5.4. See M. F. Wiles, "Origen as Biblical Scholar" (1970), esp. 462; cf. I. L. E. Ramelli, "Prophecy in Origen: Between Scripture and Philosophy" (2017). Cf. *Comm. Jo.* 28.20.171.

26 In keeping with the principle of a shared literary form between Jewish biblical narrative and Gospel narrative (Chapter 2), it is only fitting they should share a similar account of literary formation as well.

27 On the diversity of the four Evangelists' respective visions, cf. *Comm. Jo.* 1.4.22, which notes how Matthew, writing for a Jewish audience, fittingly begins his Gospel with "the book of the genealogy of Jesus the Christ, son of David, son of Abraham," whereas none of the other Gospel writers "displayed [Jesus's] divinity so absolutely as John, who presents him as saying, 'I am the light of the world'; 'I am the way, and the truth, and the life'; 'I am the resurrection'; 'I am the door'; 'I am the good shepherd,'" etc. See

matter of plain historical facticity to what had become available to them only as a kind of prophetic or spiritual vision.

Accordingly, Origen also attributes the individuation of the four Gospels, including their differences and disharmonies, to the individuation of experience, voice, and purpose natural to literary artifacts produced by four different authors. The thought experiment of the four authors "who see in the spirit" continues:

> And since there are several and they are in different places and have not been granted the same kinds of gifts in all the same ways, *each one in his own way relates what he sees in the spirit* about God and his words, as well as the ways he becomes manifest to the holy.[28]

Origen reinscribes the priority of "seeing in the spirit" now in order to ground the individuation of these narratives in the freedom of each author to relate what he has seen in his own "idiom" as it were (ἑκάστῳ ἰδίᾳ), according to the conditions of his own place and time, and subjected to the contingencies of his own experience and gifting. Thus the literary challenges Origen finds embedded within the very nature of the Gospel narratives – the features of individual pericopes that resist reduction to bare facticity, the differences and contradictions between parallel narratives – proceed from the priority of this prophetic or spiritual vision and are even intrinsic to the expression thereof.

According to the logic of the thought experiment, attributing the object of each author's experience to something divine does not render each subject's account artificially unmediated or univocal.[29] Rather, the nature of what these four hypothetical authors' writings purport to recount (divine self-revelation) becomes the very occasion for difference and individuation, since what these figures relate may be as individual and diverse as the individuality and diversity of each author's own

similarly *Comm. ser. Matt.* 92 (cf. *Hom. Luc.* 29.6), where Origen notes how Jesus's agony in Gethsemane is only recorded by Matthew, Mark, and Luke, "who also related Jesus's temptation by the devil"; John, on the other hand, "whose aim was to set Jesus forth as the divine word," does not "relate Jesus praying that the cup might pass from him, just as he does not relate Jesus's temptation" (though in counterpoint, cf. *Comm. Matt.* 12.6). See also *Comm. Jo.* 10.8.31–33 (treated in Section 3.3).

28 *Comm. Jo.* 10.4.15.

29 Cf. Strauss, *Life of Jesus*, §12. Origen's lifelong commitment to the unimpeachable freedom of every rational subject, developed so richly in *On First Principles*, remains just as richly operative here. Cf. K. A. Ecklebarger, "Authorial Intention as a Guiding Principle in Origen's Matthew Commentary" (1987), 101.

understanding and experience thereof, multiplied by what is recorded to have been variously said and done and revealed and accomplished by God in various places for various people.[30]

Let us remind ourselves of the overarching purpose of Origen's methodological digression. Upon discovering numerous inconsistencies and impossibilities throughout the Gospel narratives, Origen has set out to articulate how the Gospels can still be considered to be "true" if not with regard to pure historical facticity. For these purposes, then, his thought experiment imagines a situation even more extreme than what we find in the case of the four Gospels. Origen amplifies all occasions for historical contradiction in order to theorize (κατὰ τὴν ὑπόθεσιν) that even in such a case as this – where the narratives of four different authors are such that God is said to have become manifest to different people in various ways for diverse purposes even in far distant places *all at the same time* – there would still be a way to understand an underlying agreement.[31] That is, however much some of the things related by them "deviate from each other on other matters," the narratives can still be said to agree about "some of the things intimated to them by the spirit" – that is, they may "agree" at least insofar as they relate "true things about God and what he confers."[32]

We see, once again, how modest Origen's general principles are. It is important to remember that he has not yet returned the thought experiment to the specific horizon of the Evangelists. The hyperbole of the thought experiment asks the reader to consider a question logically one step prior to Origen's argument for the sense in which the Gospels, in

30 Cf. *Comm. Jo.* 10.4.15: "Such that one would relate certain things which were said and done by God for one righteous man in one location, and another would report things that were revealed to and accomplished for another, and another might want to teach us about a third besides the two previously mentioned. And say that there is also a fourth who does something analogous to the other three about someone else…"

31 Cf. *Comm. Jo.* 10.4.15–16 (emphasis added): Say that "God appeared to so-and-so at this time in this place, and that he has done these things to him as follows: he was made manifest to him in such-and-such a figure [τῷ σχήματι] and led him to this place where he did these things"; then "let the second [author] relate that God appeared *at the same time* as what is said to have happened in the first report, in some city, to a second person who is in a *place far removed from that* of the first, and let him record that other words were spoken, at the same time, to him whom, in the thought experiment [τὴν ὑπόθεσιν], we have taken to be a second person. Then conceive of something similar vis-à-vis the third and fourth…"

32 *Comm. Jo.* 10.4.15, 17.

particular, agree: what does it mean for any author to narrate the actions of God in history – or rather more precisely, to narrate historical events to be of God? Can attributing something to spirit arise from anything other than a spiritual vision?[33] To paraphrase Origen's answer: "we can *at least* say that these writers can agree about what they say about God and what he is and does for his people"; historical disagreement does not entail theological discord. Must the whole truth of a narrative be called into question, Origen asks bluntly, if one author depicts God standing while saying and doing something but another depicts him sitting?[34]

The absurdity of the question allows Origen to pose his alternative with more gravity: if, on the other hand, one imagines that these hypothetical authors had "intended to teach what they had perceived in their own mind by way of a figure" (χαρακτήρ), then, once one has "thoroughly grasped what is meant by what they have narrated in a historical fashion," one would no longer find any discord (διαφωνία).[35] Thus Origen furnishes his reader with another (and to the modern reader, perhaps clearer) way of articulating what he means by "seeing in the spirit": namely, that which is perceived in their own understanding.[36] In other words, one may think of

[33] In more philosophical terms: can a judgment about something non-material, something "intelligible," be anything other than a matter of one's own understanding, or "intellectual" judgment? In other words: does attributing something to God ultimately belong to anything other than a theological judgment?

[34] *Comm. Jo.* 10.4.17. [35] *Comm. Jo.* 10.5.18.

[36] *Comm. Jo.* 10.5.18: τὰ ὑπὸ τοῦ νοῦ αὐτῶν τεθεωρημένα. In the simplest sense, perceiving something "spiritually" or "intelligibly" simply means discerning something above and beyond matters of sensory observation or material facticity (see Section 4.5 for more on this subject). For Origen, νοῦς designates the whole range of what, in human experience, exceeds the merely "animate" (ψυχικός, designating the principle of movement and sensation in any "animate" thing, including humans but also, eponymously, "animals"; cf. *Princ.* 2.8.2 and 2.8.5); νοῦς can refer to the mind's discursive capacities, but also includes the whole unified experience of human consciousness (memory, judgment, understanding, vision, etc.). For Origen, the act of knowing and the objects of knowing (goodness, mercy, justice, wisdom, love, etc.) could never be construed as material phenomena (What does justice taste like? How much does wisdom weigh?); they are objects of the intellect, *intelligible* realities, the objects of what Origen calls the "intellective sense," not divorced from materiality but formative of (our perception of) it (cf. *Princ.* 1.1.7). Thus, insofar as "soul" language properly pertains to that which humans share with animal life, Origen, following a Pauline distinction, associates πνεῦμα most nearly with that which belongs to νοῦς: "For if *the animate [animalis] human being does not receive the things of the spirit of God* and, due to the fact that he is animal [*animalis*], is unable to receive an understanding [*intelligentiam*] of a better nature, that is, of the divine, it is perhaps for this reason that Paul, wishing to teach us more plainly what it is through which we are able to understand [*intellegere*] the things of the spirit [*spiritus*], that is, spiritual things [*spiritalia*], joins and associates the mind [*mentem*],

the writings of these hypothetical authors as historical narrative (ἱστορία), yes, but one that also sets out to portray what they have "seen in the spirit" by way of depicting it historically (εἰκὼν ἱστορική).[37]

Thus Origen finally returns to the Gospel writers. "It is in this way," he concludes, "that we should think of the four Evangelists." For they "made full use of many of the things that were said and done," always doing so in a manner in keeping with the "portentous and startling nature of Jesus's power," but in some places also "interweaving their writing with language that would make it seem that something made clear to them in a purely interior way was perceptible to the senses."[38] The language of "making use" (καταχράομαι) is striking on several counts. Firstly, its rather astonishing lexical range can have connotations of "misuse" and "abuse" (hardly at play here) and so can be translated as strongly as: the Evangelists "did what they liked with" the raw data of the life of Jesus available to them. Secondly, it vindicates Strauss's claim that the mythical and the allegorical views agree at least insofar as they both take each Evangelist to have "related that which is seemingly historical," but "under the influence of a higher inspiration ... *to have made use of this historical semblance*" for his own ends.[39]

Thirdly, and most importantly, Origen expresses himself here in a way nearly identical to a passage in *On First Principles*, but with one crucial difference. What he says of the Evangelists in the *Commentary on John* he first said of the divine word in *On First Principles*:

> Wherever the word found that things that happened historically could be adapted for such mysteries, *it made use of them* [ἐχρήσατο], concealing from many their

rather than the soul [*animam*], with the holy spirit. For this, I think, he indicates when he says, *I will pray with the spirit and I will pray with the mind also; I will sing a psalm with the spirit and I will sing a psalm with the mind also*" (*Princ.* 2.8.2, citing 1 Cor 2:14 and 14:14). Thus one can see the inadequacy of "mind" or "intellect" to translate all that Origen means by νοῦς; Origen himself seemed to be aware of how the term could be over-intellectualized and so identifies νοῦς with the more biblical language of "heart" (καρδία). See *Princ.* 1.1.9 on Matt 5:8: "what else is 'seeing God' in the heart than, as we have explained above, to understand and to know him with the mind? [...] That the intellect (that is, the 'intellectual') is indeed called *heart*, you will find abundantly in all the scriptures, both old and new." My translations will attempt to preserve this richer sense of νοῦς in Origen's thought (cf. *Comm. Rom.* 2.7.36–37).

[37] *Comm. Jo.* 10.4.17: Δόξει τοίνυν τῷ ἱστορίαν εἶναι νομίζοντι τὴν τούτων γραφήν, ἢ διὰ εἰκόνος ἱστορικῆς πρόσθοιτ' ἂν παραστῆσαι τὰ πράγματα. Cf. *Princ.* 4.3.1.

[38] *Comm. Jo.* 10.5.18: προσυφανάντων τῇ γραφῇ μετὰ λέξεως ὡς περὶ αἰσθητῶν τὸ καθαρῶς νοητῶς αὐτοῖς τετρανωμένον.

[39] Strauss, *Life of Jesus*, §12 (emphasis added).

deeper sense; but wherever the actions of certain individuals here – recorded for more mysterious purposes – were not suitable for the coherence of the ideas in the narrative, scripture interweaves the historical narrative with things that didn't happen.[40]

One could make too much of the fact that Book 10 of the *Commentary on John* appears to have been written sometime after *On First Principles*, though a development in Origen's thought on the matter (or at least his way of writing about it) should not be discounted.[41] In any case, the main point is that Origen was capable of accounting for the Gospels' formation from two different causal vantages, each unfolding naturally, indivisibly, yet without confusion or interruption of the other. In other words, *pace* Strauss, Origen can explain the same phenomenon – the Evangelists' freedom to make use of the Jesus tradition for their own purposes and in accordance with their own ideas – from the vantage of the absolute cause: the divine word inspiring them to do so in accordance with its own purposes.[42]

In sum, the thought experiment helps us to continue to fill out what Origen means in the programmatic passage from *Against Celsus* introduced in Chapter 2: "the whole truth" of the Gospels is not "perceived merely in the letter of what is recorded to have happened to Jesus" because the Evangelists shaped their narratives around what they had come to understand of this life – not relating the bare facts of it alone, but

40 *Princ.* 4.2.9 (cf. *Cels.* 4.44). When Origen speaks of how the narratives record the actions of certain people "for the sake of more mysterious things ... concealing from many the deeper sense" there is no more need to think of this as a "gnosticizing" tendency than there is to consider the "patterns of indirection" already intrinsic to the Gospels to be "gnostic" (cf. R. B. Hays, *Echoes of Scripture in the Gospels* [2017], 60 and throughout).

41 Cf. Watson, *Gospel Writing*, 547–50.

42 In more technical terms, Origen develops a non-competitive account of primary and secondary causality. Even if the thought experiment begins by evoking the transcendent or absolute cause of the hypothetical authors' vision(s) ("God, his words, his presence"), the thought experiment never fractures the horizon of secondary (instrumental) causes. In Origen's view, the absolute cause never interrupts the natural processes of literary formation, but rather both transcends them and remains radically interior to them, and makes itself known only *through* them. This view neither banishes nor diminishes the absolute priority of the primary cause of the Gospels, and really, all of Christian scripture, for Origen (that is, the divine spirit), while simultaneously preserving the integrity of the chain of finite causes, through which the absolute cause, in Strauss's language, "manifests itself" (cf. *Life of Jesus*, §16). There is for Origen, after all, no such thing as "unmediated" divine revelation (cf. *Life of Jesus*, §12: "unmittelbar der göttliche selbst"). Origen would find Strauss's antithesis between "divine agency" and the "spirit of a people or a community" nonsensical; the "natural process" of literary formation is itself rooted in the spirit of God (*Life of Jesus*, §12).

what they had come to perceive of "the truth about God" and what he confers on his people through and by way of this life.[43] Can a narrative only be true if it is perfectly transparent to an empirical event? If one thinks so then, Origen warns, the more familiar one becomes with the Gospels the more one will think them false.

Instead, Origen proposes that the Evangelists wrote with something more than mere historical transcripts in view – something, as he says, they had "seen in the spirit." It is this "something," to take up the language of *Against Celsus* again, of which the "things recorded to have happened to Jesus" became emblematic.[44] The life of Jesus signified something to the Gospel writers (however "inexpressible"[45]), so they composed their narratives in such a way as to capture and communicate what they had come to understand about this life, and thus, by interweaving "things that seem historical but didn't physically happen," so to "disclose certain mysteries" of this life in a figurative way (τροπικῶς).[46]

What I hope is impressed upon the reader most of all – here now and increasingly in coming chapters – is Origen's sense of the profound freedom of the Evangelists *vis-à-vis* the life of Jesus. The Evangelists looked upon the life of Jesus and came to understand it "each in his own way."[47] They, in turn, narrated his "deeds, sufferings, and words" in such a way as to communicate their significance – a manner of writing that Origen calls "figurative." And so, Origen presents the Evangelists as having been themselves "figurative readers" of the life of Jesus. They narrated what they had come to perceive in their own minds; they invested their narratives of his life with figures in order to confer what they had seen "in the spirit."[48] And the spirit in which they saw, the spirit which they sought to confer within the very form of their records, is what Christians "call the holy spirit."[49]

So even if one believes each Evangelist's consciousness was "touched, so to speak," by what Christians call the holy spirit, this touch only becomes manifest in and as a further clarifying of their own understanding.[50] But what they saw, and thus what they related, cannot be said to

43 *Cels.* 2.69 and *Comm. Jo.* 10.4.15. 44 *Cels.* 2.69: σύμβολόν τινος.

45 Or ἀπόρρητον, in Origen's language; cf. *Fr. Prov.* 1.6, and *Cels.* 5.31 and 6.2.

46 Cf. *Comm. Jo.* 10.4.15 and 10.5.18, along with *Princ.* 4.3.1: οὐκ οἶμαι διστάξειν τινὰ περὶ τοῦ αὐτὰ τροπικῶς διὰ δοκούσης ἱστορίας καὶ οὐ σωματικῶς γεγενημένης μηνύειν τινὰ μυστήρια.

47 *Comm. Jo.* 10.4.15.

48 *Comm. Jo.* 10.5.18 (and, as we will see in Chapter 5, *pace* Strauss, in the spirit of their community – that is, the spirit of the church).

49 Cf. *Cels.* 7.4. 50 Cf. *Cels.* 7.4.

have been present to them in a conspicuous totality, but disclosed itself progressively, in accord with the "seasons of their own progress."[51] There is no question of an "immediate divine agency" (as Strauss puts it) impinging upon the natural processes of literary formation here.[52] Those "who saw in the spirit" rather engaged in active reflection upon what had been seen and heard of the one whose life they shared. In and through the formation of their narratives, one finds their own progress, their own development, their own renovation and even innovation reflected in the very form of their narratives. The formation of the Gospels is the formation of the Evangelists.

Why, Origen asks of his readers, should we be scandalized by their freedom?

> But I do not condemn them, I suppose, for taking something that happened in a different way (as far as history is concerned) and changing it in some way or another for the sake of the mysterious aim they had in view; such that they have spoken of something that happened in a certain place as though it happened in another, or something at this time as though it happened at another, and so, precisely in this way, to have composed what they relate with certain alterations of their own.[53]

Origen walks back the hyperbole of his thought experiment. The agreement of the Evangelists, it seems, does not *only* subsist in a unity of spirit or harmony of ideas.[54] They all draw, in some way or another, on memories of the same life.[55] And so the substance of their narratives is derived, for the most part, from historical events – however altered and rearranged. Nevertheless, one can now recognize even more clearly how full of dimension Origen's sense of "memory"-related language is: more than a mere recollection of bare facts, the Gospels are, rather, the Evangelists' own "commentaries" (ὑπομνήματα) on the life of Jesus.[56]

51 *Comm. Jo.* 10.4.15.

52 *Life of Jesus*, §12. And so, for all its value, Strauss's "essential distinction" loses its footing.

53 *Comm. Jo.* 10.5.19: πρὸς τὸ χρήσιμον τοῦ <τού>των μυστικοῦ σκοποῦ. Cf. *Comm. Jo.* 32.2.11.

54 One may recall here Origen's discussion of the "mixed" nature of Gospel narrative in *Princ.* 4.2.9 and 4.3.4 (treated in Sections 2.2 and 2.5, respectively).

55 Cf. Section 2.5 on Origen's memory-related language.

56 Cf. R. E. Brown, *The Death of the Messiah, Vol. I*, 514: "the Gospels are in a sense commentaries on Jesus." Cf. S. Byrskog, "From Memory to Memoirs: Tracing the Background of a Literary Genre" (2012), esp. 9. For intriguing parallels in contemporary applications of memory theory to the Gospels, see J. D. G. Dunn, *Christianity in the Making, Vol. 1: Jesus Remembered* (2003); D. Allison, *Constructing*

To see in the events of Jesus's life something more than a series of empirical facts is to "see in the spirit" – or at least to have begun to. And to see in the Evangelists' narratives something more than a series of empirical recollections is to see with *their* spirit – or at least to have begun to.

"For," Origen concludes, the Evangelists' intention was "to speak the truth spiritually and materially at the same time wherever possible." Nevertheless, it is what they "saw in the spirit" that presided over all, such that "wherever it was not possible for both," they showed "a preference for the spiritual over the material, often preserving what was *spiritually* true in, one might say, the material falsehood."[57] Just as the authors in the thought experiment, the Evangelists above, before, and through all "intended to teach in figures what they had come to perceive in their own understanding."[58] For, Origen intimates, the Gospel writers subordinated their own commitments to strict historicity under the ensign of some more "mysterious aim."[59]

3.3 THE ONE AND THE MANY

"Therefore," Origen continues directly after his thought experiment on the four authors, "Jesus too is πολλά ταῖς ἐπινοίαις."[60] English resists the phrase. It means something like "therefore there are also many ways to think of" or "a multitude of ways to conceive of" Jesus, but the direct predication roots this multiplicity more nearly in the figure of Jesus himself. Ὁ Ἰησοῦς πολλά ἐστιν: *Jesus is a multitude with respect to ways of thinking of him; he is manifold in aspect.*

Moreover, this multiplicity – even to the point of disagreement – does not limit itself to the figure of Jesus alone, "but also with respect to the disciples … there is a certain discord in how they are described."[61] For the Peter of John is conceived of quite differently than the Peter of Matthew and Mark.[62] Similarly, "John the Baptist, in the Evangelist with the same name, holds out for a long time before he is cast into prison.

Jesus; and C. Keith, "Social Memory Theory and Gospels Research: The First Decade" (2015). Cf. T. Thatcher, "Why John Wrote a Gospel: Memory and History in an Early Christian Community" (2005), esp. 85.

57 *Comm. Jo.* 10.5.20. 58 Cf. *Comm. Jo.* 10.5.18.

59 *Comm. Jo.* 10.5.19: μυστικός σκοπός. Cf. B. McGinn, "Mystical Consciousness: A Modest Proposal," *Spiritus* 8.1 (2008), 44–63, esp. 46.

60 *Comm. Jo.* 10.5.21. 61 *Comm. Jo.* 10.8.31.

62 See *Comm. Jo.* 10.8.31–33: τῇ ἐπινοίᾳ ἕτερός.

In Matthew, however, he is cast into prison around the time of Jesus's temptation. For this reason too, Jesus withdraws into Galilee, to avoid being put in prison. But in John, the Baptist is not even found to have been delivered to prison."[63] Even Paul, the very one who confessed to having become "all things to all," looks different to the reader, for example, when he writes to the Corinthians compared to the way he is depicted in Acts.[64]

The heart of Origen's teaching on the "*epinoiai* of Christ" is thus, I take it, rather simpler than it is sometimes made out to be.[65] Jesus was, is, and always will be one who appears to the world as "many things." Even today, as Dale Allison remarks, "there is more than one Jesus... Jesus is not one but many ... like Odysseus in the first line of the *Odyssey*, he is πολύτροπος, a 'man of many turns,' of remarkable versatility, who appears now like this, now like that."[66] In short: ὁ Ἰησοῦς πολλά ἐστιν – Jesus is many things, a multitude. And it is from out of this very multitude of conceptions (ὧν ἐπινοιῶν), Origen goes on, that "the Evangelists seem to have recorded their Gospels, taking up differing notions while also agreeing about certain others."[67]

We now have at our disposal the conceptual resources necessary for challenging Strauss's charge of "unrestrained arbitrariness," in contrast to the mythical approach, which, he says, "searches out the ideas which are embodied in the narrative" and is "controlled by regard to conformity with the spirit and modes of representation of the people and of the age."[68] By Origen's own account, when offering exemplary expressions of his view of the Gospels' formation, he turns to paradigms from within the New Testament itself. What he means by inviting readers to "ascend from the events recorded to have happened to the things which they signified" thus remains to be seen.[69]

For this most delicate of questions, it is best to return to the very beginnings of Origen's section in *On First Principles* on "how to read

[63] *Comm. Jo.* 10.8.35 (cf. John 3:24). For Origen's extended discussion of this matter with respect to the Gospels' contradictory timelines, see *Comm. Jo.* 10.3.10–14.

[64] See *Comm. Jo.* 10.7.28–30 (citing 1 Cor 9:19–22, a favorite passage of Origen's).

[65] For more traditional ways of treating the concept, see R. E. Heine, "Epinoiai" (2004), 93–95; J. A. McGuckin, "Changing Forms of Jesus" (1987). Cf. *Comm. Jo.* 6.19.107, 6.43.222, and *Cels.* 2.64.

[66] D. Allison, *The Historical Christ and the Theological Jesus*, 45–46 (and explicitly tied to Origen on p. 47).

[67] *Comm. Jo.* 10.5.21. [68] *Life of Jesus*, §12.

[69] *Cels.* 2.69: ὧν τὰ γενόμενα ἦν σημαντικά. Cf. *Comm. Jo.* 1.7.40.

scripture" in order to discover the primordial source of his sense of the Gospels' principally figurative nature. The cause, he writes, for anyone's misapprehension of Christian belief appears to be "nothing other than scripture not being understood spiritually, but rather received only as far as the bare letter goes."[70] But note how he mounts his argument for this claim. For such readers, including many of Jesus's own day,

> accustomed to following the letter of the prophecies ... and not seeing him visibly *proclaiming release to the captives*, nor building up what they consider to be truly a *city of God*, nor *cutting off the chariots from Ephraim and the horse from Jerusalem*, nor *eating butter and honey, and before knowing or preferring evil, choosing the good*; and thinking it was prophesied that the *wolf* ... was *to feed with the lamb and the leopard to lie down with the kid, the calf and the bull and the lion to feed together, being led by a little child, and the ox and the bear to pasture together, their young ones growing up together, and the lion to eat straw like the ox* – seeing none of these things visibly happening in the advent of him believed by us to be the Christ, they did not accept our Lord Jesus, but crucified him as having improperly called himself the Christ.[71]

The basic logic of Origen's position is unmistakable, and, as a matter of his own self-presentation, the terms of his argument are indisputable. Origen's commitment to a figurative sense or "spiritual understanding" of the life of Jesus, in the first instance, has nothing to do with extrinsic philosophical pressures or with deeming any arbitrary thought "worthy of God."[72] It originates in the question of how Jesus was ever called "Christ" at all. Therefore, for present purposes, one may defer disagreements over whether Origen's approach is platonist or dualist or dissolves history or disparages the material world (etc.) in the abstract as almost entirely beside the point.[73] The fundamental claim still stands: for many, then and now, Jesus of Nazareth did not appear to be a Messiah. Origen allows even stronger phrasing: in many respects, Jesus did not demonstrably bring about what major strains of Jewish prophetic expectation seemed to await; in certain distinct ways, he was not a literal "Messiah"

70 *Princ.* 4.2.2.

71 *Princ.* 4.2.1 (citing Isa 61:1; Ezek 48:15–35; Ps 45:5; Zech 9:10; Isa 7:15; Isa 11:6–7). For a more detailed exposition of this argument (focusing on Zech 9:10), see Section 6.4 on the ascent to Jerusalem.

72 Strauss, *Life of Jesus*, §12. Though on other occasions and in other contexts Origen feels free to speculate in a more wide-ranging manner (interpretively, theologically, and philosophically), these more extravagant kinds of readings are patently not the ground of his approach.

73 Cf. Crouzel, *Origen*, 62.

at all. Suddenly the conditional *secundum litteram* makes all the difference.[74]

From the beginning, Jesus was conceived of in at least two ways: he was either confessed to be "the Christ" or he was not.[75] Yet if the former, he was destined to become an occasion for dispute, for reinterpreting the very idea of "Messiah" in a multitude of ways.[76] Put negatively: Origen freely acknowledges that Jesus cannot be said to be the "Christ" in an obviously "visible" or "literal" sense. If, having fulfilled every other prophecy, this man had literally ascended the Davidic throne, had literally released the whole people from captivity and gathered to himself all the dispersed children of Israel bodily, and had wolves literally eaten with lambs under a rule visibly "established forever," who could have doubted?[77] This is decidedly not what the Gospels proclaim. Phrased positively: Origen avows that Jesus's life brings a whole range of Jewish prophetic expectations to a kind of "fullness" only when (both become) understood – principally, though not exclusively – "spiritually."[78]

In this way, we may scatter light onto a passage that has perennially suffered a great deal of obfuscation: "What lies before us now is to

74 What Origen means by the Evangelists "preserving a spiritual truth in a material falsehood" also contains this dynamic (*Comm. Jo.* 10.5.20; cited in Section 3.2). Understanding how one can say that Jesus both is and isn't a Messiah explains the digression about Jacob and Esau in this section as well: literally speaking, Jacob wasn't Isaac's firstborn; nevertheless, he was (or became) Isaac's "firstborn" in another sense. On a kind of spiritualizing of the "messianic idea" in ancient Judaism, see I. Knohl, *The Messiah Confrontation: Pharisees Versus Sadducees and the Death of Jesus* (2022), 51–52. Cf. M. Novenson, *The Grammar of Messianism: An Ancient Jewish Political Idiom and Its Users* (2017), 187–216.

75 Cf. *Comm. Jo.* 10.5.21: ὁ Ἰησοῦς τοίνυν πολλά ἐστιν ταῖς ἐπινοίαις.

76 One cannot question the prescience of at least one New Testament prophecy, Origen notes: "Behold, this one is destined to be a sign that is contradicted" (Luke 2:34; ἀντιλεγόμενον can also be translated *disputed* or *contested*). Cf. *Hom. Luc.* 17.4–6 on how there is almost nothing narrated about Jesus's life that is not contested in some way: for instance, the narrative of the virginal conception is a "sign that is contradicted" by those who "insist that he was not born of a woman" and by those who "say that he was born of a man and a woman in the same way as we are born"; similarly, the recounting of Jesus's resurrection is "beset with various arguments and is 'a sign that is contradicted': How did he rise? Was he just as he was when he died, or did he undoubtedly rise in a body belonging to a higher reality? There is endless contention on this point." Even the idea that "he was foretold by the prophets is 'a sign that is contradicted'"; for there are many "who assert that he was simply not foretold by the prophets." In sum, "everything that the plain narrative recounts about him is 'a sign that is contradicted.'"

77 2 Sam 7:16; cf. *Princ.* 4.2.1.

78 Cf. *Princ.* 4.2.2. For a fuller treatment of Origen on prophetic "fulfillment," see Section 6.4.

translate what is immediately apparent in the Gospel into what is spiritual. For what is the narrative of something immediately apparent unless it is translated into something spiritual? It is good for nothing, or for very little."[79] What does it mean to translate what is straightforwardly "perceptible" or "empirical" in these narratives into what is "spiritual"?[80] The whole account of Origen as a reader of the Gospels hangs on this question. Yet once again, it is necessary to realize how ordinary Origen's essential point is. After all, he uses the same language (μεταλαμβάνω) when describing how one will miss the entire purpose of a parable if one does not "translate" what happens in the story into whatever the parable is meant to "indicate figuratively."[81] He is clear that one can only distinguish what is "empirical" from what is "spiritual" in the Gospels upon reflection.[82] The object remains one and the same for all: the life of Jesus – his deeds, sufferings, and words. But how does one see this life? And how was this life seen by the Evangelists themselves? As noted in the preceding section, as soon as one has begun to discern in these narratives something more than a mere recollection of facts, the translation has already begun; or rather, one has begun to recognize a translation that is already present within the Gospel writings themselves.[83]

3.4 NEW TESTAMENT PARADIGMS

The first instance of such a "translation" Origen provides could not be simpler: of all the good things the Gospels are understood to proclaim, the

[79] *Comm. Jo.* 1.8.45 (even if people commonly think, he goes on to say, they receive what is made known there without any such "translation"). For the language of "spiritual Gospel," cf. the fragment from Clement of Alexandria's *Hypotyposeis* preserved in Eusebius, *Hist. eccl.* 6.14.7.

[80] *Comm. Jo.* 1.8.45: τὸ αἰσθητὸν εὐαγγέλιον μεταλαβεῖν εἰς πνευματικόν.

[81] *Fr. Prov.* 1.6 (which, as he clarifies, does not always imply a judgment about facticity; cf. *Cels.* 5.42). On relating "allegory" vs. "parable" language vis-à-vis the Gospels (including a view of the Evangelists as "allegorical interpreters"), cf. J. P. Meier, *A Marginal Jew: Rethinking the Historical Jesus, Vol. 5: Probing the Authenticity of the Parables* (2016), 82–88. The language of *metalepsis* has made something of a comeback in contemporary New Testament scholarship, albeit in a slightly different, more narrowly defined way, via Hays' *Echoes of Scripture in the Gospels* and *Echoes of Scripture in the Letters of Paul* (1989), which draw on J. Hollander, *The Figure of Echo: A Mode of Allusion in Milton and After* (1981).

[82] Or "conceptually" (*Comm. Jo.* 1.8.44: τῇ ἐπινοίᾳ διακρίνοντες).

[83] Cf. *Comm. Jo.* 10.5.18 on how the Evangelists "interwove their writing with language that would make it seem that something made clear to them in a purely interior way was perceptible to the senses."

apostles, first of all, "proclaim Jesus."[84] The primal moment of "spiritual understanding," therefore, is as simple as coming to see this life as something good (ὡς ἀγαθόν) to begin with. The category "spiritual" therefore includes any judgment about or account of who Jesus was and what his life signified, matters which – precisely *as* judgments or accounts – are in this sense "intelligible," "immaterial," not (just) matters of sensory or empirical perception. Since the Gospels narrate, inextricably, both "what happened" and particular ways of understanding what happened, then interpreting them properly means "endeavoring to grasp" their "*whole* sense."[85]

Thereafter, Origen continues,

> it is possible to collect ten thousand times as many titles that the son of God is called in the Gospels and by the apostles ... whether it be those who wrote the Gospels *setting out their own idea of what he is* or the apostles praising him *on the basis of what they had learned.*[86]

Origen's approach, above and before all, seeks simply what the Evangelists themselves first learned to "see in the spirit," in "their own understanding." Thus, first and foremost, "translating the perceptible Gospel into the spiritual" means discerning the diverse ways of conceiving of Jesus that the Gospel writers themselves had drawn on and begun to set forth in their narratives; it means learning to see the life of Jesus with them.[87]

Even calling this approach "spiritual reading" or "spiritual interpretation" lacks something of the subtlety of Origen's expression, whose preferred phrasing also means something nearer to *receiving* the Gospel(s) as spiritual (πνευματική ἐκδοχή).[88] As noted already, merely receiving Jesus as the Christ necessarily involves, for Origen, a spiritual "translation" of certain prophetic expectations. And though ordinary Christians

84 *Comm. Jo.* 1.8.47.

85 See *Princ.* 4.3.5: "When the coherence [of a passage], literally speaking, is impossible, yet the *principal* [sense] is not impossible but even true, one must endeavor to grasp the *whole sense*, which draws together in a coherent way the account of things impossible according to the letter with things not only not impossible but even true in the historical narrative, by taking *in an entirely figurative way* whatever didn't happen in a literal sense. For our position is that with respect to the whole of divine scripture, all of it has a spiritual sense, but not all of it has a physical sense, for there are many places where a physical sense is proved to be impossible." This accords with what Origen means by coming to perceive the "*whole* truth of the things recorded to have happened to Jesus" in *Cels.* 2.69.

86 *Comm. Jo.* 1.22.136.

87 Cf. *Comm. Jo.* 10.5.21.

88 Cf. *Comm. Jo.* 10.6.27.

might think that receiving Jesus as "Lord" is a matter deducible from the letter of his life alone, Origen reminds his readers that one cannot even say this "except by the holy spirit."[89]

So in order to make a way into the great struggle of "trying to reach into the depths of the evangelical understanding and search out the bare truth of the figures therein," Origen provides several paradigmatic examples of this translation of the life of Jesus interior to the New Testament authors themselves.[90] For Origen, the Pauline *kerygma* consists in a decisively spiritualized vision of Christ's passion, death, and resurrection. Paul's writings already offer a translation of what was immediately apparent about Jesus's life into a kind of "spiritual Gospel." It is one thing to know that Jesus was crucified; it is quite another to receive "Jesus Christ and him crucified" as the "power of God and the wisdom of God." It is one thing to acknowledge the fact of Jesus's death; it is quite another to see in this death a death "to sin," a death "once for all."[91] What of proclaiming that he has become "righteousness for us from God, and holiness, and redemption"?[92] These are not empirical claims, not visibly or materially demonstrable truths; they are ways of seeing the same deeds, sufferings, and words of Jesus "in the spirit."

Even at its most extravagant, Origen's vision of the Gospels – in principle – never exceeds the breadth and depth of spiritual "reading" that he takes to be already interior to the Pauline corpus. In fact, Origen turns to this exact dynamism in Paul as he begins to explain what he means (in the programmatic passage from *Against Celsus* introduced in Chapter 2) by saying that what is recorded to have happened to Jesus was written to "signify something": what could it mean for one to be crucified, buried, and raised with Christ? For one to crucify one's passions and desires? For the world to be crucified?[93] Origen understands that Paul's entire proclamation of salvation through participation "in Christ" hangs together by understanding his passion to have implicated the whole cosmos, from the very elemental structures of reality to the innermost depths of the human heart.[94] In other words, a radically universalized and

[89] Cf. *Comm. Jo.* 1.8.45 and 32.32.399 (citing 1 Cor 12:3).

[90] *Comm. Jo.* 1.8.46.

[91] Cf. *Comm. Jo.* 1.9.58–59 (citing 1 Cor 1:23–24 and Rom 6:10) and 1.9.55–56.

[92] *Comm. Jo.* 1.9.59 (citing 1 Cor 1:30). Cf. *Comm. Jo.* 1.22.140. One could add seeing Christ as an "atoning sacrifice," "advocate," or "great high priest" (Rom 3:25, 1 John 2:2, and Heb 4:14, as referenced in *Comm. Jo.* 1.22.139, 1.33.240–41, 1.35.255, and 1.36.261). Cf. M. M. Mitchell, *Paul, the Corinthians and the Birth of Christian Hermeneutics* (2010), 51–53.

[93] See *Cels.* 2.69 (citing Gal 2:20 and 6:14, Rom 6:10, Phil 3:10, 2 Tim 2:11, and Rom 6:4).

[94] Cf. Gal 4:3–7, 5:24–25.

interiorized (that is to say, *spiritual*) vision of the life of Jesus, and particularly his death and resurrection, belongs already to the apostle Paul. One way of "translating" the perceptible Gospel into the spiritual, for Origen, is learning to see with Paul how this life could somehow be "for me," "for us," and "for the world."

But what of the Gospel writers themselves? The "translations" summarized in the first book of the *Commentary on John* are perhaps the most obvious: to say that Jesus is the "true light" of the world that enlightens all people, or the "way" and the "truth" and the "life," or the "resurrection," or the divine "word" made flesh – all of these are ways of coming to see him "in the spirit."[95] Yet even the heights of these Johannine "translations" are not without parallels in the other Gospel writers. Origen also highlights distinctly Matthean and Lukan ways of "seeing in the spirit." For when Matthew records Jesus's declaration "what you did to these, you did to me," Origen senses the entire horizon of his narrative breaking open, as "every deed we perform for our neighbor" – good or evil – "is taken up into the Gospel."[96] Or again, in a Lukan vein: why have "Judas's betrayal and the outcry of the impious people who said, 'Away with such a one from the earth!' and 'Crucify, crucify him!'" and other "things like these been included in the Gospels"?[97] So that readers may come to understand that "everyone who betrays Jesus's disciples has been counted a betrayer of Jesus. For he said to Saul, while he was still persecuting, 'Saul, Saul, why do you persecute me?' and 'I am Jesus whom you are persecuting.'"[98]

So interpreting the Gospels "spiritually" means, in one sense, not confusing what the Evangelists narrate figuratively for matters of transparent facticity. Yet in another, fuller sense, the kind of "spiritual understanding" Origen believes the Gospels ask of their readers consists in

95 Cf. *Comm. Jo.* 1.9.53–54, 57 (citing John 8:12, 1:9, 1:4, 14:6, 11:25). Similarly, in *Comm. Jo.* 1.8.47, Origen notes how John's Gospel proclaims that "the resurrection *is* Jesus in some way, for Jesus says, 'I am the resurrection.'" See also the lengthy section beginning in *Comm. Jo.* 1.24.151 on how the many titles of Christ are self-evidently "spiritual" – like "door" and "vine"; on "light" for instance, see *Comm. Jo.* 1.25.164: "The savior, however, being the 'light of the world,' does not illuminate physical things..."

96 *Comm. Jo.* 1.11.68–69 (evoking Matt 25:40). See Section 7.5.

97 *Comm. Jo.* 1.11.70 (citing Acts 22:22 and Luke 23:21), suggesting that Origen recognizes the subtle literary parallels that form between Jesus and Paul's respective trials in Luke and Acts (cf. Luke 23:18 and Acts 21:36). Cf. T. J. Cole, "Paul as Jesus: Luke's Use of Recursion in Luke-Acts" (2021).

98 *Comm. Jo.* 1.11.71 (citing Acts 9:4–5; cf. 22:7–8 and 26:14–15). See also *Comm. Jo.* 1.11.68 on a similar logic at play in Matthew: "Whatever is done to the disciples of Jesus also happens to him." Cf. *Hom. Luc.* 1 and *Cels.* 7.43.

learning to see what their writers had already come to see for themselves: that is, to receive Jesus of Nazareth, his deeds, sufferings, and words, as the divine "wisdom," "word," "life," "light," and "power," as "God with us" – a vision of his life that could not truly be called anything other than spiritual. But in its fullest sense, spiritual reading means coming to understand that, somehow, the mystery of an entire people's deliverance, even the whole world's, has been folded into the Evangelists' narratives of this life. To "translate what is immediately apparent in the Gospel into what is spiritual" therefore need not mean anything more, nor anything less, than to look upon "Joseph's son from Nazareth" and to say, "Behold the Lamb of God who takes away the sins of the world."[99]

3.5 "WOVEN OF SPIRIT"

All this talk of spirit might lead one to presume we have neared the goal of this study. We have not. We have only seen the peak from a distance, followed the path Origen himself took with our eyes, and thereby discovered its beginnings somewhere other than where Strauss (and his heirs) had thought.[100] Origen believed that the Evangelists themselves were figurative readers of Jesus's life; they had come to understand the events of and surrounding this life to have "signified something," such that their records also became "mixed."[101] But the preceding chapters' account of Origen's several ways of answering "what a Gospel is," along with his first principles for approaching them, simply serves to lay our true object before us once more: his readings of the narratives of the life of Jesus themselves and a more complete sense of "the truth of what is recorded to have happened" therein.[102] Acknowledging that the Gospel writers subordinated their narratives to some more "mysterious aim" is not the aim itself. Momentarily glimpsing the outline of a mountain's peak among the clouds does not disburden climbers from the toil of ascent, nor is it the vista that the summit alone supplies. So we set our feet at the base of the mountain and welcome the "impediments and impossibilities" that fill the way.

[99] John 1:29, 36, 45; cf. *Comm. Jo.* 1.32.228–39.

[100] In the years following the publication of *Das Leben Jesu*, Strauss himself appears to have sensed the instability of his own "essential distinction" between the mythical and allegorical views. See Beiser, *David Friedrich Strauß*, 69 and 112, which outlines how Strauss, in his reply to a review by Carl Ullmann, begins to shift away from "myth" language in favor of "symbol" and "allegory" language (cf. Chapter 6, n. 67).

[101] *Cels.* 2.69; *Princ.* 4.2.9.

[102] *Cels.* 2.69.

PART II

A SIGN FOR THIS GENERATION: READING THE GOSPELS WITH ORIGEN

PART II

INTRODUCTION

Spirit and Power

Part II of this study finds itself advantaged by Origen's presence near the epicenter of another epochal seism in the history of Gospel criticism: the controversy surrounding Gotthold E. Lessing's editing and publication of "fragments" from Hermann S. Reimarus's previously unpublished "Apology or Defense of the Rational Worshippers of God."[1] In the midst of publishing (and defending the publication of) the seminal sixth and seventh extracts,[2] Lessing composed "On the proof of the spirit and of power" (1777) – an essay that has proved, in its own way, at least equally iconic for the emergence of modern historical consciousness.[3]

[1] Lessing's word "fragment" only contributes to an ongoing mythology of Reimarus, "a figure whose fame or notoriety is entirely due to the patronage first of Lessing, then of D. F. Strauss, and finally of Albert Schweitzer" (Watson, *Gospel Writing*, 66). Reimarus and Strauss have often been portrayed as the two most pivotal figures in the history of Gospel criticism (e.g., Theissen/Merz, *The Historical Jesus*, 2-4). Schweitzer famously (if misleadingly) begins his genealogy with Reimarus: "Before Reimarus, no one had attempted to form a historical conception of the life of Jesus" (*Quest*, 14); and his "work is perhaps the most splendid achievement in the whole course of the historical investigation of the life of Jesus" (*Quest*, 22). Watson offers a rather withering critique of Schweitzer's hagiography: "Reimarus's true narrative function is to prefigure Schweitzer himself [...] Far from being an original and forward-looking thinker, [Reimarus] is at every point dependent on English deistic literature and is thoroughly ill-suited to his assigned role as founder of modern critical gospels scholarship" (*Gospel Writing*, 66 and 68).

[2] "On the Resurrection Narratives" (1777) and "On the Intentions of Jesus and His Disciples" (1778).

[3] See C. H. Talbert (ed.), *Reimarus: Fragments* (1970), 21. See also G. E. Michalson, Jr., *Lessing's "Ugly Ditch": A Study of Theology and History* (1985), 1: "Lessing's 'ugly ditch,' if not the most frequently cited nonbiblical image within Protestant theology during the past two centuries, is certainly in the running for that dubious title." Lessing's role in

It is seldom remembered, however, that the essay's primary interlocutor is Origen, and its provocation a passage from the opening of *Against Celsus*. Lessing's title belongs ultimately to the apostle Paul, of course.[4] But, hidden in plain sight, what precipitates Lessing's "ugly broad ditch" is the essay's epigraph:

> Moreover, one should add that there is a certain proof proper to the word [οἰκεία ἀπόδειξις τοῦ λόγου], more divine than that of Greek dialectic. This more divine demonstration the apostle calls a 'demonstration of spirit and power' – of 'spirit' because of the prophecies (especially those about the Christ), which are capable of producing belief in those who attend to them; of 'power' because of the portentous manifestations of power, which one may confirm to have happened by this argument, among many others, that traces of them still remain among those who live according to the will of the word.[5]

Lessing's reception of this passage quotes the letter of Origen's reply to Celsus but construes it in a manner that could not be more opposite to his spirit. Like Strauss, Lessing develops his own view of the relationship of history to the truth of the Gospels in contradistinction to Origen. Like Strauss, Lessing ultimately misrepresents Origen. And like Strauss's, Lessing's misrepresentation nevertheless grants contemporary readers a paradigmatic means of passage into Origen's own world of thought on the Gospels.[6]

Drawing on Origen's language, Lessing first develops a well-appointed distinction between miracles and mere reports of miracles (and between "fulfilled prophecies" and reports thereof): "Fulfilled prophecies which I myself experience are one thing; fulfilled prophecies of which I have only historical knowledge that others claim to have experienced them are another." Similarly, "Miracles which I see with my own eyes, and have an opportunity to assess, are one thing; miracles of which I know only

the origins of modern Gospel criticism is habitually underplayed. "Lessing is a significant figure in the development of Enlightenment Gospel scholarship, both in his own right and as editor of Reimarus" (Watson, *Gospel Writing*, 69).

4 1 Cor 2:4: "My word and my proclamation were not with persuasive words of wisdom, but with a demonstration of spirit and of power."

5 *Cels.* 1.2 (Lessing's epigraph begins with "because of the portentous manifestations of power..." I have added the preceding lines for context). G. E. Lessing, "Über den Beweis des Geistes und der Kraft" (1968); trans. H. B. Nesbit, "On the proof of the spirit and of power" (2005).

6 Cf. Watson, *Gospel Writing*, 75: "Reimarus follows in the steps of the English deist Thomas Woolston, who is in turn dependent here on Celsus." The central issues in Gospel criticism therefore have never really ceased to orbit the accusations first raised by Celsus. Cf. Strutwolf, "Kelsos und Origenes."

from history that others claim to have seen and assessed them are another."[7] Lessing is right, of course, that no one could reasonably object to these distinctions; Origen certainly wouldn't. His position, however, begs the question that we spent all of Part I negotiating: the nature of the Gospels in terms of their form, formation, and purpose. And Lessing presumes, at least for rhetorical purposes, a position vis-à-vis Origen precisely opposite to the principles detailed in Part I: the Gospels present themselves as "histories" in the most superficial sense, transparent to mere matters of fact and meant simply to report "historical knowledge" of what those who were "there" experienced and saw with their own eyes.

Concerning the character of the life of Jesus itself, Lessing proceeds: "If I had lived at the time of Christ, the prophecies fulfilled in his person would certainly have made me pay great attention to" one "whose coming had been predicted so long before"; similarly, "if I had actually seen him perform miracles" with "no cause to doubt that these were genuine miracles," then "I would willingly have subordinated my understanding to his and believed him in all matters in which equally indubitable experiences did not contradict him."[8] In other words, Lessing assumes (again, at least for the purposes of argument) that the Gospel writers present Jesus as an entirely unambiguous figure, a quality reflected – ostensibly – in their equally unambiguous chronicles of his life.

But Lessing's misrepresentation of Origen becomes particularly concentrated in a mistranslation that he picks up from J. D. Schumann's use of the passage in the opening pages of his tract against the Reimarus "fragments": *On the Evidence of Proofs for the Truth of the Christian Religion* (against which "On the proof of the spirit and power" was written). Origen himself says that one may reasonably affirm that certain "demonstrations of power" said to have unfolded in and around Jesus's life happened (ἅς κατασκευαστέον γεγονέναι) by a number of arguments, including the fact that traces of such things still remain in his day; Lessing, however, following Schumann, makes Origen say that "astonishing miracles happened in order to confirm Christ's teaching."[9] That is, a

[7] Lessing, "On the proof of the spirit and of power," 83–84, which proceeds: "It is because reports of fulfilled prophecies are not fulfilled prophecies; because reports of miracles are not miracles."

[8] Lessing, "On the proof of the spirit and of power," 84.

[9] Lessing's translation: "der Beweis der Kraft wegen der erstaunlichen Wunder so heisse, die zur Bestätigung der Lehre Christi geschehen" ("Über den Beweis des Geistes und der Kraft," 11); following J. D. Schumann, *Über die Evidenz der Beweise für die Wahrheit*

subtle but fatal reversal takes place in the process of (mis)translation.[10] The phrasing of the former remains in keeping with Origen's skepticism about the ultimate demonstrability of any historical narrative's facticity (nor is it all that clear what he means by either δυνάμεις or the present "traces" thereof).[11] The latter comes across as rather historiographically and epistemically naïve ("How do you prove the Gospels are true? Look at the miracles!"), a fact that Lessing exploits to damning effect.[12]

According to Lessing, therefore, it is only natural that Origen would have accepted the "demonstration of spirit and power" since he himself "was still in that position." For if "at his time," as he says, traces of this spirit and power "still remained," and "if he had undoubted examples of this, he had necessarily to acknowledge that proof of the spirit and of power if he did not wish to deny his own senses."[13] In other words, spirit and power become "demonstrative" for Origen not through the Evangelists' secondhand reports but because he himself was still observing miracles, as matters of indubitable empirical facticity, in his own day. "But if I," Lessing adds, "who am no longer even in Origen's position ... if I hesitate now to believe something because of the proof of the spirit and of power," it is because "the proof of the proof has now completely disappeared," and so too then the spirit of the spirit and the power of the power.[14]

The question of mediation thus comes to the fore and finally proves decisive for Lessing *contra* Origen (or Origen *via* Schumann)[15]: "this

der christlichen Religion (1778), 2: "Er heisst der Beweis der Kraft, wegen der erstaunenden Wunder, die zur Bestätigung der lehre Christi geschehen sind."

10 Since his epigraph is in Greek, we know that Lessing was using a *Vorlage* identical to the current critical edition of *Cels.* 1.2.

11 Cf. *Cels.* 1.42, treated in Chapter 2.

12 It is certainly Schumann's historiographical naivety that draws Lessing's chastisement, but since the dispute makes this passage from *Against Celsus* its battleground, Origen does not come out of the fray unscathed. See D.-M. Grube's argument that Lessing was trying to show, *contra* Schumann, that Origen "was epistemically in his right to believe because he did not ground his belief solely on historical claims, but relied on them in conjunction with other considerations" (namely, that Origen still witnessed miracles; "The Lessing/Schumann Controversy. Lessing's Stance on Contingency Compared to Kant's Stance" [2008], 102). Even still, Lessing would be defending a misshapen portrait.

13 Lessing, "On the proof of the spirit and of power," 84.

14 Lessing, "On the proof of the spirit and of power," 84–85.

15 Cf. Lessing, "On the proof of the spirit and of power," 84–85: "Prophecies fulfilled before my eyes and miracles that happen before my eyes have an *immediate* effect. But reports of fulfilled prophecies and of miracles have to act through a medium which deprives them of all their force."

proof of the spirit and of power no longer has either spirit or power, but has sunk to the level of human testimonies of spirit and power."[16] In other words, for Lessing, Origen's "spirit and power" were only ever "demonstrative" insofar as they referred to historical events that literally and obviously happened, and only retain their persuasive qualities by literally and obviously happening, in an unmediated fashion, before the observer in his or her own day. Nothing else is capable of binding one to belief in such things. Neither does believing in the "inspiration" (here reduced to meaning "factual inerrancy") of the Evangelists' reports offer anything dispositive, since saying "a miracle happened!" isn't a miracle and saying "a prophecy was fulfilled!" isn't prophetic. And so the "ugly broad ditch" gapes before him.[17]

It's as if Lessing wrote the essay as an introduction to the task before us. His argument reimposes the exact series of questions we addressed as matters of hermeneutical principle in Part I and must now address as matters of exegesis in Part II. Firstly, there is the question of what a Gospel even is, literarily speaking, for Origen: were the Gospels, as a matter of genre, ever meant merely to report events of such an obvious and empirically dispositive character that, had one simply "been there" and seen everything with one's own eyes, one could not have helped but receive them as true? Secondly, the question of literary formation: in Origen's view, were the Evangelists therefore simply "eyewitnesses" in an equally straightforward empirical sense, who composed the Gospel narratives only to convey "historical knowledge" of what took place before their eyes as a matter of "indubitable" sense-experience? In principle, "no" is the clear answer to both questions. How Origen arrives at and works from these principles in and through his actual interpretations is another matter. Only the readings themselves disclose what Origen's coupling of "spirit" with the Gospels' prophetic elements and his invocation of "traces of power" in his own day finally mean for our account of his critical capacities, specifically, and his interpretive sensibilities, more broadly, vis-à-vis the Gospels.

[16] Lessing, "On the proof of the spirit and of power," 85.

[17] Lessing, "On the proof of the spirit and of power," 87: "If I were pressed further and told: 'On the contrary! This is more than historically certain, for we are assured that it is the case by inspired historians who cannot err,' the fact that these historians were inspired and could not err is unfortunately likewise only historically certain. This, this is the broad and ugly ditch which I cannot get across, no matter how often and earnestly I have tried to make the leap. If anyone can help me over it, I beg and implore him to do so. He will earn a divine reward for this service."

Gordon Michalson has persuasively argued that there are in fact three "ditches" at play in Lessing's essay.[18] The first is *temporal*, involving the question of chronological distance between a historical event and the knower. The second ditch (or aspect thereof) Michalson calls *metaphysical*: namely, the chasm between knowledge of contingent historical facts and what Lessing calls the "necessary truths of reason."[19] Michalson identifies the third and final ditch as *existential*: what difference does historicity make for binding a believer to an object of belief?

The remainder of Part II will show how Origen anticipated each of these difficulties. Firstly, he addresses the issue of temporal distance by frequently relativizing the value of having been an "eyewitness" to the events of Jesus's life. Secondly, Origen is quite clear that the truth of the Gospels does not and truly *could* not subsist in matters of bare historical facticity alone. Finally, Origen's sophisticated conceptualization of the literary form and formation of the Gospels discloses how the mysteries of Jesus's life – their "spirit and power" – are handed on to readers of later generations precisely in and through the Evangelists' narratives thereof. In short, Origen is well aware of the three major difficulties sustaining Lessing's ditch. Origen, however, is not finally scandalized by them. He considers these "stumbling blocks" to be the very occasions not only for truly intelligent reading of the Gospels but also for ascending to the spirit of the Gospel itself. Lessing's ditch is Origen's *skandalon*.

[18] Michalson, *Lessing's "Ugly Ditch."*

[19] Perhaps the essay's most famous quote: "contingent truths of history can never become the proof of necessary truths of reason" ("On the proof of the spirit and of power," 85).

4

Between the Rivers Jordan and Chebar

Jesus's Baptism

"The heavens were opened, and I saw a vision of God."[1]

The various pericopes that introduce the life and ministry of Jesus provide the most straightforward point of entry for observing the whole sweep of Origen's first principles of Gospel reading enacted.[2] And, for an archetypal display of the "mixed" character of Gospel narrative, no sequence provides a securer first footing than his examination of Jesus's baptism in *Against Celsus*.[3] That Jesus was baptized by John is hardly problematic historically speaking.[4] But the events narrated to have taken place directly after the baptism presented no less difficulty for readers in antiquity than they do for readers today. Origen preserves Celsus's dismissal of the descent of the dove and voice from heaven as an obvious fiction.[5] Origen, however, resists the judgment. Why? His reply to Celsus puts the whole complex of first principles detailed in Part I to work.

[1] Ezek 1:1.

[2] The scope of Chapters 5 and 6 is naturally limited by the state of Origen's extant corpus. Besides scattered fragments, the first nine books of the *Commentary on Matthew* are lost. Since neither Mark nor John narrates Jesus's life prior to the beginning of his public ministry, we are left with Origen's *Homilies on Luke* alone (c. 230s CE), along with brief remarks on the baptism (and temptation) provided by *Against Celsus*, *On First Principles*, and the *Commentary on John*.

[3] Addressing certain fundamental historical and literary challenges that remain logically, if not narratively, prior to the pericopes from Luke 1–2 covered in Chapter 5.

[4] See, for example, J. P. Meier, *A Marginal Jew: Rethinking the Historical Jesus, Vol. 2: Mentor, Message, and Miracles* (1994), 105.

[5] *Cels.* 1.40: διαβάλλειν βούλεται ὡς πλάσμα ("from the Gospel according to Matthew and perhaps also from the other Gospels").

4.1 CELSUS'S OBJECTION

Celsus puts the following question to Jesus in the voice of a Jewish interlocutor: "After you were washed by John, you say that an apparition [φάσμα] of a bird flew towards you out of the air." But "what credible witness saw this apparition or heard a voice from heaven adopting you as a son of God?" Who, that is, other than Jesus, and maybe one other person who suffered a similar fate (meaning John the Baptist, hardly an impartial witness)?[6]

Origen's immediate reply occupied the closing section of Chapter 2. Here we observed Origen taking a step back in order to redirect the whole question of the Gospel narratives' historicity: given the supreme difficulty and frequent impossibility of demonstrating the facticity of "just about any historical narrative," what is the use of trying to "produce complete certainty" about an event, even if true?[7] The same goes, *a fortiori*, for "mixed" narratives with ends in view other than mere historical reporting – whether one considers literary works that are preponderantly fictional (even if they retain the possibility of some shadowy historical substrate, like the *Iliad*) or ones that draw from a richer root-system of "what happened" (though not exhaustively so, like the Gospels).[8]

In context, Origen's intervention exposes Celsus's call for "credible witnesses" for setting off on the wrong path entirely. The objection is naïve with respect to the probative powers of historiography in general and misunderstands Gospel genre specifically. Origen calls upon critical and open-minded students of the Gospels to try, rather, to discover some "means of entry" into the thought process (διανοία) underlying the narratives.[9] Then he returns to the particular challenge of Jesus's baptism.

4.2 HORIZONS OF PLAUSIBILITY

We know from Origen's earlier work that he is not opposed, in principle, to the idea that the fabric of the Gospels interweaves narrative threads that both did and didn't happen (and even couldn't have happened).[10] In fact, he advocates for the position and considers it essential for intelligent reading of the Gospels. So we may assume that Origen wouldn't find anything objectionable, again *in principle*, about postulating that what is said to have followed Jesus's baptism didn't happen, at least not exactly

[6] *Cels.* 1.41. [7] *Cels.* 1.42 (see Section 2.4). [8] Cf. *Cels.* 1.42. [9] *Cels.* 1.42.
[10] *Princ.* 4.2.9.

as narrated. Actually, he will conclude the section with this very judgment. Whence his objection to Celsus then?

Let's examine the terms of engagement more closely. Abstractly, the range of the term fiction (πλάσμα) is itself quite plastic. One can imagine a world in which Origen could have adopted a handbook definition of the term.[11] But Celsus's usage is far from neutral. He can hardly be accused of hiding his hostilities, so neither can Origen be accused of being overly defensive when he cites Celsus for deploying the term for the purposes of discrediting (διαβάλλω) the Gospels as deceptive inventions of Jesus's followers.[12] "Fiction" here is more an accusation (κατηγορέω) than a criterion.[13] But rhetoric aside, the question still stands: can one say that the events recorded to have directly followed upon Jesus's baptism "happened" in any meaningful sense?

Origen begins by asking the reader to acknowledge differing horizons of plausibility.[14] The whole question turns on how one understands the nature of the recorded appearance or apparition (τὸ φάσμα), a word as indefinite as – and playfully assonant with – "fiction" (τὸ πλάσμα).[15] Doesn't the inclusion of such apparitions render a narrative, de facto, fictional? Origen answers: it depends. If, for instance, Celsus had expressed "incredulity" in the voice of "an Epicurean, or a follower of Democritus, or a Peripatetic, the argument might have had some force."[16] For a materialist, Origen points out, apparitions of this kind cannot be anything other than fiction, at most a figment of the imagination produced by a swirl of atoms over the surface of the void. The appearance of

[11] See Section 2.5; πλάσσω appears to have had a range quite similar to *fingere* – a range preserved in the breadth of derivative English terms, from "fiction" or "fictive" (even "figment") to "figurative" (see Auerbach, "Figura"). In Greek, τροπικός and ἀλληγορικός do not share an etymological link with πλασματικός in the way "figure" does with "fiction" in English; they lack the shades of pure invention or fabrication that πλάσσω-related terms can often possess.

[12] *Cels.* 2.26 (cf. 1.40): "Celsus's Jew says the disciples of Jesus fabricated [πλασαμένους] these things: 'nor were you, in your deceit [ψευδόμενοι], able to conceal your fabrications [τὰ πλάσματα] with any plausibility.'"

[13] Cf. *Cels.* 1.40.

[14] For Origen's language of historical probability/plausibility, cf. *Cels.* 1.44 (τὸ εἰκὸς γενομένου), *Cels.* 2.26, and *Comm. Jo.* 10.25.143.

[15] Derived from φαίνω, the term can be taken as simply as "appearance," "apparition," or "phenomenon" (the way Origen takes it up), but it also bears undertones of *phantasm*, *phantom*, *hallucination*, and the like (which Celsus likely means to imply). Cf. *Cels.* 7.35, where Origen appears much less comfortable using this language for the resurrection appearances.

[16] *Cels.* 1.43. Cf. S.-P. Bergjan, "Celsus the Epicurean? The Interpretation of an Argument in Origen, *Contra Celsum*" (2001).

the dove couldn't possibly be said to have "happened" in any meaningful sense other than as a matter of Jesus's own (self-)deception, or else as a whole-cloth fabrication invented by his followers. The argument would "have some force" because it would be logically consistent within this (exceedingly restricted) horizon of plausibility. Nothing about the story in itself offers dispositive "proof" otherwise.

Conversely, nothing about the materialist view – as a strictly philosophical position – demonstrates anything about the narrative per se, particularly with respect to the more immediate concern that Celsus's objection raises for Origen: that is, a historiographically and literarily informed examination of what is recorded to have happened in the events surrounding Jesus's baptism. Celsus's first error, Origen points out, is not that he presumes an Epicurean philosophy of nature, but that he attributes this view to a Jewish interlocutor, whose own "prophetic scriptures" involve "greater and more startling things than this story about the appearance of the dove."[17] So Origen's initial move is "philosophical," one could say, but deployed only in order to establish a broader historical- and literary-critical field of play. He disallows a certain (in his view, impoverished) philosophy of nature from prematurely and facilely foreclosing the range of possibilities for determining the nature and intent of the narrative at hand. Whatever one makes of the broader philosophical questions in the abstract, reductive atomism doesn't represent the thought world of the Jewish scriptures, nor that of the authors of the Gospels, nor that of Jesus himself.[18]

[17] *Cels.* 1.43. See also *Cels.* 1.48: "The argument ascribed to him is ill-suited to the role of a Jewish interlocutor." Origen repeatedly disputes Celsus's depiction of what a Jewish interlocutor might say (cf. *Cels.* 1.45, 1.55, and 2.31, where Origen mentions his own experience debating with Jewish thinkers). Cf. J. N. Carleton Paget, "The Jew of Celsus and *Adversus Judaeos* Literature" (2017). Cf. M. R. Niehoff, "Homer between Celsus, Origen and the Jews of Late Antique *Palaestina*" (2021).

[18] For a modern analogue, see M. J. Borg, *Jesus, A New Vision: Spirit, Culture, and the Life of Discipleship* (1987), 34: "To try and understand the Jewish tradition and Jesus while simultaneously dismissing the notion of another world or immediately reducing it to a merely psychological realm is to fail to see the phenomena, to fail to take seriously what the charismatic mediators experienced and reported." Cf. D. Allison, *The Resurrection of Jesus: Apologetics, Polemics, History* (2021), 43. Cf. R. Bultmann, *Jesus Christ and Mythology* (1958), 54–55: "Every interpreter is inescapably dependent on conceptions which he has inherited from a tradition, consciously or unconsciously, and every tradition is dependent on some philosophy or other... It follows, then, that historical and exegetical study should not be practiced without reflection and without giving an account of the conceptions which guide the exegesis. In other words, the question of the 'right' philosophy arises." Origen begins to form his own response to Celsus by first attempting to expose any prejudices (conscious or not, in the broadest Gadamerian sense)

4.3 FICTION OR FIGURE? JEWISH LITERARY PRECEDENT

Once Origen has thus freed the reader to reconsider the question of historicity from within a view of the world more hospitable to that of the Gospels' own authors, the substance of his argument proceeds on more literary grounds. For the sake of discerning what one may say did and/or didn't happen in the "mixed narrative" of Jesus's baptism, Origen first invites his readers to "compare *historia* with *historia*."[19] What kind of narratives include apparitions of this sort? Here in practice (just as Chapter 2 found in principle), Origen deems it impossible to know what one is choosing to accept or dismiss prior to addressing the question of literary form.[20]

Origen's answer falls crisply into line with his consideration of Gospel genre in *On First Principles*: the story of Jesus's baptism is of a kind with the stories of Israel, particularly those of the prophets.[21] With what kind of *historia* shall we compare the *historia* of the baptism? "Your Ezekiel wrote these words: 'The heavens were opened, and I saw a vision of God.' After explaining the vision he continues: 'This is the vision of the likeness of the glory of the Lord. And he spoke to me…'"[22] Origen astutely observes the direct correspondence of Matthew's language to Ezekiel's:

<table>
<tr><td>The heavens were opened,
and I saw a vision of God…
This is the vision of a likeness
of the glory of the Lord…
And he said to me…
(Ezek 1:1, 28; 2:1)</td><td>The heavens were opened,
and he saw the spirit of God
descending like a dove and
alighting on him.
And a voice from heaven said…
(Matt 3:16)</td></tr>
</table>

that might predetermine one's sense of the reality of such an appearance (or lack thereof) and thus calling attention to the fact that one's historical-critical judgments are rarely, if ever, wholly innocent of one's philosophy of history, and one's philosophy of history is never wholly innocent of one's philosophy of nature. Note too how far such an intervention is from the clichés of Origen extrinsically imposing his "platonizing" presuppositions upon the text. His opening salvo against any hidden Epicurean assumptions is ordered toward retrieving and preserving the indelibly Jewish character of the narrative, as he perceives it, by way of comparison with other regnant worldviews in antiquity.

19 *Cels.* 1.43: τῇ ἱστορίᾳ ταύτῃ ἱστορίαν παραβάλω.

20 Cf. *Cels.* 1.43 (evoking *Cels.* 1.42 on ways of "assenting" to vs. "dismissing" a narrative).

21 *Cels.* 1.43: ἐκ τῶν προφητικῶν γραφῶν.

22 *Cels.* 1.43 (citing Ezek 1:1, 28; 2:1): «Ἠνοίχθησαν οἱ οὐρανοί, καὶ εἶδον ὅρασιν θεοῦ», ἥντινα διηγησάμενος ἐπιφέρει αὐτῇ· «Αὕτη ἡ ὅρασις ὁμοιώματος δόξης κυρίου· καὶ εἶπε πρός με.» Cf. Matt 3:16: Ἠνεῴχθησαν οἱ οὐρανοί, καὶ εἶδεν τὸ πνεῦμα τοῦ θεοῦ καταβαῖνον ὡσεὶ περιστεράν… καὶ ἰδοὺ φωνὴ ἐκ τῶν οὐρανῶν λέγουσα.

The narration of what happened after Jesus's baptism follows this exact prophetic literary trope: "the heavens are opened," there is some kind of vision of God appearing in some likeness or form, and then a heavenly voice speaks (some revelatory message) to the prophet-seer.[23] Origen's entire argument turns on preserving the record of Jesus's baptism as a narrative emerging from a distinctly Jewish visionary idiom, expressed in a distinctly Jewish literary form, which itself materializes a distinctly Jewish view of the world.[24]

For, Origen concludes, if one "presumes" that "what is recorded about Jesus is false simply because one is unable to show in a self-evident way [ἐναργῶς] how these things (seen or heard by him alone) are true ... would we not be even more justified in saying that Ezekiel was sensationalizing [τερατευόμενον] when he said that 'the heavens were opened' and so on?"[25] Similarly, "if Isaiah also asserts, 'I saw the Lord of Hosts sitting on a throne high and lifted up; and the Seraphim stood around it, with six wings on one and six wings on the other,' etc.," how could you possibly prove "that he really did see this?"[26] How, for that matter, would anyone go about "proving that the 'Lord God said'" what "he is recorded to have said" to "Adam, or Eve, or Cain, or Noah, or Abraham or Isaac, or Jacob"?[27] If it is nearly impossible to "produce complete certainty" about the facticity of "nearly any historical narrative,"[28] then the already restricted limits of historiography's probative powers impose themselves with a special severity on narratives reporting experiences of this kind.

[23] Cf. *Hom. Ezech.* 1.4.1, where Origen notes additional figural ties between the baptism narrative and the opening of Ezekiel: both figures are said to be thirty years of age at the commencement of their respective ministries, which again, for both, is marked by a visionary experience beside a river.

[24] Origen's view here corresponds well to Tzvi Novick's category of "biblicized narrative," which belongs to but is also distinguishable within a family of referential forms like allusion, echo, and rewritten Bible. See "Biblicized Narrative: On Tobit and Genesis 22" (2007), esp. 763.

[25] *Cels.* 1.43. See K. Ierodiakonou, "The Notion of *Enargeia* in Hellenistic Philosophy" (2011). Similarly, see E. Plümacher's illuminating study on τερατεία as a technical term in Greco-Roman historiography (often with connotations of embellishing or exaggerating an event in order to amplify its significance – to *romanticize* or *dramatize*): "TEPATEIA: Fiktion und Wunder in der hellenistisch-römischen Geschichtsschreibung und in der Apostelgeschichte" (1998).

[26] *Cels.* 1.43 (citing Isa 6:1–2): πόθεν, ὅτι ἀληθῶς ἑώρακε.

[27] *Cels.* 1.43. Thus the whole question of the nature of divine revelation is drawn into the balance.

[28] *Cels.* 1.42.

All the same, Origen recognizes that exposing an epistemically fallacious demand for historiographical "proof" does not resolve the literary question. Celsus doesn't simply accuse the narrative of falsehood; just prior, he "dismisses it as fiction." Even if Celsus errs in collapsing the distinction, Origen understands that "false" and "fictional" represent two different claims: the latter a literary judgment, the former a rational judgment.[29] He has already acknowledged that one can receive the epics and tragedies of Greco-Roman antiquity as true in a certain sense – figuratively, that is.[30] So invoking Jewish prophetic visionary traditions as the proper literary vantage for understanding the Baptism narrative only complexifies the question. Are these prior prophetic traditions (and the histories of Israel in general, inasmuch as they habitually narrate similar appearances in similar ways) also sensationalized fabrications? Aren't stories of torn skies, zoomorphic phantasms, and disembodied voices obviously fictional? The very definition, that is, of that narrative thread Origen identifies in *On First Principles* not only as "something that didn't happen" but also "something that *couldn't* have happened"?[31]

In formulating his response, Origen comfortably adopts Celsus's "apparition" language. He simply disputes that the depiction of a *phasma* necessarily makes the narrative a *plasma* ("fiction" in the derogatory sense leveraged by Celsus), as long as one understands that the narratives of such appearances were never meant to be taken literally (or more exactly, σωματικῶς: *physically, materially, empirically*).[32] In so doing, Origen sets

[29] See, similarly, *Hom. Luc.* 1.3: "What is true and what false" about such narratives "is not judged from visible signs and portents but by the account [λόγος]" one makes of them (cf. Section 5.2). Celsus, in short, is naïve about the epistemic reach of historical evidence in general. Cf. also M. D. Litwa on how "mythic historiography" was not synonymous with falsity in the ancient world (*How the Gospels Became History*, 1 and throughout). As already noted in Chapter 3, Strauss similarly departs from Reimarus by resisting the notion that mythical elements correspond to deception and falsehood *tout court*. Elsewhere Origen does know the terms in a looser sense, where "fiction" means "not true" and myth means "not a mystery" (*Comm. Jo.* 13.17.103).

[30] *Cels.* 1.42; these also may lay some claim to some historical substrate, as he notes. Also relevant is his notion of the "whole sense" of a narrative in *Princ.* 4.3.5 (cf. Section 3.4) and his discussion of truth, falsity, and historicity in *Comm. Jo.* 10.3.14 and 10.5.20 (cf. Sections 2.3, 3.2, and 3.3).

[31] *Princ.* 4.2.9 (cf. Section 2.2).

[32] It seems that Origen considers "appearance" language to be analogous to the Lukan language of "in bodily form" (Luke 3:22). See, for example, *Cels.* 1.41, on Celsus "dismissing" the idea that the holy spirit was "seen 'physically' [σωματικῶς], so to speak, by the savior in the form [εἴδει] of a dove." The dispute turns (just as *On First Principles* anticipates) on the qualifier "bodily." Seeing something "in bodily form" does not mean that the object of vision was itself "bodily"; there is all the difference in the

out both to resist "naïve and irrational belief" and to "show that those who approach" the Gospels with a certain "openness of mind and a great deal of critical study" may find a plausible alternative explanation to sensationalized whole-cloth fabrications – another "means of entry," that is, into the "thought-process" underlying the narrative's composition.[33]

For, Origen continues, just as we often "receive the impression [φαντασίαν] in a dream that our sense of hearing has been physically affected and that we have seen something with our eyes, though these impressions are not experienced by our physical eyes or made by any vibration in our ears" but are only "*experienced in our mind*, so also there is nothing extraordinary about such things having happened to the prophets when it is recorded that they 'saw' certain startling visions, or 'heard' utterances of the Lord, or 'beheld' the heavens opened."[34] "Many people" report having received such "impressions in their minds," asleep and awake.[35] Whether or not one receives such reports as "true" (a different question entirely), records of such visions or impressions need not be said to be, de facto, pure fabrications of the authors.

Therefore, Origen concludes,

> Neither do I imagine that the visible heaven was opened, or its physical form [τὸ σῶμα] divided, for Ezekiel to have recorded such a thing. Shouldn't the discerning reader of the Gospels therefore also take [Jesus's baptismal narrative] in a similar way? Even if this opinion may cause offense to the simplistic, who in their extreme naivety move the cosmos and rend the vast unified mass [τὸ σῶμα] of the entire heaven.[36]

By virtue of the prophetic idiom in which the throne visions of Ezekiel or Isaiah are narrated, Origen judges that there never was and never could have been any question of empirical "proof" because nothing empirical is presumed. In the same way, what is recorded to have happened on the banks of the Jordan, no less than on the banks of the Chebar, is narrated in order to depict some kind of interior prophetic vision – a view, as it

world between saying something happened physically and saying something appeared "in physical form." Origen never washes out the mediating language of subjective experience ("seen by the savior") nor the mediating language of "in the *form* of" (much like Ezekiel, where the vision is also always mediated by "likeness/form" language).

33 *Cels.* 1.42. 34 *Cels.* 1.43 (cf. 1.48). 35 Cf. *Cels.* 1.48.

36 *Cels.* 1.48. Cf. *Comm. Jo.* 1.8.45. Cf. Watson, *The Fourfold Gospel*, 175–76. Cf. *Hom. Ps.* 77(78) 4.8 on the opening of the "doors of heaven" (Ps 77[78]:23) as an obviously figurative expression. On a seemingly contradictory passage where Origen implies that Ezekiel saw what he saw with the "eyes of the flesh" (*Hom. Ezech.* 1.8), see D. J. Halperin, "Origen, Ezekiel's Merkabah, and the Ascension of Moses" (1981), 263–64 and 273–74.

happens, directly comparable to a large family of contemporary interpretations.[37]

Thus, for Origen, one can intelligently receive the narrative of the opened heaven (etc.) as something other than a pure fabrication as long as one first notices the literary tradition it invokes – and understands that this literary tradition need never have been meant to be taken literally. In Origen's view, the canonical records of Jesus's baptismal vision would be "narratives of something that couldn't happen" if one *had* to take it as some empirically observable, flatly physical event. In other words, to insist on the narrative's most superficial sense would be to make it a myth; it would render the whole prophetic tradition sensationalized fiction. But, Origen insists, it would be simplistic and critically insensitive to believe the passage required such a reading.

Origen's critical categories from *On First Principles* now demonstrate their supreme utility. Their expression is unwieldy but precise. If one were to record this kind of vision, one would find oneself obliged to use figurative language in a way that "seems historical" but "didn't physically happen."[38]

[37] See, for example, J. D. G. Dunn, *Jesus and the Spirit: A Study of the Religious and Charismatic Experience of Jesus and the First Christians as Reflected in the New Testament* (1975), 65: "*Jesus' baptism by John was probably the occasion for an experience which had epochal significance for Jesus*... The 'like a dove' may have referred originally to a vision, or it may simply have been an interpretative metaphor drawn in when the narrative was first formulated... As to the heavenly voice ... it is quite likely that Jesus was convinced that at his baptism he had heard God's voice addressing him as son and setting him apart for a special task" (note Dunn's more reserved phrasing in *Jesus Remembered*, 374–77). See, similarly, C. Rowland, *The Open Heaven: A Study of Apocalyptic in Judaism and Early Christianity* (1982), 358–63, esp. 363: "The important thing to note about the baptism of Jesus is that a vision marked the decisive moment in his life." Cf. B. Witherington III, *The Christology of Jesus* (1990), 149 and 152, and *Jesus the Seer: The Progress of Prophecy* (2014), 279. See also C. E. B. Cranfield, "The Baptism of our Lord – A Study of St. Mark I.9–11" (1955), 56: "Mark intended to record not externally objective phenomena but a vision – albeit a vision that was no empty dream but a real communication from God. That Jesus did at this time experience such a vision seems likely enough." While questioning approaches that attempt to "psychologize" the baptismal story in order to reconstruct the inner experience of the historical Jesus, there is, for John Meier, no doubt that the narrative itself presents Jesus as "the recipient of a vision" (*A Marginal Jew, Vol. 2*, 107–108 and 971 n. 9, following F. Lentzen Deis' language of *Deute-Vision* in *Die Taufe Jesu nach den Synoptikern; literarkritische und gattungsgeschichtliche Untersuchungen* [1970], 195–289). Cf. L. Baynes, "Jesus the Revealer and the Revealed" (2017), 16–17.

[38] Cf. *Princ.* 4.3.1. Cf. *Comm. Jo.* 10.5.18 on the Evangelists sometimes interweaving their writing "with language that would make it seem that something made clear in a purely interior way was perceptible to the senses."

But calling such passages "fictional" in the sense of a deceitfully sensationalized fabrication (which, in the immediate context of *Against Celsus*, πλάσσω-language seems to imply) does an injustice to the language and literary form intrinsic to the narrative. So much for Celsus's dismissal of any apparition narrative as per se fictional.

4.4 HOW THEN "TRUE"?

By "discovering commonalities between the opening of the heavens to Jesus and the voice he heard with similar things recorded in Ezekiel and in Isaiah or in any other prophet," Origen believes that one can "at least show the coherence" of receiving the narrative of Jesus's baptism as something that was recorded "without deceit."[39] But what exactly does it mean then to believe that it was "by a divine spirit not only that such things were seen by the prophet" but also "spoken about and written down"?[40] If Origen deems it impossible – and undesirable – to hang the narrative's credibility upon its historiographically demonstrable facticity (the narrative's own literary form spurns such an approach), it remains to be seen what "believing" the narrative means then. In other words: in what does the "truth of what is recorded to have happened to Jesus" subsist?[41]

Origen's argument works in three stages. Firstly, as we have seen, he accepts that one cannot prove the truth of the vision from the narrative alone. But then he takes Celsus's skepticism one step further by pointing out that neither can one prove its falsity from an appeal to historical criteria alone. In a move that Lessing could not have helped but heartily approve of (had he read beyond the second paragraph of Book 1), Origen exposes Celsus's accusation for uncritically conflating historiographical

39 *Cels.* 1.48 (cf. 1.43: ἀψευδής).

40 *Cels.* 1.43. Note how this "divine spirit" is involved not only in the vision but also in how it is passed on, whether orally or in writing. On how the tradition of Jesus's baptismal vision might have been handed on, Origen offers a few possibilities. Firstly, he suggests that Jesus himself might have "handed the vision [ὄψιν] he saw and the voice he heard on to his disciples," but he also considers the possibility that the stories were written by those who received no such tradition directly from him but rather from "the spirit" (*Cels.* 1.44). He adds a little later that openly telling his disciples about this vision also wouldn't be entirely "consistent with the character of one who said to his disciples after the vision [ὀπτασίᾳ] on the mountain, 'Tell the vision to no one. . .'"; for it was his "constant habit to avoid speaking about himself" (*Cels.* 1.48, citing Matt 17:9).

41 Cf. *Cels.* 2.69.

truths and truths of reason.[42] The truth or falsity of such things is not a matter for historical criticism to decide.[43] So Celsus is not skeptical enough. The story can't be *proved* to be self-evidently "true," but Origen does not cede that it is thus self-evidently false, since even classical myths and tragedies can be true in a certain sense.[44]

Secondly, Origen still questions the sufficiency of Celsus's literary designation: "fiction" (here construed as a misleading fabrication of something that didn't happen). As the previous section showed, he disputes the idea that a narrative of someone experiencing a vision is per se fictional – a quite simple historiographical point that, once noted, should be obvious enough to anyone. But what then of the claim of self-deception? Even if one need not presume the narrative was invented whole cloth, what prevents one from indexing this "apparition" to more hallucinatory overtones? If the narrative is not unworthy of some kind of belief, the last step is to understand how one might still receive the vision as "true."

It is only then that Origen turns to argue for the coherence of the idea that such visions arise from some transcendent ground. "Many people," he says, across all ages and from many religious and philosophical persuasions, have believed that they "received certain impressions (whether clear or enigmatic) in their minds – some about divine things, others about things that are about to take place in their lives."[45] The whole history of the human race – with those of Jewish and Christian faith no exception, at every stage of their respective traditions – is riddled with accounts of people who are said to have experienced such things. Moreover, that such things should happen is "self-evident to all who accept the idea of providence."[46] That is, Origen notes, for those many and various religious or philosophical communities that align such experiences with some true movement of "providence" in the world, such an experience is "nothing strange."[47]

Therefore, Origen briefly invokes a providential philosophy of history in the very broadest sense – inclusive of Judaism, Christianity, Stoicism, and various forms of Platonism, among others – only to expose any latent presumptions in favor of philosophies of history alien to the world of the

[42] Cf. Lessing, "On the proof of the spirit and of power," 85. [43] Cf. *Hom. Luc.* 1.3.

[44] Cf. *Cels.* 1.43.

[45] *Cels.* 1.48. Cf. D. Allison, *Encountering Mystery: Religious Experience in a Secular Age* (2022).

[46] *Cels.* 1.48. [47] *Cels.* 1.48.

New Testament (e.g., an Epicurean or Democritean atomism or certain non-providential construals of Aristotle[48]) and to deflect them from surreptitiously inflecting one's approach to the Gospel narratives. If one remains open to the idea that nature, including the human *psyche*, may be receptive and yielding to phenomena irreducible to vacant materiality (that is, receptive and yielding to spirit), then one's literary judgment may remain open, as well as one's rational judgment regarding the possibility that this vision belonged to a real disclosure of something truly providential moving in the world.

In sum: it is almost laughable to think that Origen arrives at this particular judgment regarding the narrative of Jesus's baptism because of "platonizing" predilections for "dissolving history" or disparaging (avian?) "embodiment" in the abstract. Even Origen's more philosophical intervention here is clearly intended only to underwrite a meaningful appropriation of this narrative *as true* – a real disclosure of the real God – in a way that approximates how the Gospel writers likely would have thought of their own expositions of the event. As Origen notes, the prophetic idiom the Evangelists' own language evokes should draw the reader to conclude that nothing empirically observable, nothing *corporeal*, "happened" on the banks of the Jordan, which is not to say that what is depicted in the narrative "didn't happen" at all (note how indispensable the κατὰ τὸ σωματικόν qualification becomes – there was no astrophysical catastrophe, no feathers to be gathered), but rather that the narratives depict the mystery of Jesus's "messianic consciousness" (to use a modern phrase) in a figurative way.[49]

4.5 "A CERTAIN KIND OF DIVINE SENSE"

This historiographically astute and literarily sophisticated exposition of the Baptism account(s) gives rise to Origen's most decisive exposition of a kind of "divine" or "spiritual" sense intrinsic to narratives of this kind. In contrast to those who presuppose a naïve literalist approach to the

[48] Cf. *Cels.* 1.43. One could say that, for Origen, the prophetic visionary tradition itself stands as a challenge to such preconceived notions of what "history" even is in the first place.

[49] Cf. *Princ.* 4.3.1. With this phrase, I do not mean to call to mind certain psychologizing obsessions with this topic in previous (and outmoded) generations of Gospel scholarship, only Origen's position that the event is depicted as a prophetic vision and recorded "as (if) it happened, but not as having literally happened" (ibid.).

narration of such matters (rent skies, heavenly speech, and animal-like appearances), "anyone who examines this subject more deeply will say that there is, as the scripture calls it, a certain kind of 'divine sense.'"[50] The phrase, for Origen, evokes a kind of perception that one finds narrated in "many forms" throughout the vast and variegated expanse of the scriptural tradition: a "seeing" of something that obviously exceeds what belongs to purely physical observation (a vision of angelic creatures, for instance) or a "hearing" that appears to apprehend sounds or voices that nonetheless lack any "real existence in the air."[51] Such things (and more) are not only interior to but even constitutive of every major narrative in Christian scripture.[52] And this, by Origen's own unambiguous account, is what he means first and foremost by the "spiritual sense" of scripture.[53]

Therefore (at the risk of trading one obscurity for another), what Origen means by a "divine sense" shares a crucial tract of conceptual territory with what a number of scholars now designate under the category of "apocalyptic vision"; that is, a revelatory understanding or revealed wisdom, often but not exclusively expressed in a visionary idiom, disclosive of some divine mystery[54]:

50 *Cels.* 1.48: θείας τινὸς γενικῆς αἰσθήσεως (citing an otherwise unattested textual tradition of Prov 2:5; cf. Z. Schwáb, "The Value of a Curious Translation: Revisiting Proverbs 2:5" [2014]).

51 *Cels.* 1.48.

52 Besides the more obvious examples of "seeing" and "hearing" something transcendent in, say, the stories of the patriarchs or prophets (or "tasting," as in Ezekiel's "eating" of a scroll), Origen also calls to mind Paul's language of "smelling" a "sweet savor of Christ unto God" – an obviously non-physical (that is, "spiritual") sense of "smelling"; or the author of 1 John describing what he "touched with [his] hands concerning the word of life" (is this meant in a purely physicalist sense?); or the kind of "taste" John's Gospel evokes when proclaiming that one must "feed on living bread that has come down from heaven" (*Cels.* 1.48, citing Ezek 3:1–3, 2 Cor 5:15, 1 John 1:1, and John 6:51). See *Princ.* 1.1.9 on Matt 5:8: "For the names of the organs of sense are frequently applied to the soul, so that it may be said to 'see' with the eyes of the heart" when it means "to understand or to know" (and so forth vis-à-vis the other senses). Cf. D. Lee, "The Gospel of John and the Five Senses" (2010).

53 The most accessible collection of passages on spiritual perception in Origen remains H. U. von Balthasar (ed.), *Origen: Spirit and Fire: A Thematic Anthology of His Writings* (1984), 218–57. For a helpful negotiation of the last century of scholarship on the topic, see M. J. McInroy, "Origen of Alexandria" (2012). Cf. J. Heath, "The Beginnings of a Christian Doctrine of the Spiritual Senses before Origen" (2023), esp. 25.

54 Following the broad definition of Rowland, *The Open Heaven*, 70–71: "Apocalyptic seems essentially to be about the revelation of the divine mysteries through visions or some other form of immediate disclosure of heavenly truths" (such as heavenly ascents or

> The blessed prophets found this divine sense, both seeing "divinely" and hearing "divinely" ... with a sense which was not sensory, so to speak... In this way they "saw" what they record that they saw, and they "heard" what they say they heard.[55]

Readers will risk misunderstanding every subsequent step of this study without internalizing that what Origen means by "divine sense," above and before all, is (1) something directly akin to what belongs to prophetic vision or discourse and (2) something already woven into the Gospel narratives as a constitutive element of their own literary content and character.[56] Thus, this "divine sense" (or "seeing in the spirit") is recorded to have belonged first, "at least, to Jesus."[57]

But Origen continues:

> *In the same way*, "John bore witness saying, I have seen the spirit descending as a dove from heaven and remain on him. And I myself did not know him, but the one who sent me to baptize in water said to me, 'He on whom you see the spirit descend and remain, this is he who baptizes in a holy spirit.' And I have seen and have borne witness that this is the son of God."[58]

So Origen also identifies John the Baptist's own witness with this divine sense; his confession partakes of this same prophetic-apocalyptic visionary idiom. And while, "on the one hand, no one other than John is recorded to have seen the heavens opened at that time" (in the fourth Gospel), on the other hand, Jesus, "foretelling this 'opening of the

verbal revelations; cf. pp. 14 and 76). Rowland draws a direct analogy between these sorts of visionary experiences and allegorical exegesis in "Visionary Experience in Ancient Judaism and Christianity" (2006), 56.

55 *Cels.* 1.48: αἰσθήσει οὐκ αἰσθητῇ.

56 Corresponding to the two basic principles outlined in Chapter 2. See, for example, *Princ.* 4.3.1 (citing Matt 4:8), where Origen takes up the story of the devil leading Jesus up "to a high mountain" to show him "the kingdoms of all the world and their glory" as one example among "countless" (μυρία) passages in the Gospels narrated *as if* they happened, but that didn't occur (at least not "literally"): "For who (of those who do not read such passages carelessly) would not criticize those who suppose that the kingdoms of the Persians, Scythians, Indians, and Parthians ... were seen with the eye of the flesh?" (as if this were possible if one were only "up high" enough). Similarly, see *Fr. Matt.* 66: "It is irrational to understand the 'mountain,' the 'going up,' and the 'kingdoms' in a sensory way [αἰσθητῶς]," rather than depicting, perhaps, some kind of interior vision (θεωρητός); see also *Fr. Luc.* 97. Cf. Theodore of Mopsuestia, who also says that the descent of the dove "appeared in a kind of spiritual vision [πνευματικὴν θεωρίαν], after the manner of the prophets" (*Commentary on John* Fr. 14 [on John 1:32]), and that the "high mountain" of the Temptation narrative was simply "imagined" (φαντασία) (*Commentary on Luke*; PG 66 722A); cf. Strauss's citations of both in *Life of Jesus*, §§50 and 55.

57 *Cels.* 1.48: Καὶ τῷ Ἰησοῦ γε ἠνοίχθησαν οἱ οὐρανοί.

58 *Cels.* 1.48 (citing John 1:32–34).

heavens' for his disciples, says to those who will see the same thing come to pass: 'Truly, truly, I say to you, you all shall see heaven opened [ὄψεσθε τὸν οὐρανὸν ἀνεῳγότα] and the angels of God ascending and descending upon the Son of Man.'"[59]

Origen could not be clearer. When he identifies a "certain kind of divine sense" in the Gospels, he is simply supplying an overarching terminology for those dimensions of certain narratives that – for all of the historiographical, literary, and logical reasons marshaled above – remain resistant to a literalist reduction: the non-physical or non-empirical dimensions of the Gospels' "mixed" narratives. This sense includes heavenly apparitions and divine voices, but also terminates in the confession: "I have seen and borne witness that this is the son of God." The pictorial or figurative language with which this "perception of what is imperceptible" is communicated becomes the medium by which others may come to share in this same "divine sense" – meaning that others may experience similar apocalyptic visions, perhaps,[60] but more fully (as the remaining chapters will continue to unfold) that they may share in the revelatory confession: "this is the son of God."[61]

Origen doesn't address the meaning of the figures of the dove and opened heavens here,[62] since "the argument does not demand that this be explained now. For our object is to prove [ἐλέγξαι] that Celsus wrongly attributed to a Jew incredulity about this matter expressed with such arguments as these."[63] The loss of most of Origen's commentaries on the Baptism narratives leaves us with only a few suggestive fragments: "the spirit comes down in the form of a dove, because where there is reconciliation with God there is a dove, as on the ark of Noah"[64], and: "The appearance of the dove reveals the deliverance from the flood and

59 *Cels.* 1.48 (citing John 1:51).

60 *Cels.* 1.48 (citing 2 Cor 12:2 and alluding to Acts 9): "So also Paul was caught up to the third heaven, having seen it opened before." Cf. *Cels.* 1.46. On sharing in a prophet's vision, cf. *Hom. Isa.* 5.2 and *Hom. Ezech.* 1.8.

61 See Sections 5.2–5.4 especially. In *Comm. Jo.* 2.36.221, Origen notes, similarly, that every reader is meant to share in Andrew's confession, "we have found the Messiah" (John 1:41).

62 *Cels.* 1.48: leaving to others to "explain the reason for the opening of the heavens and the form of the dove, and why the holy spirit did not appear to Jesus in the form of any other living being than this."

63 *Cels.* 1.44.

64 *Fr. Matt.* 56: "Even now the spirit comes in the form of a dove proclaiming the mercy of God to the world." See also *Hom. Luc.* 27.5–6.

the regeneration [παλιγγενεσία] of the world below, as it once did, for the first things bear an image of the second."[65]

In any case, all of the above vindicates the claim in Chapter 2 that when Origen says the truth of the Gospels doesn't only consist in their "corporeal" features, he frequently employs such distinctions for historical- and literary-critical purposes.[66] According to this reading of the Baptism (and of much of the Lukan infancy narrative, as Chapter 5 will show), we find that when Origen judges that some narrative – or some aspect of a narrative – in the Gospels didn't physically happen or that its truth doesn't consist in the "bare letter," he is often simply suggesting that what is narrated wasn't meant to depict some empirically observable fact alone: which is to say, as in the case of the Baptism narrative, it *represents some truth of Jesus's (and/or the disciples') interior vision or subjective understanding*. And yet, according to Origen's own order of argument, it is precisely by virtue of this critical precision that the narrative may then open into a "spiritual understanding" in a more directly theological sense. It is this very "perception of the imperceptible" or "sense of what isn't sensory" – a "seeing in the spirit" – that both produces the form and inspires the formation of the Gospels. Transposing Ernst Käsemann's dictum that "apocalyptic was the mother of Christian theology"[67]: for Origen, this kind of "divine sense," in all of its many forms, was the mother of the Gospels.

4.6 DISPELLING CARICATURES

I have suggested that Origen's figurative sense of the Gospels arises, in principle, from rather straightforward historical- and literary-critical judgments. In Part I's summary of his first principles for Gospel reading, and now in his direct reading of Jesus's baptism, Origen's interpretive approach bears no hint of taking each narrative "as a cryptogram for an idea, so that the whole has to be decoded term by term."[68] Nor does this

[65] *Fr. Matt.* 57 (evoking Matt 19:28). Cf. J. Dunn on how the image of the dove may be an "allusion to the epochal role ascribed to the Spirit in creation and to the dove after the flood" (*Jesus and the Spirit*, 65). Cf. W. D. Davies and D. Allison, *Matthew 1–7* (1998), 332–33, and J. A. Fitzmyer, *The Gospel According to Luke I–IX: Introduction, Translation, and Notes* (1982), 484.

[66] Cf. *Comm. Jo.* 10.3.14.

[67] E. Käsemann, "Die Anfänge christlicher Theologie" (1960), 180 (English translation, "The Beginnings of Christian Theology" [1969], 102).

[68] C. H. Dodd, *Parables of the Kingdom* (1978), 13. In fairness, Dodd is critiquing Augustine's reading of the parable of the Good Samaritan here (though the tradition to

consummate expression of what he means by the divine or spiritual sense of the Gospel narratives here in *Against Celsus* "completely destroy the truth of the historical narrative."[69] A satisfactory portrait of Origen as a reader of the Gospels simply cannot accept such reductions of his figurative view to stereotype.

Origen's motives and criteria for judging what in the Gospels was written symbolically – especially in cases where this judgment involves deeming that (parts of) a narrative didn't literally happen – have suffered from similarly misguided caricatures through two major stages in the modern development of Gospel criticism. A brief review of two particularly instructive misrepresentations of Origen's position should go far in showing the degree to which this study has already obviated slippage into such false starts and dead ends.

The first, extended by Thomas Woolston (1668–1733), construes Origen as a kind of proto-rationalist.[70] Directly citing *On First Principles* toward the beginning of his *Six Discourses on the Miracles of Our Saviour* (published between 1727 and 1730), Woolston writes:

> Origen says, that in the historical Part of the Scriptures, *There are some Things inserted as History, which were never transacted, and which it was impossible should be transacted; and other Things, again, that might possibly be done, but were not.* This he asserts of the Writings of the *Evangelists* … and gives many Instances to this Purpose … that is, that the Story of many of Jesus's Miracles is literally absurd, improbable, and incredible.[71]

which Augustine's reading belongs stretches back to Origen and, as Origen indicates, prior to him as well; cf. *Hom. Luc.* 34). As it happens, Dodd thinks this sense of allegory is what best characterizes the narratives in John's Gospel (*The Interpretation of the Fourth Gospel* [1953], 133–43), so my quotation does not really amount to a critique of Dodd; the phrase is simply an especially clear expression of a common stereotype of allegoresis.

69 Richard Simon, *Histoire critique des principaux commentateurs du Nouveau Testament, depuis le commencement du Christianisme jusques à nôtre tems* (1693), 47. Cf. Section 6.5.

70 Cf. Baird, *History of New Testament Research*, I:45–49. Origen, of course, considered Christian belief, including belief in the Gospels, to be thoroughly and unequivocally λογικός – that is, capable of being believed "rationally" (cf. *Cels.* 3.16: μετὰ λόγου πιστεύειν) – but such "rationalism" had little patience for presuming the sort of reductive materialism that Origen perceived Celsus slipping in and out of (with some analogy to disputes among various philosophies of nature in Woolston's own day). Cf. *Comm. Jo.* 2.16.114 and *Comm. ser. Matt.* 134.

71 Thomas Woolston, *Six Discourses on the Miracles of our Saviour* (1727), 8–9 (emphasis original). Cf. pp. 19–20, where Woolston theorizes (citing *On First Principles* Book 4 again, p. 21) that the miraculous elements of Jesus's life, as recorded by the Evangelists, "imply Improbabilities and Incredibilities … consequently, they, in whole, or in part,

Woolston himself has been subject to caricature as a crypto-Deist, and I wish to avoid over-reading his argument while citing him for over-reading Origen's.[72] He cannot be accused of saying Origen denies the historicity of miraculous events in the Gospels unequivocally (though his own rhetoric clearly tends in this direction).[73] Nevertheless, the effect of Woolston's citations simplifies Origen's sophisticated argument about the literary form of the Gospels to the question of miracle. The rather icy calculus becomes: when Origen says the Gospel narratives interweave things that "couldn't have happened" he means "miracles." Given the skeptical milieu of late seventeenth- and early eighteenth-century England, one can appreciate Woolston's motives (and his sincerity: he died in prison over controversies surrounding this work). But they are not – and could never be construed as – Origen's. The scandals, impediments, and impossibilities of the Gospel narratives, for Origen, are not reducible to the scandals, impediments, or impossibilities of miracle *tout court*.[74]

Chapters 1 and 3 have already made note of how, a little over a century later, David Strauss presented Origen as a progenitor of the mythical view. Yet, Strauss concludes, Origen's inability to overcome his "prepossessions in favor of the supernatural" prevented him from finally attaining a completely critical understanding.[75] However, Strauss's construal of the "supernatural" betrays his own "prepossessions in favor" of a "materialist twist on romantic monism"[76] – a position whose terms Origen would never embrace and which, for that matter, appears retrograde even in view of Strauss's own German Idealist patrimony.[77] Origen's religious

were never wrought, but are only related as prophetical and parabolical Narratives of what would be mysteriously and more wonderfully done by him."

72 Cf. W. H. Trapnell, *Thomas Woolston: Madman and Deist?* (1994); see pp. 33 and 84 for more on Woolston's devotion to Origen.

73 See, for example, Thomas Woolston, *Defence of his Discourses, Part II* (1730), 18–20.

74 Cf. Section 6.3.

75 Strauss, *Life of Jesus*, §4. For Strauss on Woolston, see *Life of Jesus*, §5.

76 T. Fabisiak, *The "Nocturnal Side of Science" in David Friedrich Strauss's* Life of Jesus Critically Examined (2015), 26.

77 See P. Tzamalikos, *Origen: Philosophy of History and Eschatology* (2007), 414–15: "Origen makes no distinction between 'natural' and 'supernatural' evidence, which is rather an invention of the centuries which followed." See Meier, *A Marginal Jew, Vol. 2*, 874 (and throughout) on avoiding "nature" language in historical criticism. Origen might not have unequivocally disputed "that an account is not historical ... when the narration is irreconcilable with the known and universal laws which govern the course of events" (*Life of Jesus*, §16), but would question the merits of Strauss's purely theological-philosophical stipulation that "the intermingling of the spiritual world with the human is found only in

philosophy is not so wooden.[78] A philosophical openness to the ontological subordination of matter to spirit is altogether different from a facile "prepossession in favor of the supernatural" and remains an intellectually honest position, even to the present day.[79] Anyway, Origen clearly attends to such a priori issues when he acknowledges that a Democritean or Epicurean might naturally come to different judgments about the ultimate "truth" of the Baptism narrative than a Jew, Christian, or any thinker disposed to a providential view of the world would, while also insisting that one must be wary of allowing such presumptions to inflect one's critical judgments.[80]

Be that as it may, Strauss is a better reader of Origen than Woolston. But his judgment regarding the limits of Origen's critical capacities relies

unauthentic records and is irreconcilable with all just conceptions" (*Life of Jesus*, §14), whether Strauss sufficiently interrogates the categories of "prophecy" and "miracle," and if his sense of "unmediated" divine causality is actually what the narratives imply by "divine apparitions, voices from heaven, and the like" (*Life of Jesus*, §16).

78 Some have argued that Strauss's "criteria of the unhistorical" are extricable from his philosophical commitments (see, e.g., M. Borg, "David Friedrich Strauss: Miracle and Myth" [1991]), even if this position directly contradicts Strauss's own self-understanding: see esp. his *Streitschriften* III, 55–126 (trans. *In Defense of My "Life of Jesus" against the Hegelians* [1983]). See also Fabisiak, *The "Nocturnal Side Of Science"*, 126–38. Cf. J. Breuss, "Das 'Leben Jesu' von David Friedrich Strauss und die Hegelsche Philosophie" (1972), esp. 399–400.

79 To be fair, Strauss had in view the more naïve "supernaturalists" of the generations preceding him; the subtleties of Origen's religious philosophy of nature (and that of his broader late-antique milieu) were simply not in view. On the question of the miraculous in Gospel criticism, see Meier, *A Marginal Jew, Vol.* 2, 514–15: "the historian may conclude that an event claimed by some people to be miraculous has no reasonable explanation or adequate cause in any human activity or physical force. To go beyond that judgment and to affirm *either* that God has directly acted to bring about this startling event *or* that God has not done so is to go beyond what any historian can affirm in his or her capacity as a historian and to enter the domain of philosophy or theology." Cf. Theissen/Merz, *Historical Jesus*, 312 for a "possible interpretation" of Jesus's healings "which is neither supernaturalistic or naturalistic." On the theological-philosophical intelligibility of the subordination of nature to spirit in a contemporary key, see S. Bulgakov, "On Miracle" (2011).

80 Strauss's other critique in *Life of Jesus* §4 regarding Origen's "fear of giving offense to the Orthodox Church" also oversimplifies matters, since Origen never intimates any avoidance of expressing his "true" opinion for fear of offending the "orthodox" (acknowledging that some "simpler" readers might find some of his critical judgments scandalous is decidedly not the same thing) and goes so far as to say that the presence of historical impossibilities in the biblical records are attributable to the very "economy" of the divine word and proper to the spirit's self-expression. Some may hold that Christian belief is incompatible with, or at least only ever adjacent to, the exercise of higher criticism; Origen himself clearly did not think so.

on presumptions just as detrimental to his vision of Origen's own interpretive criteria, with the question of miracle, once again, the determinative factor.[81] Woolston's and Strauss's over-readings, paradigmatic as they are of their respective eras, serve to deflect any notion that Origen's many evocations of "impossibilities" and "things that couldn't have happened" consist merely in the question of miracle – mostly by calling into question the usefulness of the category of the "miraculous" itself. For Origen, there is good reason (philosophically, logically, and otherwise) to believe nature and history are receptive and yielding to spirit; yet, as his reading of the Baptism narrative shows, he feels himself just as free to judge, for other reasons, that an event depicted as a physical phenomenon in the Gospels didn't happen (and really couldn't have). His position thus finds itself ill-suited for tidy typologies.

In sum, Origen's comparative work allows his readers to see how one can receive the appearance (φάσμα) of the dove as something other than a purely sensationalized fiction (πλάσμα) of the Evangelists. "Fiction" is too imprecise a category for what amounts, in Origen's view, to fairly self-evident historical- and literary-critical reasons and not theological ones alone – at least not theological reasons artificially imposed from outside the text, but rather evoked to account for a vision of the world and of history welling up from within this kind of prophetic literary tradition. Any similitude between Jesus's vision of the opened heavens and, say, Oedipus's encounter with the Sphinx, in the end, admits a much greater dissimilitude.[82]

According to Origen's view, what is recorded in the Gospel(s) is true inasmuch as the narrative depicts, in a figure, Jesus's own interior inspiration at the commencement of his public ministry. In short, it is entirely real, and can be thought of as "historical" even, precisely insofar as it is entirely spiritual. Thus, Origen roots his own "spiritual understanding" of the passage, first and foremost, in *Jesus*'s spiritual sense – *his* vision of the opened heavens, committed to writing in such a way as to preserve

[81] Cf. Schweitzer, *Quest*, 11 (emphasis added): "the critical study of the life of Jesus ... falls, immediately, into two periods, that before Strauss and that after Strauss. *The dominant interest in the first is the problem of miracle.* What terms are possible between a historical treatment and the acceptance of supernatural events? With the advent of Strauss this problem found a solution, viz., that these events do not belong in a historical account, but are mythical elements in the sources. The way was thus thrown open."

[82] Cf. *Cels.* 1.42.

this very sense. Or, as Origen phrases it in the *Commentary on John*, the Evangelists are themselves those who had come to share the same kind of vision that Jesus is recorded to have "seen in the spirit" at his baptism and set out to teach, "in figures," what they too "perceived in their own understanding."[83]

[83] Cf. *Comm. Jo.* 10.4.15.

5

Seeing the Word

The Lukan Infancy Narrative

"Many have tried to draw up a narrative of what has come to pass among us."[1]

Origen's homilies on the Lukan infancy narrative provide the next waypoint for our passage from his view of the Gospels in theory to his interpretation of them in practice.[2] Luke's prologue itself raises the question that occupied Part I ("What is a Gospel?") by way of pressing the subject into new territory. When first introducing Origen's understanding of the term "Gospel," we established that, in the strictest sense, the title is reserved for the four works devoted to narrating the life of Jesus. However, while accounting for how Origen compared the Gospels to other forms of writing in Christian scripture and the broader Greco-Roman milieu, a more restricted but highly consequential set of texts was left out of consideration: the many other writings that variously recorded Jesus's life and/or teachings *not* included in the New Testament canon. Many of them also accrued the title "Gospel," generally conformed to the definition supplied by Origen in Part I, and populated the literary landscape of early Christianity into Origen's own day. How, according to Origen, is one to distinguish the four received Gospels from the many others?

[1] Luke 1:1.

[2] The *Homilies on Luke* provide our only extant sequential commentary on either infancy narrative until Hilary of Poitier's *Commentary on Matthew* and Fortunatianus of Aquileia's *Commentary on the Gospels* (both c. 350s CE). Furthermore, they remain our only commentary on Luke prior to Ambrose's *Exposition of the Gospel according to Luke* (390–91 CE), the first two books of which borrow heavily from Origen.

5.1 THE LUKAN PROLOGUE: OTHER GOSPELS

Origen recognizes that the opening of Luke's prologue already invites the question of Gospel plurality. "Since *many* have attempted" to write such narratives (Luke 1:1), how is one to discriminate among them?

> Just as formerly among the Jewish people, many professed to prophesy, but some were "false prophets" (Hananiah, son of Azzur for instance) while others were truly prophets, and the people had a gift for discerning spirits, according to which they received some as prophets and rejected others (like "well-trained money changers"), so also now… "many have tried" to write Gospels, but not all have been received.[3]

Origen is fond of beginning works with dense comparisons of this kind.[4] The analogy anticipates the dominant theme of the first homily and captures something of the spirit of the whole collection. Just as in *On First Principles* Book 4 where Origen identifies the literary qualities shared by Jewish biblical narrative and Gospel narrative alike, so also here one immediately notices the continuity Origen sets out to establish between the reading communities before and after the time of Jesus. The trying task of discerning one voice from another – even of receiving one as authoritative instead of another – is not novel to Christ believers. There have always been "many" who claim to speak for God. Yet inasmuch as one can discern any continuity whatsoever among the scriptures of Israel, however great their diversity and development, one has already tasted something of the "discernment of spirits" with which Origen believes the Jewish people were gifted.

So too with the Gospels. Many were written (and still in the process of being written). Some were received by the newly forming churches; some were not.[5] Origen makes note of a number of other Gospels still in circulation: one "*According to the Egyptians*, another *According to the Twelve Apostles*. Basilides, too, dared to write a Gospel and give it his own name … one Gospel called *According to Thomas*, and another

[3] *Hom. Luc.* 1.1 (citing Luke 1:1 and evoking 1 Cor 12:4, 10; cf. Jer 35:1 LXX). On this unwritten saying of Jesus ("be well-trained money changers"), see also *Comm. Jo.* 19.44 and 32.215, *Comm. Matt.* 12.2, and *Comm. ser. Matt.* 33. Cf. *Hom. Ezech.* 2.2. Cf. J. Vos, "Das Agraphon 'Seid Kundige Geldwechsler!' bei Origenes" (1997) and C. Hutt, "'Be Ye Approved Money Changers!' Reexamining the Social Contexts of the Saying and Its Interpretation" (2012).

[4] Often with the construction ὥσπερ… οὕτω (*sicut… ita*); see, for example, *Comm. Jo.* 1.1.1 and *Hom. Lev.* 1.1.

[5] *Hom. Luc.* 1.1: "Not only four Gospels, but a great many, were written." Cf. 1.2: "The church has four Gospels, the heretical sects a great many."

According to Matthias, and many others."[6] Since Luke himself indicates that the proliferation of accounts of Jesus's life occasioned his own work ("many have tried to draw up a narrative of what has come to pass among us..."), Origen invites his readers to wonder: why were four – and these four in particular – "chosen from among them and handed on by the churches?"[7] What distinguishes the received Gospels from any other life of Jesus, which "many wrote"?

Origen suggests that Luke's phrasing ("many have *attempted*") "perhaps implies a subtle censure" of any who set about writing without a certain "charism" (χάρισμα) shared by the four received Evangelists, whose writings, Origen says, were all in keeping with or find their origins in a "holy spirit."[8] What Origen means by this exactly will take the remainder of the chapter to unfold. For now, one must simply deflect what we identified in Chapter 3 as the great Straussian misreading: namely that the only distinction between the allegorical and the mythical "modes of explanation" is that the allegorical "attributes the narrative to a supernatural source," an "immediate divine agency," while the mythical "ascribes it to the spirit of a people or a community," that "natural process by which legends are originated and developed."[9] This is no *spiritus ex machina* that Origen invokes in order to sidestep issues of true

6 *Hom. Luc.* 1.2. Origen just as often references noncanonical Gospels (and related literature) open-handedly, such as the "Gospel according to the Hebrews" in *Comm. Jo.* 2.15.87 (cf. *Hom. Jer.* 15.4), the "Acts of Paul" in *Princ.* 1.2.3 and *Comm. Jo.* 20.12.91, the "Gospel according to Peter" and "Book of James" in *Comm. Matt.* 10.17, and the "Preaching of Peter" in *Comm. Jo.* 13.17.104 and *Princ.* pr.8. On a certain "Gospel of the Nazaraeans," see the Latin translation of *Comm. Matt.* 15.14. On other "unwritten" sayings, see the Latin version of *Hom. Jer.* 3.3 and *Or.* 2.2. Cf. A. van den Hoek, "Clement and Origen as Sources on 'Noncanonical' Scriptural Traditions during the Late Second and Earlier Third Centuries" (1995). See also *Comm. Cant.* pr.4.

7 *Hom. Luc.* 1.1 (citing Luke 1:1).

8 *Hom. Luc.* 1.1, following the phrasing of the Greek fragment (all cited fragments drawn from M. Rauer [GCS 49], checked against the palimpsest catena of *Codex Zacynthius* with no differences of note). Cf. J. A. Fitzmyer, *Luke I–IX*, 291 on the possible "pejorative nuance" of ἐπεχείρησαν, citing Acts 9:29 and 19:13, as well as Josephus (*Life* 9.40 and 65.338) and Herm. Sim. 9.2.6. See also R. Helms, *Gospel Fictions* (1988), 13: "Luke was obviously writing during a time when literature about Jesus was flowering, and some of it was unacceptable to him." Cf. Keith, *The Gospels as Manuscript*, 125–29 and 233–34. The phrase ἀπὸ ἁγίου πνεύματος remains firmly in keeping with the argument developed in Chapter 3. The choice of preposition continues to deflect a notion of "immediate divine agency" (in Strauss's language) since ἀπό, more than other prepositions, carries an air of indirect or mediated causality (cf. Smyth 1684c on ἀπό vs. ἐκ or ὑπό).

9 Strauss, *Life of Jesus*, §12.

arbitration among the many Gospels. Inspiration is not, for Origen, just some detached dogmatic a priori, stipulated and then left behind.

Instead, Origen's "charism" language compels the reader to remember his opening comparison to Israel's reception of the prophetic writings. The Jewish people had "a gift [χάρισμα] for discerning spirits, according to which they judged some to be true prophets and some to be falsely so called."[10] So too, "like well-trained money changers," the churches discerned a certain spirit shared by these four Gospels – however diverse their respective voices – and received them accordingly. Moreover, Origen presents this election not only as a dogmatic *credendum* (it is this too[11]), but also as a true judgment or act of criticism (διάκρισις; κρίνω). Like the Jewish people's own processes of discernment that ultimately received the words of some prophets while rejecting others', so too it became the collective judgment of the churches that these four writers shared a certain "charism" or spirit distinguishable from other Gospels in circulation. What then is the nature of this "gift" of discernment that the four share?

For the sake of naming more distinctly what it is about the received Gospels that produced such a judgment, Origen turns to the succeeding phrase of the Lukan prologue: "just as they were handed on to us by those who from the beginning themselves saw, and became attendants of, the word."[12] Origen's interpretation involves a delicate question of translation. Contemporary Bibles almost universally translate Luke's *autoptai* as "eyewitnesses." Jerome's Latin translates the passage with a slight but ever-so-significant difference in emphasis: *ipsi viderunt* (both in Origen's homily here and in the Vulgate).[13] The English word "eyewitness" implies, almost invariably, a simple act of observation dependent on "being there"; similarly, eyewitness testimony generally asks for "just the facts" (Was the thief wearing red or blue? Did the victim have brown or blonde hair?). *Autoptēs* can occasionally mean "eyewitness" in this empirical or forensic sense, but Jerome's translation better preserves the word's more literal, and more ambiguous, sense: simply to "see (for)

[10] *Hom. Luc.* 1.1, following the phrasing of the Greek fragment.

[11] Cf. *Hom. Luc.* 1.2: "But in all these matters we approve of nothing but what the church approves of, namely only four Gospels are to be received."

[12] Luke 1:2.

[13] Upon moving to Rome, Jerome began the edition that was to become known as the Vulgate in 382; his revision of the Gospels was first published in 384 (cf. H. A. G. Houghton, *The Latin New Testament: A Guide to its Early History, Texts, and Manuscripts* [2016], 31–35). The *Homilies on Luke* were translated after Jerome moved back to Bethlehem, c. 390–93 CE (see FC 94, xxxiv).

oneself" – which includes *seeing with one's own eyes*, but can also extend to something like a *personal experience* or *vision* (even of divinity or divine manifestation).[14] As with the English "seeing" (or "perceiving" or "sensing") ὁρᾶν may mean "looking" *and/or* "understanding." Only context determines which is meant (or both). The prefix lays additional emphasis on one's personal involvement (*ipse*/αὐτός).[15]

Origen's interpretation of the phrase both confirms and tests the ambiguity of *autoptai*. What kind of "seeing" is handed on by those who themselves, as Luke says, became "attendants of the word?" The apostles were deemed *autoptai*, Origen says, "not only because they had 'looked at' Jesus (in a physical sense), but because they had also 'seen' the word of God."[16] For if merely "looking at Jesus physically" was all it took to come to "see the word for oneself" then "Pilate, who condemned him, was an '*autopēs* of the word,' and so was Judas the betrayer, and all those who cried out," "Crucify, crucify him!"[17] Pilate, Judas, and the mob were all "eyewitnesses" of Jesus's final hours (in a banal empirical sense[18]). Does this qualify them for inclusion among Luke's tradents? They saw

[14] Cf. LSJ on αὐτοπτέω and related nouns (αὐτόπτης, αὔτοπτος, αὐτοπτικός). See L. Alexander, *The Preface to Luke's Gospel: Literary Convention and Social Context in Luke 1.1–4 and Acts 1.1* (1993), 120: "Eyewitnesses" has "misleading associations for modern readers. For us, the word has forensic links: an eyewitness is characteristically a witness who was present *at the time when an accident or a crime took place*, very often a passer-by whose connection with the incident is accidental. The Greek word is hardly ever used in this way." Ibid., 124: "the *autoptēs* is one who knows what s/he is talking about from personal experience." Cf. R. Bauckham, *Jesus and the Eyewitnesses: The Gospels as Eyewitness Testimony* (2006), 116–24, with counterpoint from J. N. Collins, "Rethinking 'Eyewitnesses' in the Light of 'Servants of the Word' (Luke 1:2)" (2010). On the range of the term in Origen, see *Comm. Jo.* 6.49.253 on how John the Baptist "sees Jesus for himself" (αὐτόπτης) but precisely *as* the "lamb of God who takes away the sins of the world"; cf. *Comm. Jo.* 20.7.46–48 on what it means to share in Jesus's own vision (αὐτόπτης) of the Father (similarly, see *Comm. Jo.* 13.53.352 on "seeing the word").

[15] Luke shows no interest in "mere hearsay," Origen adds (*Hom. Luc.* 1.6).

[16] *Hom. Luc.* 1.4, following the phrasing of the Greek fragment. Another analogy is drawn to the people of Israel in this section (citing Exod 20:18: "The people saw the voice of the Lord"): "Obviously a voice is heard rather than seen. But the scripture says this to show us that it is with different 'eyes' that those who are worthy of 'seeing God's voice' see." Cf. *Cels.* 6.62. See also Philo, *Decal.* 32–35. On the connection between vision and the word of God in both patriarchal and prophetic narratives, cf. Gen 15:1 and Isa 2:1. On ὁ λόγος as "word of God" here, cf. Fitzmyer, *Luke I–IX*, 295 and F. Bovon, *Luke 1: A Commentary on the Gospel of Luke 1:1–9:50* (2002), 21.

[17] *Hom. Luc.* 1.4 (citing Luke 23:21), following the phrasing of the Greek fragment. Cf. *Cels.* 7.43. See also *Hom. Lev.* 1.1 on "what was seen" vs. "what was understood" about Jesus (cf. *Hom. Isa.* 6.3).

[18] *Hom. Luc.* 1.4, Greek fragment: τὸ ἑωρακέναι τὸν Ἰησοῦν κατὰ σῶμα.

Jesus for themselves. But this was not enough to make them "attendants of the word." The apostles also physically looked at Jesus (κατὰ σῶμα). Yet, Origen argues, Luke's *autoptai* simply cannot mean *only* this. Some may have themselves seen "what has come to pass among us," but "being there" guaranteed nothing.

So we find ourselves passing into territory made familiar in the preceding chapters. The canonical Gospels, as Origen has said all along, do not narrate matters of mere empirical facticity alone. In view of the Lukan prologue, Origen disputes that anything could have been materially probative for receiving the proclamation that what had "come to pass" belonged to the word of God. Whether consciously intended or not, Rudolf Bultmann's comments on John 1:14b ("we have seen his glory...") may as well have been written as a penetrating exposition of Origen on Luke's *autoptai*. Such a vision, Bultmann writes, "clearly does not occur, as some might naively wish to imagine, in a divine demonstration, visible to the natural eye of the body or the soul and with the power to fascinate and convince the natural man."[19] Rather, "the notion of the vision of the glory has been historicized," and this kind of "'seeing' is not concerned with eye-witnessing in a historical or a legal sense." "For in this sense" others "were also eye-witnesses, yet they saw nothing."[20] Since "what faith sees ... has never been perceived as an empirical event by any man," such "sight is not limited to the contemporaries" of these events, "but it is passed on by them to all the succeeding generations."[21] Therefore, just as the "we have seen..." in John 1:14

> could not have been spoken only by "eye-witnesses," so too it could not have been spoken outside the history which is founded on the believing eye-witnesses and the tradition passed on by them ... the "eye-witnesses" as such are considered not as those who stand guarantee for some later generation for the truth of the revelation, but as those who confront every generation anew.[22]

For Origen, neither can Luke be said to rely simply on "eyewitnesses"; he draws from material passed on by those who had both seen these things for themselves *and* had come to perceive them in a particular

[19] R. Bultmann, *The Gospel of John: A Commentary* (1971), 68.
[20] Bultmann, *The Gospel of John*, 68–69. [21] Bultmann, *The Gospel of John*, 70.
[22] Bultmann, *The Gospel of John*, 70: "the old dispute whether the speakers are eye-witnesses or those who see in a 'spiritual' sense is based on a false alternative, inasmuch as the precise character of 'spiritual' sight is not defined." Bultmann proceeds to define "spiritual" sight in a way that contrasts with what he means by "what faith sees" (a distinction that does not apply to Origen's sense of the term "spiritual") and in the process ironically fashions another "false alternative."

way.[23] They "signified something."[24] Luke's tradents are those who had come to conceive of the life of Jesus as a definitive pronouncement, even embodiment, of the word of the Lord. And this perception, for Origen, does not consist in simply having observed "what happened" as prophecies plainly "fulfilled *before my eyes*."[25] Luke, rather, composes a narrative of those things of which he and his community had become "fully convinced" – or, as Jerome explains the phrase (breaking the translator's fourth wall): a narrative of "that which has become manifestly clear to us."[26]

Luke therefore intends, Origen says, not merely to relate what transpired as a matter of fact (there is nothing here decisively "convincing" to the naked eye), but a particular "understanding" and "account" of these things, since the reality or significance of them, "what is true and what false, is not judged from visible signs and portents but by one's account" thereof.[27] To borrow one of our programmatic formulations from Part I: Luke narrates what those "from the beginning" had come to "perceive in their own understanding" about the events of (and surrounding) this life – that is, what those "among us" had come to see, in a manner utterly and terribly clear to them, "in the spirit."[28] In Origen's view, therefore, Luke sets out to compose a narrative whose literary form is ordered according to the spirit of those who had seen this life in such a way that they discerned God's own word at its heart, devoted their lives to the service of this word, and handed on their vision of "what had come to pass among" them in precisely this way – that is, "just as those who from the

[23] See Fitzmyer, *Luke I–IX*, 289–90. Cf. D. P. Moessner, "Luke as Tradent and Hermeneut: 'As one who has a thoroughly informed familiarity with all the events from the top' (παρηκολουθηκότι ἄνωθεν πᾶσιν ἀκριβῶς, Luke 1:3)" (2016).

[24] *Cels.* 2.69. [25] Lessing, "On the proof of the spirit and of power," 84–85.

[26] *Hom. Luc.* 1.3 (on Luke 1:1): "Latin cannot express 'πεπληροφορημένων' in one word." Jerome paraphrases it several ways in his translation of the first homily (*Hom. Luc.* 1.1: *quae manifestissime cognitae sunt in nobis*; 1.2: *quae confirmatae sunt in nobis… quae nobis manifestissime sunt compertae*; 1.3: *in nobis manifestissime sunt ostensae*). The exact meaning of πληροφορέω is still a matter of some debate (cf. Fitzmyer, *Luke I–IX*, 293); Origen leans into its epistemic dimensions, though not to the occlusion of a sense of "fulfillment" (things have "come to pass" among us, about which we have become "fully convinced").

[27] *Hom. Luc.* 1.3, Greek fragment (from which Jerome's translation differs slightly): ὄφις γαρ οὐ πληροφορει, ἐπει οὐκ ἀπὸ σημείων καὶ τεράτων ὁρατῶν κρίνεται τὰ πράγματα, ἀλλὰ λόγῳ κρίνεται, ποῖα τὰ ἀληλθῆ καὶ ποῖα τὰ ψευδῆ (a distinction hardly opposed to the spirit of Lessing's sensitivity to confusing truths of history with truths of reason).

[28] Cf. *Comm. Jo.* 10.4.15.

beginning themselves saw, and became attendants of, the word handed these things down to us."[29]

From the very first lines of the *Homilies on Luke*, therefore, one can already see Origen's first principles of Gospel reading fully in play. Rather than allowing the spiritual to relativize the critical or the critical to relativize the spiritual, Origen immediately establishes the non-competitive, even coinherent, character of the two categories. We have already seen Origen establish his sense of the principally spiritual or figurative character of Gospel narrative on historical- and literary-critical grounds; here, conversely, Origen deems that Luke's own self-proclaimed literary *modus operandi* subsisted in a series of judgments about the traditions he was receiving and ways of handing them on, a "discernment of spirits." Similarly, readers cannot come to a judgment concerning what is distinctive about his Gospel (or any of the others) apart from the same process of critical discernment. As Francis Watson puts it:

> The four Gospels did not simply impose themselves on the Christian community, marginalizing all other Gospel literature by their sheer presence. Early Gospels looked broadly similar, sharing many of the same generic conventions. There was no prior reason to suppose that some would be counterfeits, that precisely four would prove genuine, and that a Gospel attributed to Matthew would be included in that number whereas one attributed to Thomas would not. Informed critical reading of all early Christian Gospels was required, and it was informed readers who chose the texts that would henceforth be normative, just as their predecessors in ancient Israel chose Jeremiah at the expense of Hananiah.[30]

In other words, the four were not chosen merely due to historical proximity or degree of factual accuracy. They were chosen because a shared spirit was discernible within and among them – discernible, that is, precisely in and through attentive reading.

In sum, Origen takes the Lukan prologue to mean that the Evangelist orders his narrative not only according to *what* his tradents saw, but also according to *how* they saw it. In other words, this "discernment of spirits" belonged originally to those who had "themselves seen and become attendants of the word." The Gospel writer, in turn, conforms his narrative (ἀνατάξασθαι διήγησιν) according to this selfsame spirit and passes on this "spiritual" understanding precisely under the form of his narrative (καθὼς παρέδοσαν), so arranged to preserve and confer what those who preceded had "perceived in their own understanding."[31]

[29] Luke 1:1. [30] F. Watson, *Gospel Writing*, 514 (commenting on *Hom. Luc.* 1).
[31] Cf. *Comm. Jo.* 10.5.18.

In short, the spirit *is* the form of the narrative. And the narrative is formed to hand on this spirit, *their* spirit. Luke's Gospel, for Origen, is, in this very precise sense, an inspired narrative.

5.2 VISION IN THE TEMPLE: THRESHOLDS OF THE NARRATIVE

The first event recorded by Luke immediately re-raises the question of the kind of vision the Evangelist conforms his narrative to: "*then there appeared to* [Zechariah] *an angel of the Lord* standing at the right side of the altar of incense."[32] What sort of "seeing" does one find depicted here? And what kind of *historia* narrates such an event?

Zechariah's vision in the Temple is, for Origen, the definition of a narrative *skandalon*; any reader approaching the text with a superficial sense of historicity will stumble over the threshold of the narrative. The very nature of what it depicts impedes a reduction to matters of purely empirical facticity. Origen's caution from *On First Principles* thus finds direct application here: attentive readers must feel the impediment, lest they be "thrown off by the enticing simplicity of [Luke's] style" to such a degree that they, never "stirred from the letter," might "doubt that anything besides the obvious could be meant."[33] One may also recall Origen and Strauss's shared opponents: those who "sacrifice all divine meaning" either, on the one hand, out of a misguided obligation to a simplistic sense of historicity or, on the other hand, because they presume any story that narrates an apparition of this nature is *per se* false (or worse, deceptive).[34] Yet, like the events narrated to have happened following Jesus's baptism, Origen also does not presume that telling the story of such a vision automatically makes the narrative a pure fabrication.

So what is the historical status of the angelic apparition, in Origen's view? He first deflects any presumption that the appearance is recorded as a matter of simple sensory perception, as if all it took to see what Zechariah is said to have seen was healthy eyesight.[35] This is not the kind of perception at play here, or anywhere in the whole sweep of the scriptures, when something divine or angelic is said to have appeared to someone.[36] As Origen understands the kind(s) of visions narrated in Luke

[32] Luke 1:11: ὤφθη δὲ αὐτῷ. [33] *Princ.* 4.2.9.

[34] See *Life of Jesus*, §12 as discussed in Section 3.1.

[35] *Hom. Luc.* 3.1 (cf. *Hom. Luc.* 4.1): ὑγιὴς ὀφθαλμός. [36] *Hom. Luc.* 3.2. Cf. *Cels.* 6.4.

1–2, even if other people were to have been in the exact same place – here, even if someone had been standing right next to Zechariah – one might "see" something and the other(s) nothing at all.[37] Appearances of this kind rather belong, Origen says, to those who have been prepared (or *prepared themselves*) for this sort of vision.[38] In the case of Zechariah in the Temple, the kind of "seeing" that Luke narrates was never a matter of simply having been "there" to gape at some physical spectacle, but rather of interior vision.[39] In the language of the preceding chapters, it depicts a "seeing in the spirit," a "certain kind of divine sense," or perhaps, in more contemporary parlance, a prophetic-apocalyptic vision.[40]

With the near total loss of the first books of both the Matthew and Luke commentaries, one can only speculate about how Origen might have dealt with a detailed comparison to Matthew's infancy narrative in a different context – i.e., in a commentary proper and not a series of short sermons, where he never engages in the kind of lengthy critical examinations of parallel narratives that often appear in his commentaries.[41] Origen's brief excursus on the nature of Zechariah's vision nevertheless serves to underscore several crucial questions raised in Part I. Firstly, it shows that Origen's historical-critical intuitions neither trade in the naïve "supernaturalism" that Strauss accuses him of nor, on the other hand, does he find anything unhistorical or inauthentic per se about narratives that report someone's mystical experience or interior vision. He simply looks to present a coherent way to receive the story of a divine or angelic vision like this as something that happened. At the same time, and in view

37 *Hom. Luc.* 3.3: "Even if in the same place, the place itself will not be able to help or hinder them," because "seeing God" is a matter of the heart (evoking Matt 5:8).

38 *Hom. Luc.* 3.3: παρεσκευάσθαι.

39 Cf. *Princ.* 1.1.9 on Matthew's language of "purity of heart" pertaining to interior vision or understanding.

40 Cf. *Comm. Jo.* 10.4.15 (Chapter 3) and *Cels.* 1.48 (Chapter 4); in *Hom. Luc.* 3.3, Origen directly compares the way such things appear in this "present age" with the kind of vision that characterizes the "age to come." For contemporary scholarship on angelic apparitions as apocalyptic visions in Luke-Acts, see K. P. De Long, "Angels and Visions in Luke-Acts" (2017). Cf. C. Rowland and C. R. A. Morray-Jones, *The Mystery of God: Early Jewish Mysticism and the New Testament* (2009), 99–104.

41 See Chapter 6 (though one finds the occasional exception: for example, *Hom. Luc.* 28.1–4 and 35.1–2). Cf. *Hom. Lev.* 7.1.1, along with Rufinus's "epilogue" appended to his translation of Origen's *Commentary on Romans*, where he confesses his habit of changing the style of Origen's homilies in order to make them more like commentaries, a difference Jerome appears to have preserved better in his translation of the *Homilies on Luke*. On the difficulties of harmonizing Matthew and Luke's timelines in their respective infancy narratives, cf. P. Tzamalikos, *Origen: New Fragments from the Commentary on Matthew, Codices Sabaiticus 232 & Holy Cross 104, Jerusalem* (2020), 15–17.

of such an opening pericope, we see quite clearly why Origen's reading of the prologue so strongly relativizes a reflex to "eyewitnesses" in any superficial sense. Such things "don't appear to everyone."[42]

Still, since Origen's openness to attributing a certain kind of facticity to Zechariah's vision finds fewer friends among contemporary scholars, perhaps the reader will permit a modern analogy. Stories of divine or angelic apparitions are, of course, not a uniquely ancient phenomenon. In fact, appearances of this sort are narrated in an unbroken chain from the beginning to the end of the scriptures of Israel, in every stratum and genre of the New Testament writings, and in innumerable testimonies through every age of the Christian era since. In more recent generations, the most instructive (and widely known) examples are the Marian apparitions of Guadalupe, Lourdes, and Fatima. In a study of the history and effects of Lourdes, for instance, Ruth Harris writes:

> No amount of documents can "prove" that Bernadette saw anything at all. Silent and invisible to everyone but the young shepherdess, the apparitions were believed because of the ardent faith of the visionary and her witnesses ... while I hope that nothing will offend the faith of believers, I cannot engage with the question of whether or not Bernadette Soubirous saw the Virgin Mary: it is not a matter an historian can decide.[43]

Historical criticism cannot decide, empirically, whether Bernadette "really" saw the Blessed Virgin and heard her Provençal "que soy era Immaculada Councepciou" or if her tale "was a fabrication" or "hallucination" as some believed from the very beginning.[44] As Origen himself puts it: "What is true and what false" about such matters "is not judged from visible signs and portents but by the account" (λόγος) one makes of them.[45]

[42] *Hom. Luc.* 3.3.

[43] R. Harris, *Lourdes: Body and Spirit in the Secular Age* (1999), 21 (a project that, as Harris herself observes, did not ultimately dissuade her from her own "Jewish secularism" [p. xv]).

[44] Harris, *Lourdes*, 55 and 62. Yet, as Harris points out, the immense historical effects of this event on France, the world, the millions who still make pilgrimage to the shrine every year, and the millions more who regularly devote themselves in prayer to Notre Dame de Lourdes, can hardly be overstated.

[45] *Hom. Luc.* 1.3. The methodological difficulties Harris draws out in her study share remarkable parallels with perennial questions in historical criticism of the Gospels (cf. Meier, *A Marginal Jew, Vol. 2*, 514–15; cf. Allison, *The Resurrection of Jesus*, 294–300). Must Origen be considered more critically naïve (for implying that such an apparition could have happened in the way outlined above) than, say, a Strauss or Bultmann, who frequently take their own philosophical/theological judgments for what is "critical" in a strictly historical sense? Cf. Strauss, *Life of Jesus*, §14: "narratives of angels and of devils,

Using the grammar developed in Chapters 2 and 3, then, one could say that Origen finds a historical narrative here, yes, but one which interweaves things that "didn't *physically* happen," one that sets out to portray historically (εἰκὼν ἱστορική) what was "seen in the spirit."[46] What can only have been made clear to Zechariah in a "purely interior way" is composed "with language that would make it seem that it was perceptible to the senses,"[47] all while, for Origen, relating an event no less wondrous and startling – and real – for it.

In a more literary register, the particular phrasing of "there appeared to him..." recalls similar divine or angelic appearances to Abraham and to the other saints and prophets of old.[48] By invoking the divine

of their appearing in human shape and interfering with human concerns, cannot possibly be received as historical." See also *Life of Jesus*, §16: "Even admitting the existence of angels, we cannot suppose them capable of manifesting themselves to human beings, since they belong to the invisible world, and spiritual existences are not cognizable by the organs of sense; so that it is always advisable to refer their pretended apparitions to the imagination." Cf. R. Bultmann, "New Testament and Mythology" (1961), 5: "It is impossible to use electric light and the wireless and to avail ourselves of modern medical and surgical discoveries, and at the same time to believe in the New Testament world of spirits and miracles." Origen, instead, points out that what many other religious and philosophical traditions call "good daemons" Christians call "angels" (*Cels.* 4.24; cf. Philo, *Gig.* 6). See also *Cels.* 1.66 on the angelic appearances to Joseph in dreams: "That it should be indicated to certain people in a dream that they ought to do certain things is an experience which happens to many others also, whether an angel or any other agent brings the suggestion before the soul."

46 See *Princ.* 4.2.9 and *Comm. Jo.* 10.4.17. 47 See *Comm. Jo.* 10.5.18.

48 *Hom. Luc.* 3.1 (Luke 1:11: ὤφθη αὐτῷ). Origen's appeal to Jewish literary precedent is reminiscent of his treatment of the baptism narrative, as we saw in Section 4.3. See Fitzmyer, *Luke I–IX*, 324: Luke uses the form *ōphthē* "again in 24:34; Acts 2:3; 7:2, 26, 30, 35; 9:17; 13:31; 16:9; 26:16 to denote various epiphanies or appearances. It is also used frequently in the LXX in the same sense (e.g., Gen 12:7; 17:1; 18:1)"; cf. R. E. Brown, *The Birth of the Messiah: A Commentary on the Infancy Narratives in the Gospels of Matthew and Luke* (1999), 260. One might add Gen 22:14; 26:2, 24; 35:9, and Exod 3:2, all the way through the divine appearance at Sinai (Exod 16:10) and in the tabernacle (Lev 9:23; cf. Exod 25:8 LXX: "you shall make a sanctuary for me and I shall appear [ὀφθήσομαι] among you). See also 1 Cor 15:5–8 (cf. 9:1) on the appearances of the resurrected Christ. The judgment of the people outside upon Zechariah's delayed reappearance (Luke 1:22: "they realized he had seen a vision [ὀπτασίαν] in the sanctuary") similarly situates the narrative within a deep bed of visionary parallels: see Acts 26:19 (τῇ οὐρανίῳ ὀπτασίᾳ) and 2 Cor 12:1 (εἰς ὀπτασίας καὶ ἀποκαλύψεις κυρίου), both concerning visionary experiences of Paul (note how in 2 Cor the question of whether or not the vision was "bodily" is specifically raised twice). Based on Josephus *Ant.* 13.10.3 §§282–83 (and y. Yoma 5:2, 42c; cf. b. Yoma 39b; cf. b. Berakhot 7a), both Brown (*Birth of the Messiah*, 263) and Fitzmyer (*Luke I–IX*, 329) mention the possibility of a longer tradition of appearances in the sanctuary. It is possible Luke intended some connection between Zechariah's vision and the way Paul self-narrates being caught up

appearances to Abraham (among others), Origen recalls a whole network of *historiae* whose narrative coherence subsists essentially in such appearances.[49] Stretching from the call of Abram, the rest of the patriarchal narratives, and the Exodus, through the diverse historical and prophetic writings of Israel, on into the variously recorded experiences of the earliest Christians, divine-angelic appearances of this kind populate a literary tradition that constitutes the entire sweep of Christian scripture. Such visions become the *axis mundi* around which the whole movement of the life and history of Israel and early Christianity turns. Origen senses Luke's language invoking this tradition and invites his readers to read the angelic appearance to Zechariah in the same spirit.

Thus we find here in the *Homilies on Luke* that everything Origen says in the *Commentary on John* regarding the nature of the Gospel writers as "those who see in the spirit" extends from the literary formation of the Gospels to the formation of any traditions – written or otherwise – that precede.[50] The spirit in which Luke sees is not only his spirit but also (involves the tradition of) the "spirit" of the subjects of his narrative, who are said to have themselves come to see "what has come to pass among us" in the spirit.

It is only fitting then that Origen makes Zechariah's vision in the Temple an occasion for returning to the larger motif he developed in his first homily on the Lukan prologue: "One also ought to think about Christ in a similar way, because not everyone who saw him saw him as the Christ."[51] Sure, they "saw his body," but "Christ, *insofar as he was the Christ*, they did not see."[52] Anyone could have stood in the sanctuary with Zechariah and not seen what he is recorded to have seen. It would not have been any different, *mutatis mutandis*, for one to have stood before Jesus himself. "Neither Pilate nor Judas saw Christ as the Christ; nor did the crowd which pressed around him." He was seen *as such* "only by those who were worthy."[53]

in an "ecstatic" vision while "praying in the Temple" directly after the Damascus experience (Acts 22:17); see O. Betz, "Die Vision des Paulus im Tempel von Jerusalem: Apg 22,17–21 als Beitrag zur Deutung des Damaskuserlebnisses" (1970), esp. 114. Cf. Dan 9:23, 10:1, 7–8, 16 (Θ) and Mal 3:2.

49 Cf. *Hom. Luc.* 3.2: "Thus, wherever scripture says 'God appeared' to someone or other ... understand it as I have explained here."

50 Cf. *Cels.* 1.43, as covered in Section 4.4.

51 *Hom. Luc.* 3.3 (following the phrasing of the Greek fragment).

52 *Hom. Luc.* 3.4. These passages directly recall several lines from *Hom. Luc.* 1.4 on "seeing Jesus physically" vs. "seeing the word" (cited in Section 5.1).

53 *Hom. Luc.* 3.4.

In other words, *this* is the kind of vision that Luke's tradents are said to have handed on and to which the Evangelist conforms his narrative: seeing Jesus as the Christ. This is what it ultimately means, in Origen's view, for Luke to have ordered his narrative according to the spirit of those who had "themselves seen, and become servants of, the word" (Luke 1:1). The narrative of the angel's appearance in the sanctuary is a subspecies of a far more expansive sensibility – a "charism" – Origen finds embedded within the very nature of Luke's Gospel (and, in their own way, the other three that have been received), inclusive of but not reducible to this particular kind of visionary experience alone. Origen's analysis of the nature of Zechariah's Temple vision, in sum, continues to unfold how his conception of "seeing in the spirit" or "spiritual understanding" or a "certain kind of divine sense" becomes a universally applicable criterion for coming to terms with both the form and formation of Gospel narrative.[54]

Moreover, it is a vision somehow no less available to the present reader of the narrative: "Let us too, therefore, labor so that God might appear to us at this moment."[55] Origen concludes the homily here, leaving what it might mean for God to appear "at this moment" wrapt in reverent silence. Nevertheless, it is our first taste of a recurring motif in Origen's ever-so-subtle translations of the "perceptible Gospel into the spiritual": the simple addition of "even now."

5.3 IN SPIRIT AND POWER: JOHN THE BAPTIST

What would it mean for Luke's audience – as well as Origen's – to share in Zechariah's vision? Why narrate such a thing at all? Let us turn our attention to the object of the appearance: the angelic prophecy regarding Zechariah's son. "He will go before him in the spirit and power of Elijah ... to make ready a people prepared for the Lord."[56] Here we stumble upon the troubled pairing – "spirit and power" – from *Against Celsus* and Lessing's (mis)representation thereof. For Origen, the spirit and power that mark the life of the Baptist are embedded within and

[54] Cf. *Comm. Jo.* 10.4.15, 10.6.27, and *Cels.* 1.48, respectively. See also *Hom. Lev.* 1.1 on the distinction between what was seen (*quod videtur*) vs. what was understood (*quod intelligitur*) about Jesus (cf. B. Lonergan, "Cognitional Structure" [1988], esp. 206).

[55] *Hom. Luc.* 3.4 (cf. 3.2).

[56] Luke 1:17 (construing John's relationship to the figure of Elijah in terms of "spirit and power" is unique to Luke).

remain unrecognizable apart from Israel's prophetic tradition.[57] To be endowed with the "spirit and power of Elijah" means to participate in a certain "spiritual charism" which all of the prophets shared; "in the spirit of" simply means to share a "prophetic charism."[58] Just so, in ways evocative not only of Elijah, but also Isaiah, Amos, and Jeremiah, "the word of God" comes to "John the son of Zechariah in the wilderness" with "portentous force."[59] In other words, in the Baptist's ministry we find a kind of "demonstration of spirit and power" – one "proper to the word" – utterly in keeping with Origen's open-ended evocation of this doublet in *Against Celsus* but utterly at odds with Lessing's reductive construal.[60]

So one can already describe much more precisely what, for Origen, marks this "spirit" John is to be possessed of and what kind of "power" he is to "go forth before" the Lord in. Dazzlingly demonstrative displays find no home here. "John performed no signs."[61] Rather, he is said to be

> the voice of one crying in the wilderness: Prepare the way of the Lord, make his paths straight. Every valley shall be filled, and every mountain and hill shall be brought low, and the crooked shall be made straight, and the rough ways shall be made smooth; and all flesh shall see the salvation of God.[62]

To whatever extent this Isaian imagery was ever meant literally, in the Gospels it becomes deeply, if not utterly, figural.[63] "What way is prepared for the Lord?" Origen asks, "surely not a physical one? Or can God's word go on such a journey?"[64] Origen continues to press his listeners: if,

[57] *Hom. Luc.* 4.5: "Spirit and power were upon Elijah, as in all the prophets ... the spirit that had been in Elijah was in John as well, and the power that was in Elijah also appeared in [John]."

[58] *Hom. Luc.* 4.5 (Greek fragment).

[59] *Hom. Luc.* 21.1–2 (citing Luke 3:1-2): τεράστιος δύναμις. Cf. *Cels.* 1.2: διὰ τὰς τεραστίους δυνάμεις.

[60] Cf. "On the proof of the spirit and of power," 83–85.

[61] John 10:41.

[62] Luke 3:4–6 (citing Isa 40:3–5). For Origen's presentation of the four Evangelists' varying receptions of and editorial adjustments to this prophetic tradition, see *Comm. Jo.* 6.24.127–6.26.138.

[63] See K. Baltzer, *Deutero-Isaiah: A Commentary* (2001), 54–55. See also S. Moyise, "The Wilderness Quotation in Mark 1:2-3" (2005), esp. 84. Cf. N. Perrin, *What Is Redaction Criticism?* (1969), 36 (with reference to W. Marxsen, *Mark the Evangelist: Studies on the Redaction History of the Gospel* [1969], 37–38). Cf. Wis 9:17–18. See also the use of Isa 40:3 in the Community Rule (1QS 8:13–15, 9:19–20; cf. the Aramaic Levi Document 2:5), especially in light of D. Dimant, "Not Exile in the Desert but Exile in Spirit: The Pesher of Isa 40:3 in the *Rule of the Community* and the History of the Scrolls Community" (2014).

[64] *Hom. Luc.* 21.5.

in the Gospels, the way of the Lord is prepared neither by paving literal roads through the Judean desert nor by earthmoving among its foothills, then how else does John begin to "make straight his paths" than "from *within*"?[65] In what way does the Gospel represent these paths, valleys, mountains, and rough or crooked ways other than "spiritually"? That is, the decisive new advance of the word of God which John heralds and ushers into the world begins in this "way": by passing first through the cry of his voice and then into the hearts of a new community that begins to form around his preaching – that is, through a "baptism of repentance for the forgiveness of sins." "This is the way by which God's word enters: in the spaces of the human heart."[66]

"Yet not only then, but also now," Origen goes on, "'a burning and shining lamp' comes first, 'preaching a baptism of repentance for the remission of sins'; then the 'true light' follows."[67] So the crucial supplement reappears once more: the candescently understated *even now* (καὶ νῦν), in which Origen's whole vision of the "eternal Gospel" lies latent.[68] Origen found himself, at that very moment, standing before a group of catechumens whose own hearts, by the selfsame word, had been moved to repentance and who also were then, so many generations later, preparing for baptism.[69] Thus:

> The mystery [*sacramentum*] of John, I think, is filling the world *even to this day*. If anyone is going to believe in Christ Jesus, John's *spirit and power* first comes to her soul and "prepares a perfect people for the Lord." It makes the roads in the heart's rough places level and straightens out its paths. Not only at that time were the roads made ready and paths straightened; *even today John's spirit and power* precedes the coming [*adventum*] of our Lord.[70]

John is certainly a historical figure for Origen, and his preaching a fact of history. Yet, precisely as a historical figure, the Baptist becomes an archetype of those who "see in the spirit," those for whom it seemed the words and presence of God drew near.[71] Luke, in turn, arranges his narrative of what had "come to pass among us" so as to hand on the spirit and power of John's proclamation. In and through the Lukan account, Origen suggests, the Baptist's spirit continues to fill the world.

65 *Hom. Luc.* 21.5. 66 *Hom. Luc.* 21.5.
67 *Hom. Luc.* 21.3 (citing Luke 3:3; John 1:9, 5:35).
68 Cf. *Comm. Jo.* 1.7.40 (citing Rev 14:6; cf. *Comm. Jo.* 1.14.84). See the Conclusion.
69 See *Hom. Luc.* 21.4, where he addresses catechumens directly with the same language.
70 *Hom. Luc.* 4.6. 71 Cf. *Comm. Jo.* 10.4.15.

One can see then how flat Lessing's reading of Origen falls: "this proof of the spirit and of power no longer has either spirit or power, but has sunk to the level of human testimonies of spirit and power."[72] For Origen, the "demonstration of spirit and power" subsists precisely in and through "human testimony" – here, at least, having nothing whatsoever to do with a trivialized sense of either "power" as empirically astonishing miracles or "spirit" as clairvoyant predictions whose fulfillment would have been readily recognizable to any who had just "been there." Rather, it is the very record of this "voice" in the wilderness that both preserves and hands on the spirit and power of John's witness, which, for Origen, still goes forth and prepares "the way of the Lord." Or to transpose the point into the language of *Against Celsus*: By way of the Evangelist's figurally inflected narrative – that is, by way of the selfsame "roads" and "paths" Luke presents as figures of this call to repentance – John's prophetic spirit still proves "capable of producing belief in people who attend" to his preaching, and "traces" of the power of his proclamation still "remain among those who live according to [his] word."[73]

Here again, Origen leaves what he means by the advent of the Lord "even today" veiled in the closing doxology.[74] What his treatment of John the Baptist offers now is what we lacked at the close of the preceding section: a concrete illustration of how a particular vision preserved in the Gospel might also "appear to us at this present moment," "even now."[75] Origen presents Luke as having arranged his portrait of John the Baptist for this exact purpose: narrating his ministry in such a way as to hand on John's "prophetic charism," his spirit, his word, his very life, as a sign (*sacramentum*) that even now runs about the world "preparing the way of the Lord." If anyone – Origen includes his own catechumens – comes to receive the proclamation of this coming kingdom, repents, and is baptized, (s)he comes along the way the Forerunner prepared, and in fact still prepares, within the hearts of all who heed the word of the Gospel, that "all flesh might see the salvation of God."[76]

[72] Lessing, "On the proof of the spirit and of power," 85.

[73] *Cels.* 1.2 reapplied: This word may not be "demonstrative" according to the canons of "Greek dialectic," but it clearly does retain, for many, a persuasive power of its own. In any case, what Origen means by τεράστιοι δυνάμεις here ultimately shares precious little ground with Lessing's gloss of "erstaunliche Wunder."

[74] *Hom. Luc.* 4.6. [75] *Hom. Luc.* 3.4.

[76] Luke 3:6. This "sacramental" reading of John establishes the basic pattern to which Origen will return repeatedly in subsequent homilies. So *Hom. Luc.* 12.2: "Do you think that the words of the scriptures signify nothing else, nothing more divine, but only say

5.4 RECEIVING THE CHRIST CHILD: THE PRESENTATION

Part I established how, for Origen, the process of discerning something more than a recollection of bare facts in the narratives of Jesus's life is to have already begun to "see in the spirit"– of their authors, of the traditions they were receiving, and ultimately of the divine spirit they shared.[77] Similarly, perceiving the events of Jesus's life as a "sign of something" begins by recognizing a kind of spiritual vision already interior to the form and formation of the Gospel writers' narratives. There is perhaps no purer display of this dense matrix of "spiritual understanding" (πνευματικὴ ἐκδοχή) than Origen's reading of Jesus's Presentation in the Temple. Origen says that Simeon's astonishing pronouncement over the child was the "summit" or "pinnacle of the things that were being said" about him.[78] And Origen's interpretation of the Presentation itself rises to become a kind of peak overlooking this cycle of homilies, drawing all of the surrounding landscape into itself and allowing us to survey the whole length of the preceding path.[79]

Rather than simply citing the spirit as the "Lukan motivation" for Simeon's arrival and then leaving it behind,[80] Origen allows it to mark the whole nature and purpose of the story. The figure of Simeon abides in spirit: we are told at the beginning of the pericope that a "sacred spirit was upon" a certain man in Jerusalem, that this holy spirit had disclosed to him that he would not "see death before he had seen the Christ of the Lord," and that he comes to the Temple "in the spirit."[81] But why introduce Simeon in this way? For it does not simply say that "he entered the Temple by chance ... he 'came to the Temple in the spirit of God.'"[82] And what, Origen asks, was Simeon to gain from seeing him? "Did he have only this promised to him, that he would see him? And that nothing

this, that an angel came to shepherds and spoke to them? [...] Listen! His angel always comes down from heaven and proclaims to you, 'Today a savior is born for you, who is Christ the Lord.'" And *Hom. Luc.* 13.5: "The angels spoke these words to the shepherds. They spoke not only at that time, but in the present day also." And *Hom. Luc.* 22.3 (on Luke 3:5): "His coming touched our souls; whatever was 'crooked' is now 'straight.' For what profit is it to you if Christ once came in the flesh unless he also comes into your soul? We should pray that he will come to us each day." Cf. Angelus Silesius, *Cherubinischer Wandersmann*, 61: "Wird Christus tausendmal zu Bethlehem geboren / Und nicht in dir, du bleibst noch ewiglich verloren."

[77] See Section 3.2. [78] *Hom. Luc.* 16.2 (citing Luke 2:33). [79] Cf. *Hom. Luc.* 16.1.

[80] *Pace* Fitzmyer, *Luke I–IX*, 427. [81] Luke 2:25-27a. [82] *Hom. Luc.* 15.3.

worthwhile would follow from seeing him?"[83] Why should the Evangelist narrate any of this anyway?[84]

As we might have now learned to anticipate, in Origen's view the narrative itself originates in – and directs its readers toward – a kind of spiritual or prophetic vision. Inasmuch as Luke narrates that the "holy spirit was upon him," so also Simeon does not simply look at the child Jesus, he sees (him as) "the Lord's anointed."[85] That is, in the language of Origen's first homily on Luke, Simeon does not simply perceive Jesus "physically," he "sees the word of God."[86] "He sees Christ as the Christ."[87] For Simeon to have looked on this infant and have found himself able to say, "My eyes have seen your salvation,"[88] means for him to have seen something "in the spirit" – a perception irreducible to anything empirically manifest before him, and so, quite precisely, a *spiritual* vision, "a certain kind of divine sense."[89] Simeon, like Zechariah, like John the Baptist, "sees in the spirit," but "since they are several and are in different places and haven't been granted the same kinds of gifts in all the same ways," Luke narrates what each one, "each in his own way, sees in the spirit" regarding "God, his words, and the ways they become manifest to the holy."[90]

The one who "comes to the Temple in the spirit," however, does not simply look on the child; he also "takes him into his arms" (Luke 1:28). Is that all? Does the author intend nothing more than to narrate the bare fact that Simeon picked the infant up?[91] To forestall such a reduction, Origen asks the reader to recall the woman, a little later in Luke's Gospel, who merely "'touched the fringe of Jesus's garment and was healed.' If she gained so much from the outermost edge of his garment, what is one to make of Simeon, who 'received' the infant 'into his arms'?"[92]

83 *Hom. Luc.* 15.1.

84 Cf. *Hom. Luc.* 15.1. Cf. Chapter 3 on Strauss's accusation that "the allegorical interpreter … may with the most unrestrained arbitrariness separate from the history every thought he deems to be worthy of God, as constituting its inherent meaning" (*Life of Jesus*, §12). Is the interpretation that follows Origen's own call to "seek an account worthy of God" (*Hom. Luc.* 15.1) so arbitrary here, so "separated from the history," so alienated from "the ideas which are embodied in the narrative," without any "conformity with the spirit and modes of representation of the people and of the age" (*Life of Jesus*, §12)? The force of Origen's repeated "why?" throughout these homilies has just as much to do with the kind of questioning he believes one ought to subject all literature to (see Section 2.4).

85 Luke 2:26. Cf. *Hom. Luc.* 15.1. 86 *Hom. Luc.* 1.4. 87 *Hom. Luc.* 3.4.

88 Luke 2:30. Cf. *Hom. Luc.* 15 (Greek fragment): "What does he see? 'Your salvation…'"

89 *Cels.* 1.48: "a sense of what isn't sensory." 90 Reapplying *Comm. Jo.* 10.4.15.

91 Cf. *Hom. Luc.* 15.1. 92 *Hom. Luc.* 15.1 (citing Luke 8:44).

Having spent his life "awaiting the consolation of Israel," now he gazes upon the infant that he bears in his arms and joyfully prays: "now Lord, you are releasing your servant in peace." He not only sees the child, he "receives him" *as* this promised consolation.[93] That is, Simeon holds to his breast the very salvation God himself has prepared; somehow, as he gazes upon the little one wrapped in his arms he confesses, behold, "a light": "for the glory of your people Israel," yes, yet not of "Israel only," but also "for a revelation to the nations," such that the deliverance God has prepared now appears "before all people."[94] What does this child offer to Simeon's physical eyes?[95] What of this moment recommends itself as plainly messianic? Once again, we find here no dazzling spectacles of power, no *erstaunliche Wunder* in Lessing's sense – only this infant, his parents, and the spirit. How does one receive what Simeon receives, the heights and depths of this vision, but "in the spirit"?

And this is precisely how Origen's spiritual "understanding" (ἐκδοχή) works: it attempts to partake in, to make one's own, to "receive" (ἐκδοχή) that spirit already present within and (in)forming the narrative. Simeon is presented as one who sees in the spirit, and it is this same vision that Luke's narrative is composed to hand on. And it is in this selfsame spirit that Origen understands himself to be reading, that his listeners too might not only "see" but "receive" this child as their own light and salvation.

> If you wish to hold Jesus and to embrace him with your arms and to be made worthy of departing from captivity, you too must struggle with every effort to possess the guiding spirit and come to God's Temple... If you come "to the Temple in the spirit," you will find the child Jesus. You will lift him up in your arms and say, "Now you are releasing your servant, Lord, in peace, according to your word."[96]

Everything that "spiritual understanding" or "reception" (πνευματική ἐκδοχή) means for Origen is contained in this turn: "you too..." Here in his homily on the Presentation, to the questions left lingering from the

[93] Luke 2:28: ἐδέξατο αὐτό. Cf. *Hom. Luc.* 15 (Greek fragment), where δέχομαι language appears playfully throughout: Simeon "receives" this sight, he "receives" the promise, he "receives" Jesus into his arms, etc. Cf. *Comm. Jo.* 10.43.304.

[94] Cf. *Hom. Luc.* 15 (Greek fragment, citing Luke 2:30–32).

[95] *Hom. Luc.* 15 (Greek fragment, citing Luke 2:30: "for my eyes have seen your salvation"): "What once I believed in my heart and knew in thought alone, now I behold even with my bodily eyes; so my life is complete [ὡς τετελείωμαι]." Notice the total coinherence of physical and spiritual sight here; what Simeon "sees in the spirit" is this very particular, very concrete child.

[96] *Hom. Luc.* 15.3–4.

previous two sections (What would it mean for "God to appear to us at this present moment"? What would it mean for "John's spirit and power to precede the coming of our Lord even today"?) we find an answer by way of one more question: What would it mean for us to take up and hold the child Jesus in *our* arms? It means to share in Simeon's own vision, to share in the spirit in which he sees, and with him to receive and embrace this little one, the child Jesus, as "your salvation," as the "glory of Israel," as a "revelation to the nations" – to come to understand, to "see," with Simeon that this is the Christ in whom God will "reconcile the world to himself."[97]

Yet Origen's language compels us to say more. This passage also betrays, one might say, a certain mystical or sacramental depth.[98] One senses that Origen means, somehow, that it is the little child Jesus himself, quite really and truly, who comes to "you too." That is, as one learns to acknowledge and receive – and in the depths to which one learns to acknowledge and receive – this Jesus as one's "salvation," "light," and "consolation," in this very recognition, in this very spirit, in this very reception, the Christ child himself may come and dwell in your embrace, if only for a moment. To press into the passage as far as I dare without betraying Origen's own spirit of reverential reserve, perhaps I might transpose what he says – a little more daringly, a little more revealingly – elsewhere, although perhaps "this is something impossible to understand unless one has experienced it oneself":

> God is my witness that I have often perceived [him] drawing near me and being most intensely present with me; then suddenly he withdraws and I cannot find him, though I sought to do so. I long, therefore, for him to come again, and sometimes he does so. Then, when he has appeared and I hold him in my arms, he slips away once more; and, when he has so slipped away, my search for him begins anew. So does he act with me repeatedly, until I truly hold him and ascend, "pressing my beloved near… "[99]

Now we may follow the full length of the golden concatenating thread of spiritual readings out of which Origen's whole vision of Luke's infancy narrative becomes seamlessly woven. Simeon is recorded as one of the

[97] *Hom. Luc.* 15.4 (citing 2 Cor 5:19): "And thus he is dismissed 'in peace' to go on to the holy fathers, to whom Abraham also went forth" (also citing Gen 15:15, which Luke 2:29 appears to be evoking).

[98] By "sacramental" I do not (only) mean "eucharistic," at least not quite as strongly as H. Crouzel suggests (though the reference is certainly possible; cf. SC 87, 234 n. 1).

[99] *Hom. Cant.* 1.7. Cf. Bernard of Clairvaux, *On the Song of Songs* Sermon 74.2.5–7.

first to have "spiritually received" (πνευματικῇ ἐκδοχῇ) this Christ, or to have seen and received ("in the spirit") this infant as the Christ, as the "word" of God; it is in this same spirit, handed on by Luke's tradents (those who "saw for themselves, and became attendants of, the word"), that the Evangelist also comes to see, as he then looks to confer this same kind of vision under the form of his narrative (according to what he had "come to perceive in his own understanding"); finally, the very form of the narrative thus calls for readers to receive this selfsame word in the selfsame spirit, so that "even today" those who learn to see this word might also find themselves able to pray with Simeon, "My eyes have seen your salvation."[100]

In this way, like John the Baptist, the figure of Simeon also becomes a kind of sign for Origen, as the *sacramentum Simeonis* still "fills the world even to the present day" and prepares a way for the coming of the Lord for all who receive the little child Jesus in their arms, for all those who live in the hope that his spirit, his life, he himself might become so completely present and enfolded in one's own, that one might even dare to say, "now not I, but Christ lives in me."[101] It is this kind of seeing that Origen himself seeks to hand on in his homily, so that, precisely by attending to the form of the narrative, his hearers might receive its word "in the spirit" of Simeon, which remains present even now with all those who continue to pray in his voice: *nunc dimittis*...

> Therefore let us pray that we too, standing in the Temple and holding the son of God and embracing him, might be worthy of release and of departing to better things. Let us pray to almighty God, and let us pray to the little child Jesus himself. We long to speak to him and hold him in our arms, to whom is glory and power unto the ages of ages. Amen.[102]

5.5 APPEARANCE OF HISTORY, HISTORY OF APPEARANCES

Origen cannot accept that Luke's own language allows one to reduce his intent with these narratives to matters of plain facticity. He is not an impartial historian (if there is such a thing). Something, as he says, had "come to pass among us," something of which he and his tradents had become fully convinced, something that had made of them all servants of

[100] Luke 2:30; cf. Luke 3:6: "all flesh shall see the salvation of God."
[101] *Hom. Luc.* 15.5 (citing Gal 2:20), and reapplying Origen's language from *Hom. Luc.* 4.6.
[102] *Hom. Luc.* 15.5.

its proclamation: "attendants of the word." In other words, the very writing of the Gospel becomes, in this view, a form of "spiritual reading" of Jesus's life.

By extension, then, the other Gospel writers too, like "well-trained money changers," each in their own way possessed a similar "charism for discerning the spirits" of the traditions *they* were receiving (or rejecting) and developing.[103] According to Origen, moreover, the spirit in which these four authors wrote, or which they received and sought to hand on in and through their writing, is not ultimately separable from the "charism" by which the churches discerned their underlying agreement and received "the four," even as they judged against the "many other Gospels" that others had "attempted" to write.[104]

Origen's own intertwined language thus serves to expose the indivisible matrix of a people made by the discernment of the Gospels and Gospels received by the discernment of a people, both proceeding from the gift (χαρίσμα) of one and the same spirit: the one that Christians call the holy spirit. Learning to receive these four Gospels oneself means learning to participate in this people's own "discernment of spirits," and this process of discernment remains indissoluble from the critically nuanced reading Origen exemplifies for his listeners in each of these homilies. From the opening lines of this collection, then, Origen invites them to join him in becoming "well-trained moneychangers" as well, to discern the word that those before them had already come to see, and so become servants of it themselves.

[103] Cf. *Hom. Luc.* 1, particularly 1.4 where Origen suggests that "seeing the word" expresses something not unlike Jesus's saying in John, "whoever has seen me has seen the Father" (John 14:9; cf. *Hom. Luc.* 3.4 and *Cels.* 7.43).

[104] See *Hom. Luc.* 1.1. Cf. *Fr. Luc.* 9 (*Hom. Luc.* 1.2), which preserves a tradition that John himself, sometime during the reign of Nero, "collected the written Gospels," and that he "accepted" (ἐνκρῖναι) and "received" (ἀποδέξασθαι) some while rejecting others. See I. L. E. Ramelli, "John the Evangelist's Work: An Overlooked *Redaktionsgeschichtliche* Theory from the Patristic Age" (2016). Moreover, it is no great mystery how Origen might express this "underlying agreement" among the four, for all their diversity, in more concrete summary: what finally expresses their inner unity and harmony of spirit is nothing other, in Origen's view, than what is expressed in the *regula fidei* (see, e.g., his own summaries of the faith in *Princ.* pr.2 and *Comm. ser. Matt.* 33, among others, helpfully gathered by A. C. Outler in "Origen and the Regulae Fidei" [1939]). For a contemporary analogue, cf. S. Gathercole, *The Gospel and the Gospels: Christian Proclamation and Early Jesus Books* (2022).

6

Difference and Discord

Ascending To Jerusalem

"The Son of Man will be a sign for this generation."[1]

The two preceding chapters ought to have made the interpretive judgments underlying Origen's understanding of the nature of the Gospels increasingly evident: it is a particular vision of Jesus – certain ways of seeing his life and its significance – that ultimately shapes the literary form and formation of each narrative. The present chapter will now forge ahead by illustrating how Origen's sense that the principal aim of each Gospel writer was to hand on what they had "perceived in their own understanding" also becomes the ground for his account of Gospel difference.

Up to this point, Part II has considered Origen's approach to particular Gospel passages entirely by virtue of their individual voices – without, that is, invoking parallel narratives from more than one Gospel. In the process, it has become clear that Origen's figurative understanding of the Gospels doesn't originate merely in noticing discrepancies among the four received Gospels. Having established this more fundamental point, we may now attend to the occasions where his reading does proceed by way of comparative reading of parallel pericopes.

The cluster of narratives surrounding Jesus's ascent(s) to Jerusalem provides an especially textured model of Origen's approach to Gospel difference. At least in the extant remains of his corpus, Origen's most developed engagement with critical issues that arise directly from comparing the four Gospels is to be found in his treatment of events associated

[1] See Luke 11:30. Cf. Ezek 12:11, 24:24, 27; Isa 8:18. Cf. *Comm. Matt.* 12.3.

(by most of the Evangelists) with Jesus's final days. The pericopes of the healing of the blind, anointing, Temple demonstration, and entry into Jerusalem thus precipitate Origen's most muscular demonstrations for why one must receive the Gospels as "otherwise than mere history" alone if one wishes to receive them as true.[2]

Before beginning, it may be useful to recall Origen's pithy conclusion to his analogy of the four authors in the *Commentary on John*, a thought experiment immediately occasioned by the challenges attendant to the narrative of Jesus's visit to Jerusalem near the beginning of John's Gospel. There are a "multitude of ways of conceiving of Jesus," he writes, and this plurality finds itself mirrored in each of the Evangelists' records. Jesus *is* (the occasion of) this multiplicity of ways of receiving him, and it is from out of this very plurality of conceptions, Origen concludes, that "the Evangelists seem to have recorded their Gospels, taking up differing notions while also agreeing about certain others."[3]

A profound intimacy thus discloses itself between the first and second moments of Origen's logic of Gospel formation, as his consideration of the character of the Gospel writers (first moment) finds its vanishing point in the character of their primary subject (second moment). Those who shaped their narratives figurally echo one who appears himself to have spoken and acted in figures. It is to this second moment that this chapter (and the next) will finally turn, but by way of attending first to Origen's negotiation of the "differing notions" preserved in, and productive of, the Evangelists' differing narratives.

6.1 A DEEPER EXPLANATION: HEALING THE BLIND

Origen begins his examination of the healing of the two blind men in Matthew 20 by collecting parallel pericopes into what amounts, functionally, to a Gospel synopsis: "Now since some think that Mark and Luke relate the same historical narrative [as Matthew] but others that it is another parallel one, it is worthwhile to look at each of them."[4] The

[2] *Comm. Jo.* 10.5.19. [3] *Comm. Jo.* 10.5.21 (see Section 3.3).

[4] *Comm. Matt.* 16.12. In a pattern repeated throughout his commentaries on John and Matthew, Origen provides the beginning and end of each parallel pericope, thus defining the boundaries of comparison and (re)creating a synopsis for the reader. It is quite possible that Origen had a tabular synopsis of the four Gospels at hand (after the manner of the *Hexapla*), but he never says as much. In any case, Helmut Merkel's comment that Origen's comparisons of parallel narratives are so thorough "one could almost believe that [he] had Aland's *Synopsis Quattuor Evangeliorum* in front of him" still holds (*Die Widersprüche*

Three (Origen's shorthand for Matthew, Mark, and Luke) all share in "common" a healing of some blind person(s) somewhere around Jericho during Jesus's final approach to Jerusalem; at the same time, Origen insists, one must also compare "what is distinctive and unique" to each.[5] Matthew and Mark agree that the healing occurred when Jesus was *departing* from Jericho (though they disagree on whether it was one or two blind men, and Mark may locate it within the city limits); Luke, however, places the episode during the *approach* to Jericho.[6] In Matthew, Jesus stops when he hears them and asks the two blind men directly what they want him to do for them, but in Mark and Luke, the crowd intervenes. In Mark and Luke, Jesus's words alone effect the healing, but Matthew adds that Jesus touched their eyes.[7]

Since Mark alone, moreover, records the name of the blind man (Bartimaeus), Origen wonders whether it could be that the Gospel writer "had something deeper in mind in this passage"? Perhaps, Origen grants, Mark "added the name out of necessity as a part of the historical record," but "one might also say that he did so for his own purposes."[8] Similarly, Mark alone includes the detail that at the disciples' beckoning ("take heart, rise, he is calling you"), Bartimaeus "threw off his cloak, sprang up, and went to Jesus."[9] Did Mark "mean nothing" by writing this? Were any of these details simply "tossed into the Gospel at random"? "For my part," Origen adds, "I do not consider one iota or a single serif to be empty in the divine teachings – though I do think, to light upon the meaning, the interpreter requires a great deal of understanding due to how much these matters resist interpretation."[10]

zwischen den Evangelien: Ihre polemische und apologetische Behandlung in der Alten Kirche bis zu Augustin [1971], 98). Cf. H. Merkel, *Die Pluralität der Evangelien als theologisches und exegetisches Problem in der Alten Kirche* (1978), 18–50. Cf. M. R. Crawford, "Ammonius of Alexandria, Eusebius of Caesarea and the Origins of Gospels Scholarship" (2015).

5 *Comm. Matt.* 16.13: τὰ δὲ καίρια καὶ ἴδια. Cf. *Comm. Jo.* 6.32.162.

6 *Comm. Matt.* 16.13.

7 *Comm. Matt.* 16.13.

8 *Comm. Matt.* 16.12. Χρήσιμος (to *make use of* for some purpose) falls among the several χράω-related terms (e.g., συγχράομαι, καταχράομαι) Origen employs to describe the Evangelists' literary agency. Cf. *Comm. Jo.* 10.5.18–19 (treated in Section 3.2).

9 *Comm. Matt.* 16.12 (citing Mark 10:49–50).

10 *Comm. Matt.* 16.12 (on Mark 10:49–52 and evoking Matt 5:18): διὰ τὸ δυσερμήνευτον. He suggests that "they indicate, perhaps, the trappings" of blindness and poverty that "Bartimaeus had been bound up in" and then "threw off upon hearing, 'Take heart, rise, he is calling you'"; and though Jesus then simply told him, "Go," he "did something even better than this," for "he did not go away, but 'immediately' upon 'regaining his sight' he 'followed' Jesus 'on the way.'" Here then is a revealing instance of Origen's literary

This synopsis of the narratives of Jesus's healing of the blind on the way to Jerusalem makes it clear to Origen that one of the current opinions – that these depict the same historical narrative (ἡ αὐτὴ ἱστορία) – is impossible; it is rejected almost without comment. Origen, however, doesn't think that merely invoking the second opinion – that these are different narratives that resemble each other (ἡ ἑτέρα παραπλησία ἱστορία) – resolves all remaining critical questions. The synopsis thus prompts him to compose a miniature dialogue between two contrasting ways of holding this second opinion.

Option 1: Someone "disposed to the bare historical narrative alone and who doesn't want the Evangelists to disagree" will say that

> what is in Matthew and what is in Mark did not happen at the same time. Instead, what is related about the two blind men who received their sight again happened on one visit to Jericho, what is related about this single son of Timaeus ("Bartimaeus") on another, and what is related in Luke on still another. For since we believe that the Gospels have been recorded with precision (together with the cooperation of the holy spirit), and that those who wrote them did not err in what they were memorializing, it is clear that, since it couldn't possibly be true that the two blind men and the one were healed during one and the same visit, two different visits have been presented by Matthew and Mark, and indeed yet still another by Luke – a fact that, by virtue of this disagreement with the rest [of the Gospels], can be confidently shown to anyone who gives their attention to it. After all, it is no wonder that someone in Jericho who had observed the prior healing should look to be healed in the same place by way of the same language and a similar request. One could say then, too, that the blind man in Luke is another who was healed in this way.[11]

There are several ways of saying that the various and variously related healing stories are "different narratives that resemble one another." One approach insists on a certain (at least attempted) transparency to history.[12] In this case, it could be that one (or more) of the Gospel writers is simply wrong; the differences arise from inaccuracies and mistakes. For someone, however, who both insists on factual transparency *and* will not dismiss any disagreements as mere flaws in the records, some acrobatics are required. Since the divergent details make it clear that it simply isn't possible (μὴ δυνατόν) for the different Gospels to be narrating an identical historical event, then one would have to imagine that the reason the

approach to the Gospels – or, rather, of his account of the Gospels that takes the Evangelists seriously as literary agents: the details particular to Mark's version of the narrative are not interwoven solely to inform (nor merely to entertain) but are a sign of Mark investing the story with certain figurative qualities (cf. *Cels.* 1.42). Cf. Collins, *Mark*, 510–11.

11 *Comm. Matt.* 16.12. 12 *Comm. Matt.* 16.12: τῇ ἱστορίᾳ ψιλῇ παριστάμενος.

healings look so similar is because word got out about one blind man's good fortune, and so at least two others, on at least two other occasions (each picked up uniquely by individual Gospel writers), thought they would try a similar technique in roughly the same location (roadside in the vicinity of Jericho). In brief, the first option looks to harmonize all the accounts historically.

So Origen turns to Option 2: "On the other hand, anyone looking for a deeper explanation of all this will say that one and the same matter is being depicted by differing texts."[13] That's it. Option 2's razor-like simplicity slices through the knots Option 1 ties itself up in. As with many approaches that he considers a little simplistic, Origen is not utterly dismissive of those disposed to both transparent facticity and historical harmony – even if the contrast between "being disposed to the bare historical narrative" and "seeking a deeper explanation of these matters" tenders a slightly disapproving air.[14] The history-harmonizing approach develops an inchoate historical-critical sensitivity (acknowledging the simple impossibility that the Gospels are recording the same event) and even literary sensitivity (since a synoptic comparison has disclosed fundamental differences between the stories) and so remains at least possible in theory. For Origen, Christian belief only forswears ascribing Gospel differences to flawed records.[15] Nevertheless, Origen himself will follow the "deeper explanation," which naturally entails that these "differing versions of one and the same thing" are intentionally shaped by the Gospel writers "for their own purposes."[16]

[13] *Comm. Matt.* 16.12: ἓν καὶ τὸ αὐτὸ πρᾶγμα διαφόροις λέξεσι παρίσταται.

[14] To be perfectly clear, the μέν ... μέντοιγε construction that governs this entire passage is not progressive (as some translations seem to imply). While not necessitating a total exclusion of the prior position, μέντοιγε is most often used for an adversative effect – that is, to introduce, in contradistinction, a strongly corrective position (see J. D. Denniston, *The Greek Particles* [1954], 412–13). Origen is presenting two possible but contrasting positions. He does not completely dismiss the first (as he does those who think the same story is being narrated); he allows it, but then points out what one would have to say to hold it, and then redirects the reader by offering his preferred approach. Significantly, the way Origen puts "Option 1" is not entirely dissimilar from a position he seems to express in *Comm. Jo.* 6.34.171–172 (cf. 6.13.20), signaling, perhaps, a development in his own thinking on this issue. I am not sure that the movement from *Comm. Jo.* Book 6 to *Comm. Jo.* Book 10 suggests quite as "radical" of a self-criticism as F. Watson proposes (*Gospel Writing*, 547–50), especially in light of how strongly *On First Principles* affirms the presence of non-factual narratives in the Gospels. But I certainly allow that the subtlety with which he discusses this topic increases in later writings like *Comm. Matt.* and *Cels.* (cf. similarly *Cels.* 4.44). Cf. M. M. Mitchell, "Gospel Optics" (2019), 198–99, and F. Watson, *What Is a Gospel?* 302–303.

[15] Cf. *Comm. Matt.* 16.12 and *Comm. Jo.* 6.34.171.

[16] Cf. *Comm. Matt.* 16.12 (and *Comm. Jo.* 10.5.18–19).

6.2 BORN FROM HISTORY: THE ANOINTING

One of Origen's more magisterial performances of the "deeper explanation" outlined above occurs in his exposition of Jesus's anointing(s). Later in the *Commentary on Matthew*, Origen goes about an exhaustive comparison of the various anointings narrated in the four Gospels.[17] He first acknowledges that "many think the four Evangelists have told of one and the same woman, because they have all written something about a woman, and all alike have mentioned an 'alabaster box of ointment.'"[18] Matthew, Mark, and John, moreover, all locate the event in Bethany, include some complaint about how the unction "could have been sold and given to the poor," and conclude with Jesus referring the anointing to his burial. Matthew, Mark, and Luke, on the other hand, also agree that the house belonged to a certain Simon. "Therefore," Origen grants, "it seems that there is a lot of similarity and a certain kinship" among these passages "about a woman in the four Evangelists."[19]

Nevertheless, Origen directly turns to the more numerous inconsistencies and divergences among the various narratives. Luke, for instance, narrates no complaint about the cost, no statement about "always having the poor with you," and no mention of preparation for burial.[20] Though Matthew, Mark, and John all locate the narrative in Bethany, in John, the hosts are Mary, Martha, and Lazarus, while in Matthew and Mark, the meal takes place in the house of "Simon the Leper." Luke's host is also named Simon, but he is identified only as a Pharisee, with no mention of leprosy.[21] In Matthew, Mark, and John the event takes place during

[17] Matt 26:6–13; Mark 14:3-9; Luke 7:36–50; John 12:1–8. Preserved in the (so-called) *Series Commentariorum*, an anonymous Latin translation (from around the sixth century perhaps), which includes much of the remainder of the *Commentary on Matthew* (through Matt 27:66) after the extant Greek concludes (Book 17, through Matt 22:33). Though the quality of translation is still something of an open question, it remains our only witness to Origen's maturest work on the Gospels. For a helpful overview, see Heine, *Matthew*, I:29–30. On the anointing, cf. *Comm. Cant.* 2.9 and *Hom. Cant.* 1.4.

[18] *Comm. ser. Matt.* 77; *Fr. Matt.*: δοκεῖ μέν τισι μία εἶναι καὶ ἡ αὐτή παρά τοῖς εὐαγγελισταῖς ἅπασιν.

[19] *Comm. ser. Matt.* 77: *multa ergo similitudo et cognatio quaedam.*

[20] *Comm. ser. Matt.* 77: "In Matthew and Mark the disciples are indignant ... but in John, only Judas ... and in Luke no one grumbles" (about the cost). Throughout this section, Origen appears to notice the special closeness of Matthew and Mark in their respective narratives of Jesus's final days, and that similarity among the Gospels is not relegated only to the three we now call "synoptic"; in the case of the anointing, John is in many ways closer to Matthew and Mark than Luke is. See also *Comm. Matt.* 16.8, where Origen notes that juxtaposing the Gospels shows that in "many passages" Matthew and Mark preserve a similar "order."

[21] *Comm. ser. Matt.* 77.

Jesus's final days; Matthew and Mark say "two days before Passover," though, and John "six days."[22]

The act of anointing, along with its occasion, also differs quite drastically. "Do you think," Origen asks, "that this woman who 'poured' expensive ointment 'on the head' of Jesus, as Matthew and Mark say, herself also 'anointed his feet with myrrh,' as Luke and John say?"[23] For in Luke, the woman, who remains unnamed and is identified (uniquely among the four) only as a sinner, won't even face Jesus. She is said to have stood behind him, wept at his feet, and then to have begun to wash "'his feet with tears' as if scarcely even worthy of his feet"; she dries them with her hair, kisses them, and finally anoints them. Is it merely "accidental," Origen asks, that the sinful woman in Luke's version never dares to lift herself above Christ's feet (which she merely "daubs"), while the woman in Matthew and Mark's who *isn't* "recorded to have been a sinner" rather approaches Jesus directly and lavishly pours out the whole container upon his head – such that the disciples complain of "waste" here, but not in Luke?[24] Similarly, the "'Mary' who is mentioned in John is introduced neither as a sinner nor as weeping."[25] As a matter of emphasis, Origen resists even calling the four passages narratives of "Jesus's anointing." Luke's is a quintessentially penitential narrative – the woman's self-abasing act of foot washing simply happens to conclude with a gentle application of ointment (which is hardly the featured act).[26]

What then explains how these narratives, "as similar and related as they are contrary and different," came about?[27] In light of these passages' clear resistance to harmonization (literary or historical), Origen maintains that one must either say that the contradicting stories are due to the Gospel writers "lying" or – "if it is impious to believe this" – that "all the Evangelists have not written about the same woman, but about three or four."[28] As far as

[22] *Comm. ser. Matt.* 77 (Luke's narrative takes place during the Galilean ministry).

[23] *Comm. ser. Matt.* 77.

[24] *Comm. ser. Matt.* 77: *non "unxit" sed "effudit."*

[25] *Comm. ser. Matt.* 77.

[26] *Comm. ser. Matt.* 77 (evoking 2 Cor 7:10): *prae tristitia "paenitentiam in salutem stabilem" operante.*

[27] *Comm. ser. Matt.* 77.

[28] *Comm. ser. Matt.* 77 (or writing under "false pretenses"; *mentior* may also have notes of *self*-deception, thus to be "mistaken"). On a purely literary level, he allows that one could say there are four stories about four different women, but he himself "favors the view that there are three" (with Matthew and Mark writing about the same figure "in unison [συνᾴδοντες], as in many other places"). As a matter of historical plausibility, however, Origen suggests that though there may be three distinct *literary* figures here (i.e., three distinct *stories*), it is unlikely that they correspond to three *historical* figures: for instance, "if Matthew and Mark wrote of one woman and John of another and Luke of a third, how have the disciples, once rebuked by Christ about one woman (for being wrongly

strict facticity is concerned, he notes that someone "with a little more daring" could say that there was only "one woman who did something like this" (and adds "you can argue for a second or a third, if you like").[29] In any case, Origen forcefully concludes, the Evangelists' overarching intent was not merely to narrate matters of historical fact; their "principal" aim, rather, was to "expound the mysteries of things that were born from history."[30] For this reason, "they also wove in certain things convenient to and consonant with their understandings of the mysteries" arising from Jesus's life.[31]

There is perhaps no more succinct expression of Origen's understanding of the relationship of the Gospel narratives to history, on the one hand, and their intrinsically figurative nature, on the other. In the case of the anointing pericopes, the Evangelists may well preserve some memory of a historical event as the ground of their vision (whatever exact form it took), but they also "did what they liked with what was said and done," at times "interweaving things that didn't happen" (or at least "adjusting" certain details) for the sake of "the mysterious aim they had in view."[32] In sum, their ultimate intent was to teach "what they had come to perceive in their own understanding by way of figures." Perfectly in line with the general principles outlined in Part I, Origen's account of the Gospels' literary formation thus comfortably accounts for both the nature of individual Gospel passages and differences among parallel stories in the four received Gospels.

His figural interpretation of this particular set of texts similarly roots itself in his view of the Evangelists as "figurative readers." In the case of the anointing, Origen suggests, the "differences between these women represent differences among the faithful."[33] The Lukan version becomes, in his view, a kind of penitential type-scene, wherein even the lowliest of "sinners," those yet incapable of the extravagant "waste" of an entire jar of expensive "genuine spikenard," those who feel themselves unworthy of even lifting themselves above his feet, are nevertheless found "acceptable before Christ."[34] Were all the narratives collapsed into a single

indignant about what she did), not corrected themselves so that they would not become indignant about another woman who acts in a similar way?"

29 *Comm. ser. Matt.* 77.

30 *Comm. ser. Matt.* 77: *et non satis curaverunt ut secundum veritatem historiae enarrarent, sed ut rerum mysteria quae ex historia nascebantur exponerent.* Cf. *Hom. Gen.* 10.4. Cf. *Princ.* 4.2.7.

31 *Comm. ser. Matt.* 77.

32 See *Comm. Jo.* 10.5.18–19 and *Princ.* 4.2.9.

33 *Comm. ser. Matt.* 77. Cf. *Comm. Matt.* 11.4.

34 Cf. *Comm. ser. Matt.* 77. See also a little later: "Notice how carefully in [Matthew and Mark], who do not refer to her as a sinner, her ointment is praised as 'expensive.' But in Luke, who represents her as a sinner, the ointment is simply mentioned, and labelled

harmonized account, without a sensitivity to the figurations proper to each scene, one would never discern the simple lowliness of the Lukan woman's sorrowful penitence, nor the prophetic-symbolic heights of the woman's bold act in the other Gospels, which (Origen notes) Jesus binds directly to the coming paschal events.[35] In other words, by refusing an artificial reduction of the voices of each Evangelist into a single one-dimensional harmony, Origen preserves the figure of each woman in each narrative (however many there may have "really" been, he does not finally decide) precisely by preserving them *as* figures of those who approach the Lord – those whom, for all their differences in worthiness, Christ receives as his own.

The collective effect of these differences, Origen concludes, becomes an "exhortation to all of us." For it is only in the Matthean and Markan version(s) that Jesus says the woman did a "beautiful" thing for him.[36] Only for her does he promise that "wherever this Gospel is preached in the whole world, what she has done will be told in memory of her."[37] If therefore "we too wish that what we have done for Jesus be told about us," then "let us progress" from merely "'daubing' his feet to 'pouring out' expensive ointment 'on his head.'"[38]

6.3 PERFORMING SIGNS: TEMPLE DEMONSTRATION

Origen's account of Jesus's provocative demonstration in the Temple adds one further degree of complexity to his account of Gospel difference. In the introduction to this chapter, I noted that Origen's phrasing suggests that differences among the Gospels not only arise from the "multitude of ways of conceiving of Jesus" but were somehow occasioned by the character of Jesus himself.[39] Turning to Origen's reading of the Temple expulsion narrative(s), one may begin to discern the continuities between his view of the figurative character of the Gospels and his view of Jesus's own characteristic manner of teaching by way of symbolic actions.

Following his thought experiment about the four authors in the *Commentary on John*, Origen proceeds to draw together another

neither expensive nor 'genuine spikenard' ... but the fact that she was still able to anoint the Lord's feet with ointment was great."

35 *Comm. ser. Matt.* 77 (cf. Mark 14:8, Matt 26:12, John 12:7).

36 *Comm. ser. Matt.* 77 (Matt 26:10 and Mark 14:6).

37 *Comm. ser. Matt.* 77 (Matt 26:13 and Mark 14:9).

38 *Comm. ser. Matt.* 77. Cf. *Fr. Luc.* 113.

39 Cf. *Comm. Jo.* 10.5.21.

synopsis of the relevant passages ("at very great length," he acknowledges) for the sake of "establishing the discord" among them "as far as their express sense is concerned."[40] The series of events that "the Three say happened during one and the same visit to Jerusalem is thought, by many, to be identical [τὰ αὐτὰ] with what is recorded in John."[41] But they "are related by John to have happened during two ascents to Jerusalem, separated by many deeds and a great deal of journeying to different places clearly set in between."[42] John records the Temple incident as the second major event of Jesus's public ministry, "but the rest place something similar [τὸ παραπλήσιον] nearly at the end" of the cluster of events leading up to the Passion.[43] Additionally, one should observe that "after many other things had taken place – and during another visit of his to Jerusalem besides the present one – John recorded things parallel [τὰ παραπλήσια] to those said by the Three to have happened during the Lord's ascent to Jerusalem when he did these things in the Temple."[44] Furthermore, Mark and Matthew have Jesus driving out both buyers and sellers, but Luke the sellers only. "In John, however, they are all cast out *together with the sheep and oxen* – with a 'whiplash plaited from cords'" no less.[45] Jesus's rebuke in John is also phrased differently than the others.[46] "Therefore," Origen concludes, "as far as I am concerned, it isn't possible for those who understand nothing beyond the historical narrative in these passages to show that the apparent discord is an agreement."[47]

Beyond disagreements among the four, Origen remains skeptical that the Johannine version makes much sense as a purely historical narrative in its own right, considering it "implausible for what is reported to have taken place according to the avowed 'historical' sense" for a number of reasons.[48] For instance, why would Jesus drive out the animals at all? If they were the

[40] *Comm. Jo.* 10.22.129. Cf. *Comm. Jo.* 10.26.152 on the need to consider what, in the other Gospels, is "related to [τὰ συγγενῆ] this passage on the expulsion from the Temple." Cf. *Comm. Jo.* 10.27.167 where he invites his readers to pick up the puzzling (ἐπαπορέω) aspects of this pericope again.

[41] *Comm. Jo.* 10.22.129. [42] *Comm. Jo.* 10.22.129. [43] *Comm. Jo.* 10.20.119.

[44] *Comm. Jo.* 10.21.123 (referring presumably to the Triumphal Entry in John 12:12–15 and possibly the anointing; cf. *Comm. Jo.* 10.22.128).

[45] *Comm. Jo.* 10.31.199. Cf. *Comm. Jo.* 10.27.168, which may preserve a slight slip on the matter of who exactly is cast out (buyers and/or sellers) in the different accounts. Cf. *Comm. Matt.* 16.22 and *Hom. Luc.* 38.5.

[46] See *Comm. Jo.* 10.27.170–71: "For John says that Jesus said to them, 'Do not make my Father's house a marketplace!' But in the [other Gospels] they are rebuked for having made the house of prayer a 'den of bandits.'"

[47] *Comm. Jo.* 10.22.130, where he happily invites alternative proposals.

[48] *Comm. Jo.* 10.25.143: ἀπίθανος ἂν ἦν ἡ γραφὴ κατὰ τὴν ἐνδεχομένην ἱστορίαν γεγονέναι ἀπαγγελλομένη.

animals set aside for sacrifice, there would be nothing offensive about their presence, and it simply isn't possible (for cultural/cultic reasons) that other animals would have been brought into the Temple purely for commercial purposes.[49] "On account of which – in my opinion – the Evangelist used what was customarily done by vendors during the Jewish feasts (when they brought these animals into the outer court of the Temple) and availed himself also of an act which had occurred."[50]

Origen then reflects on Jesus's socioeconomic status as a further occasion for historical skepticism – not to mention the sheer physical impracticability of expelling so many people along with tens of thousands of uncooperative livestock:

> And indeed any who take an interest in a more thoroughly critical examination will consider whether it was in keeping with Jesus's position in life – since he was supposed to be the son of a carpenter – to venture to do so great a thing as driving out a multitude of vendors who had come up to the feast to sell the sheep which were to be sacrificed to such a mass of people (numbering in the tens of thousands) ... there were also oxen available for those who were wealthier and had vowed larger animals, and there were doves which many would purchase as they were assembling for the feast.[51]

There is, moreover, the difficulty of how the story seems to imply a wordless and even docile acquiescence on the part of the vendors:

> And when the moneychangers saw their money being poured out and their tables overturned would they not have accused Jesus of an outrage? And who – if he were being struck with a whip of cords and driven out by someone supposed to be of such low estate – would not have apprehended him, called for help, and subjected him to mob justice, especially since he would have had such a great multitude of those who would have thought themselves to have suffered the same outrage to help?[52]

In the end, any "who still wish to preserve" the story's perfect transparency to some historical event have "one last defense to fall back on": namely, that the narrative indicates some manifestation of divine power, in no way inferior to any of the other miracles associated with Jesus's life – "if, again, it even happened."[53] Such an achievement, Origen adds (perhaps a little wryly), would have been even greater than the changing of water to wine.[54]

49 Cf. *Comm. Jo.* 10.25.143.
50 *Comm. Jo.* 10.25.144: ἐχρήσατο ὁ εὐαγγελιστής, ὡς οἶμαι, καὶ γεγενημένῳ συγχρησάμενος πράγματι.
51 *Comm. Jo.* 10.25.145. 52 *Comm. Jo.* 10.25.145–46. 53 *Comm. Jo.* 10.25.148.
54 *Comm. Jo.* 10.25.149. Origen makes the same point a little later in *Comm. Jo.* 10.27.169. Cf. E. P. Sanders (*Jesus and Judaism*, 69–70), U. Luz (*Matthew 21–28* [2005], 11), and P. Fredriksen (*When Christians Were Jews: The First Generation* [2018], 46), among

In light of the disagreements between John's version of the demonstration and those of the other three, the historical implausibility of the event having taken place exactly as narrated (given the sheer practical unfeasibility of having such an effect on such a mass of people and animals), issues of realism with respect to matters of class prejudice and the kind of outrage this sort of act would have naturally provoked before it could have ever had hope of completion, not to mention inconsistencies in the presentation of Jesus's own character,[55] Origen concludes by asking his readers to "consider carefully if it is possible to untangle the alterations and disagreements of these writings by way of referring them to something higher"[56]: that is, by attributing any divergences to the different ways the Evangelists depict what the word of God is bringing to pass.[57] "*Only in this way* is it possible to retrieve the apparent rift between Jesus's ascents to Jerusalem" in John and what is recorded differently by the other three.[58]

Once again, then, Origen makes sense of Gospel difference by way of a theory of literary formation that bears a distinct resemblance to what is more commonly known today as redaction criticism.[59] Each Gospel writer "made use of an event that occurred" (in some form or another) for their own purposes, which were not concerned principally with historical transparency but rather with interpreting (*expono*) that history in a way "convenient to and consonant with their own understandings" of the "mysteries born" therefrom.[60]

others, who similarly note that this would have had to have been a fairly small symbolic demonstration for it not to have resulted in immediate violence and/or arrest.

55 See *Comm. Jo.* 10.25.147: Doesn't the fact that he "takes cords and plaits a whip for himself and drives them out of the Temple point to one who is bad-tempered, rather insolent, and undisciplined"?

56 *Comm. Jo.* 10.31.199: παρὰ τὸν τῆς ἀναγωγῆς τρόπον. Cf. *Comm. Jo.* 10.3.10.

57 *Comm. Jo.* 10.31.199. 58 *Comm. Jo.* 10.31.200.

59 Cf. I. Boxall, "Origen's *Commentary on Matthew* and the Reception of Matthew's Gospel" (2022), 335, and *Discovering Matthew: Content, Interpretation, Reception* (2015), 19–20, which draw certain strands of allegorical reading into parallel with Günther Bornkamm's seminal essay in the history of redaction criticism, "The Stilling of the Storm in Matthew" (1963). Bornkamm himself ties his approach – wherein "Matthew is not only a hander-on of the narrative, but also its oldest exegete" – to early Christian reading practices (ibid., 55). Cf. Merkel, *Die Widersprüche zwischen den Evangelien*, 109–111 and 121. Cf. M. Müller, "Were the Gospel Authors Really 'Simple Christians Without Literary Gift' (Albert Schweitzer)?: Arguments for the Quest for the Sources Behind the Gospels" (2018), esp. 94–96.

60 See *Comm. ser. Matt.* 77 (and *Comm. Jo.* 10.25.144). Cf. *Comm. Jo.* 10.5.18: "Once the *meaning* of what has been narrated in a historical fashion (by those who wanted to teach

Yet Origen ultimately orders these critical considerations under the graver matter of Christian belief: "I have made all these comments about the manifest disagreements of the Gospels out of a desire to present" a kind of harmony that emerges "by way of receiving them spiritually."[61] Because "when the discord is left unresolved, many have dismissed belief in the Gospels," thinking them therefore "untrue" (and certainly not "written by a divine spirit") or that the Gospels are simply deficient in recording the memory of these events, "for their composition is said to have involved both."[62] The question naturally becomes: in what does Christian belief in the Gospel narratives consist? Is what the Evangelists memorialize (ἀπομνημονεύω) a perfect transparency to "what happened"? Is factual inerrancy alone what makes them "true," the privileged mark of their divine origin?[63] If so, then by virtue of the numerous inconsistencies, implausibilities, and outright contradictions outlined above, Origen believes anyone who attentively examines the Gospels may either reject their credibility as a whole or have to choose one of them at random.[64]

Accepting the four received Gospels then, in Origen's view, means accepting that neither their truth nor their "success" as remembrances (ἀπομνημονεύματα) of Jesus's life consists wholly in their transparency to history.[65] Disagreements among parallel narratives need not render them unqualifiedly "untrue" – no less than employing figurative language ("interweaving things that didn't physically happen") to depict some interior vision or understanding renders the kinds of narratives studied in the previous two chapters unqualifiedly "untrue." Nor need one conclude that the differences arise from failures in recording the memory of his life properly; the Gospels' status as "memoirs" does not mean such a slavish attachment to facticity. On the contrary: "those who accept the four Gospels" ought to "think the apparent discord" may be "resolved by reference to something higher"– that is, by holding "that the truth of these accounts lies in their ideas."[66]

us what they had perceived in their own understanding by way of figures) has been thoroughly grasped, one would no longer find any discord."

61 *Comm. Jo.* 10.6.27: ὁδῷ τῆς πνευματικῆς ἐκδοχῆς.

62 *Comm. Jo.* 10.3.10: ὡς οὐκ ἀληθῶν οὐδὲ θειοτέρῳ πνεύματι γεγραμμένων ἢ ἐπιτετευγμένως ἀπομνημονευθέντων. Notice the similarity to *Comm. Matt.* 16.12 (treated in Section 6.1 above), particularly with respect to questions regarding the relationship between inspiration and memory.

63 See Lessing, "On the proof of the spirit and of power," 87.

64 Cf. *Comm. Jo.* 10.3.14 (cited in Section 2.3).

65 Cf. *Comm. Jo.* 10.3.10.

66 *Comm. Jo.* 10.3.10: τὴν περὶ τούτων ἀλήθειαν ἀποκεῖσθαι ἐν τοῖς νοητοῖς. Cf. *Comm. Jo.* 10.31.199. See also *Comm. Jo.* 10.4.15, 17 (treated in Section 3.2).

Such a conclusion may conjure, for some, the specter of "platonizing." But the preceding sections should make it obvious that what drives Origen to the position described above is not any extrinsic philosophical prejudice but rather a series of hard-won critically informed judgments about the literary nature of the Gospels and the literary activity of the Evangelists. The question that historical discord among the four Gospels puts to Christian belief is: how one can accept the four and simultaneously hold them all to be true. Origen's answer? Whatever the discord on a narrative level, and however diverse the Gospel writers' "notions" of Jesus that gave rise to these differences, one may still discern a harmony – notice he does not say univocity – in the realm of how the significance of this life is thought of, conceptualized, or understood.[67] Meaning: the "*whole* truth of what is recorded to have happened" in the Gospels lies elsewhere than in transparently literal facts alone.[68] "Only in this way," Origen concludes, "is it possible to retrieve" the many apparent discrepancies among the four received Gospels.[69]

Given the often censorious caricatures of Origen as a "destroyer of history," it is worth reemphasizing that his position does not subject any historical substrate of the Gospels to erasure anyway.[70] For their narratives of the Temple expulsion (one may add the anointing, etc.), the Evangelists "made use of an event that occurred."[71] As Part I established in principle, and Part II now bears out in practice, Origen believes a majority of the Gospel narratives arise from something that happened in some form or another.[72] Nevertheless, for Origen,

[67] Cf. *Comm. Jo.* 10.3.10. Strauss, not Plato, is the more valuable interlocutor here, as one readily recalls his definition of the "evangelical *mythus*" as an "idea" of Jesus "invested with imagery" (*Life of Jesus*, §14); see also his dialogue with C. Ullmann, where, on this very question of the relationship between ideas and history in the matter of religious truth, Strauss himself moves toward "symbol" and "allegory" language over "myth" language (*Streitschriften* III, 153, 156–57; cf. Beiser, *David Friedrich Strauß*, 112–13).

[68] *Cels.* 2.69. See similarly *Princ.* 4.3.5: "When the coherence [of a passage] is impossible, as literally described ... one must endeavor to grasp its *whole sense*, which draws together in a coherent way the account of things impossible (literally speaking) with things not only not impossible but even true in the historical narrative, by taking in an entirely figurative way as many things as didn't happen in a literal sense."

[69] Cf. *Comm. Jo.* 10.31.200.

[70] Cf. Simon, *Histoire critique des principaux commentateurs du Nouveau Testament*, 47. See this chapter's conclusion.

[71] See *Comm. Jo.* 10.25.144.

[72] See *Princ.* 4.3.4, treated in Section 2.5. Cf. *Comm. ser. Matt.* 77 on how the Evangelists' principal concern was to exposit "the mysteries" of things born from that history.

one does not – indeed cannot – discover any ultimate "harmony" among the Gospels by way of historicizing acrobatics but rather by recognizing that they are already a kind of "spiritual" literature, that the "things of history" have already been figuralized by the Evangelists in view of these ideas.[73] He is committed to preserving what is "distinctive and unique" to each of their voices and equally committed to showing a deeper harmony that still rings therein.[74]

A fortiori, Origen believes that much of what is narrated to have been done by Jesus was, in the vanishing point of history, already figurative – that is, already charged with symbolic significance, a "sign of something." On the Temple expulsion, he concludes:

> I think that he has also performed a deeper sign through what has been mentioned, so that we might understand that these events have occurred as a symbol of the fact that the ministry related to that Temple … would soon no longer be able to be performed.[75]

Here the quotation from *Against Celsus* that Part I took up as a provocation for considering Origen's view of Gospel genre now unfolds as a complete thought. The general claim that the various events recorded in the Gospels "show themselves, to those who approach them more attentively, to be a sign of something as well" now takes on a definite referent (viz., a symbolic act warning that Temple service, as it had been known, would soon be rendered impossible), offering the reader another concrete expression of what it means, for Origen, to "ascend from the events recorded to have happened to the things which they signified."[76]

[73] See *Comm. Jo.* 10.6.27: "I have said all this about the manifest disagreements of the Gospels out of a desire to present" a kind of "harmony" that nevertheless emerges "by way of receiving them spiritually."

[74] Cf. *Comm. Matt.* 16.13.

[75] *Comm. Jo.* 10.24.138. Cf. Sanders, *Jesus and Judaism*, 75: by overturning the tables in the Temple, Jesus is not simply "cleansing" it; rather, he intends it as a "symbolic gesture" or "demonstration" in miniature of the (eschatological) destruction of the Temple (see also Sanders, *The Historical Figure of Jesus* [1993], 107, 113, 124, 253–64). Cf. J. Dunn, *Jesus Remembered*, 636–40 on the favorable reception of this view (and expansions thereof). See also C. H. Dodd, *The Interpretation of the Fourth Gospel*, 301 n. 2 for an approving nod to Origen's interpretation here. Cf. M. Barber, *The Historical Jesus and the Temple: Memory, Methodology, and the Gospel of Matthew* (2023), 101–104 (cf. 71–74).

[76] *Cels.* 2.69. On the broader dynamic of prophetic-symbolic actions in the Gospels, see M. D. Hooker, *The Signs of a Prophet: The Prophetic Actions of Jesus* (1997), as well as S. McKnight, "Jesus and Prophetic Actions" (2000).

The passage from *Against Celsus* thus works as a programmatic précis of Origen's view of the Gospels both on a literary level and with respect to how Jesus's own actions are depicted. In the case of the Temple demonstration, Origen believes the reader encounters (to borrow a phrase from E. P. Sanders) "historicity of a curious kind: the historicity of a symbol."[77] So, with a slight transposition, the quotation from *Against Celsus* also serves to summarize Origen's sense of how the Gospels present Jesus's *modus operandi* as a whole.

> The truth of the records of *Jesus's deeds* cannot be fully seen in the mere letter and historical narrative; for each of them shows themselves, to those who approach them more attentively, to be a sign of something as well.[78]

Jesus's actions throughout the Gospels – and particularly in the narratives of these final days – are intrinsically symbolic.[79] Just as the physical expulsion is performed as a sign of the Temple's imminent destruction, the various narratives of healing also (which Origen freely embraces as having "happened at that time") are set down as "symbols of what Jesus's power is ever bringing to perfection"[80]; they both signify and embody the advent of the kingdom, like shadows cast back into this present age by the

[77] Sanders, *Jesus and Judaism*, 101 [78] *Cels.* 2.69 (altered words emphasized).

[79] See *Comm. Jo.* 10.24.138; cf. *Comm. Matt.* 16.20 where Origen also refers to Jesus as one who "performed signs" (σύμβολα ποιήσας) vis-à-vis the Temple demonstration (cf. De Lubac, *History and Spirit*, 235). For a similar comment on the act of foot washing in John 13, see *Comm. Jo.* 32.6.65 (cf. *Hom. Isa.* 6.3–4).

[80] *Comm. Matt.* 11.17 on the request of the Canaanite woman (Matt 15:21–28). In this way, Origen simultaneously holds that these sorts of healings really did take place and proleptically addresses Lessing's misgivings over whether narrating such things matters for contemporary readers: he acknowledges that though these "portentous manifestations of power" might have been able to "summon those who lived at the time" of Jesus to faith, they "do not retain their impressiveness [ἐμφαντικόν] and are presumed to be myths" (*Comm. Jo.* 2.34.204; even if, as Origen believes, such things may still happen: cf. *Comm. Jo.* 6.33.166 and 20.36.329). Origen allows (for instance) that the narrative of the raising of Jairus's daughter and the healing of the bleeding woman "still edifies, even when understood physically," but then invites his readers to consider a "subtler" vision of this story, which "sees that 'these things happened to them as types, and they were written for our sake'" (*Fr. Luc.* 125, reapplying 1 Cor 10:11 to the Gospels). Cf. *Comm. Jo.* 13.64.452 on John 4:48 ("unless you see signs and portents...") vis-à-vis the healing of the royal official's son (Jesus's "second sign" in John): "there isn't any startling event in scripture that is not a sign and symbol of something else." *Fr. Prov.* 1.6 preserves a similar vision of miraculous events in Israel's history (citing Ps 77[78]: 2, 12–13): "How is the saying '*I will open my mouth in parables*' to be harmonized with this? For that which [the Psalm] brings up did happen: he '*performed wonders before their ancestors*'; and he '*split the sea asunder and led them through it*' as described. For all these things happened, even if they are [also] symbols ... received in the same way as the Gospel parables" (cf. H. J. Vogt, *Origenes als Exeget* [1999], 56–57).

more radiant sun of the life of the age to come.[81] The symbolic qualities of the Gospel narratives therefore reflect their primary subject, whose primary mode of proclamation consisted in figurative discourses and symbolic acts. The Evangelists thus take up and make use of this exact quality within the very form of their narratives, "each in his own way," according to their own purposes, and "for the sake of the mysterious aim they had in view."[82]

6.4 TYPE OF THE PAROUSIA: ASCENT TO JERUSALEM

The pericope of Jesus's final ascent into Jerusalem (the "Triumphal Entry") provides the most direct passage from Origen's view of the Evangelists as figurative readers to his vision of Jesus's own figurative ways of speaking and acting; the character of the Evangelists' literary activity becomes bound indissolubly to the figure of Jesus himself. Origen's initial approach ought to be familiar by now. He collects the parallel versions of Jesus's final ascent to Jerusalem and attends to their disagreements[83]: in addition to the major chronological and structural discrepancies outlined above "when parallel events intersect," he also notes how John has Jesus himself find the young donkey, whereas the Synoptics have him send two disciples ahead to retrieve the animal(s)[84]; there are even differences about the kinds of branches involved in the acclamation and how the crowds employ them.[85]

Yet then, in a manner that readily recalls the comparative literary approach developed in *Against Celsus*, Origen turns to concentrate on an even more fundamental interpretive matter: the simple fact of writing. Why even record this event? In his attempt to redirect Celsus's reduction of Gospel interpretation purely to matters of facticity (much less to

[81] See *Or.* 17.1; cf. *Hom. Ps.* 77 3.1–2 and *Hom. Isa.* 6.3–4. Cf. J. P. Meier, *A Marginal Jew*, Vol. 2, 450–54.

[82] Cf. *Comm. Jo.* 10.5.19.

[83] See *Comm. Matt.* 16.14 (citing Matt 21:1–5 par.).

[84] *Comm. Jo.* 10.31.200 (Τοῖς παραπλησίοις πράγμασιν ἐπιπεσόντος) and *Comm. Jo.* 10.31.201, where he notes: "in this way [John] has presented something additional with respect to the more figurative significance of the young donkey" in keeping with Jesus's increased autonomy in John's Gospel (for a similar note about why Jesus is depicted bearing the cross alone in John but shares the burden with Simon of Cyrene in the Synoptics, see *Comm. ser. Matt.* 126; cf. *Comm. Matt.* 12.14).

[85] *Comm. Jo.* 10.31.200 (on John 12:13): "in place of branches [κλάδων] cut from the trees [Matt 21:8], or leafy branches [στιβάδων] cut from the fields [Mark 11:8] and spread on the road, John says the large crowd had taken up palm branches [βαΐα τῶν φοινίκων]."

"proofs" thereof), Origen had set out to "anticipate the whole question of the story of Jesus in the Gospels" by calling more "open-minded" readers instead to approach these narratives just as they would any work of literature: to seek out some "means of entry into the intention of the writers in order to discover" the purpose or thought-process underlying any given passage, both freeing oneself *from* any artificial restraints imposed by purely historiographical concerns and freeing oneself *to* consider the narrative from a more literary – which is to say "figurative" – standpoint.[86] In the same way, Origen believes that "it is especially worthwhile" in the case of the story of Jesus's ascent to Jerusalem "to focus on the intent of what was written and its purpose. What did [the Evangelists] have in mind when, in addition to the startling and portentous signs brought about by the savior, they recorded things which display nothing of the kind?" "What did they intend with the passage before us?"[87]

When examining Matthew's version of the ascent, Origen first levies a lengthy inquiry against those "who think that Matthew set forth nothing beyond the historical when he wrote his Gospel," especially in view of the numerous interpretive dead ends such a reduction produces.[88] What, for instance, "was so pressing that two of the disciples be sent into the village opposite Bethphage to find a donkey tied and a colt with her, to loose and bring to him? And what happened worth recording in someone sitting on a donkey and a colt and entering into the city?"[89] It couldn't be a matter of mere geographical exigency ("if they should allege that it is because it was a long way"). For, Origen replies, "in the first place, those who draw on" John's note that Bethany was about "fifteen stades" (less than two miles) from Jerusalem, "which is a short distance, do not provide any reasonable defense for this way of reading at all. And secondly, let them tell us why he needed *two* beasts for so short a journey?"[90] Moreover, the large crowd's scattering of garments on the way makes very little sense "if nothing else is indicated by them" – not to mention the fact that "cutting branches from the trees to scatter in the way of the donkeys passing by would seem to be more of an obstacle for the one being crowded than a thoughtful reception."[91]

[86] See *Cels.* 1.42 (Section 2.4). [87] *Comm. Matt.* 16.14.

[88] *Comm. Jo.* 10.26.159 (see *Comm. Jo.* 10.26.152–27.166 for the full scope of this rhetorical broadside). For the phrase πέρα τῆς ἱστορίας, see also *Comm. Jo.* 10.22.30.

[89] *Comm. Jo.* 10.26.159–60. [90] *Comm. Jo.* 10.27.164 (see John 11:18).

[91] *Comm. Jo.* 10.27.166.

Origen's "means of entry" into the story rather foregrounds Matthew's own direct invocation of a prophetic figuration: "The prophet Zachariah intensifies our inquiry into this passage, because he uttered a prophecy related to these things that is worth pausing to consider"[92]:

> "Rejoice greatly, daughter of Zion!
> Proclaim, daughter of Jerusalem!
> Behold, *your king is coming* to you,
> just and saving is he,
> meek and mounted on a beast of burden and a young colt."[93]

Origen notices the adjustments both Matthew and John make to the prophecy, as their alterations only further raise the question of how prophetic evocations of this kind function for the Gospel writer(s) in the first place.[94] "For if this prophecy only predicts the physical event indicated by the Evangelists, let those who are fixated on the literal meaning maintain for us how this coheres with the rest of the prophecy, which goes like this":

> "And he shall utterly destroy the chariots from Ephraim,
> and the cavalry from Jerusalem,
> and the bow for war shall be destroyed,
> and there shall be an abundance and peace from the nations,
> and he shall reign over the waters as far as the sea,
> and the rivers at the exits of the earth..." etc.[95]

Origen's point is clear: Jesus doesn't fulfill the prophecy, not in any plain way. Yet Matthew relates that this "prophecy was 'fulfilled' through what took place."[96] But "fulfilled" in what sense? How, in a purely

[92] *Comm. Matt.* 16.14; cf. *Comm. Jo.* 10.26.160.

[93] *Comm. Matt.* 16.14 (citing Zech 9:9).

[94] *Comm. Jo.* 10.26.162: "One must note, however, that Matthew did not cite the text as it is found in the prophet. For instead of 'Rejoice greatly, daughter of Zion; proclaim, daughter of Jerusalem,' he has rendered it as '*Tell* the daughter of Zion,' thus *abbreviating* [ἐπιτεμνόμενος] the prophecy. And he also *omitted* [παρεσιώπησεν] the phrase 'just and saving is he' and says (leaving as is) 'meek and mounted,' but instead of 'on a beast of burden and a young colt' he has written 'on a donkey, and on a colt, the foal of a beast of burden.'" Cf. *Comm. Jo.* 10.31.202 (emphasis added): "Neither did John cite the exact words [αὐτολεξεί] of the prophecy. Instead he has 'Fear not, daughter of Zion, behold your king is coming, *sitting* [καθήμενος],' instead of '*mounted* [ἐπιβεβηκώς] upon a donkey's colt' or 'upon a beast of burden and a young colt.' And it does not say '*Fear not*, daughter of Zion' at all."

[95] *Comm. Jo.* 10.26.161 (citing Zech 9:10). On Origen's text of Zech 9 here, note Heine, FC 80, 292 n. 213.

[96] *Comm. Jo.* 10.26.155 (alluding to Matt 21:4).

historical or literal sense alone, could one say that Jesus fulfilled this prophecy in any way whatsoever? Such a claim, Origen holds, would be nonsense, so long as one presumes that Matthew's intent was to record "nothing beyond the historical," to set forth some "physical" event that fulfilled a prophecy he himself took to predict a plainly observable event.[97] Thus Matthew's own use of the prophecy (including his alterations and abbreviations) problematizes a purely literal reading of the passage as a whole. In other words, for Origen, the prophecy – and thus also the event to which it is bound – has *already* been spiritualized in the scene.

Chapter 3 studied how, in *On First Principles*, Origen locates the primordial source for his sense of the Gospels' principally figurative nature in the Evangelists' own translation of prophetic expectation. Origen's argument for reading the Gospels "spiritually" therefore rests upon the simple fact that relatively little of a whole host of Jewish prophetic expectations literally or "*visibly* happened in the advent of him believed by us to be the Christ."[98] Thus "translating what is immediately apparent in the Gospel into what is spiritual" is already interior to the literary formation of the Gospels. In this section of *On First Principles* Origen mentions Zechariah 9 in passing; now, in the *Commentary on John*, he completes the thought. "The Jews too, when we closely examine together the connection of this prophecy to the things recorded about Jesus, exert no negligible pressure on us when they inquire how Jesus 'destroyed the chariots from Ephraim' and the 'cavalry from Jerusalem,' and how he 'destroyed the bow for war' and has done the things which follow."[99]

The stakes could not be higher. In *On First Principles*, Origen identifies the "cause" for anyone's "disbelief in our savior" as *nothing other* than

[97] Cf. *Comm. Jo.* 10.26.159, 161. Also note *Fr. Matt.* 97 (on Matt 5:17) where Origen judges that Matthew's "fulfill" language is analogous to making one's way into adulthood – not by one's form of life being dissolved or destroyed but rather by a growth or maturation from within that very form. So, for Origen, πληρόω means to bring something to a kind of *fullness*, not just "fulfillment" in a more simplistic sense. Cf. J. R. D. Kirk "Conceptualising Fulfilment in Matthew" (2008).

[98] *Princ.* 4.2.1. Though relatively "little" does not mean "none" for Origen (see, e.g., *Comm. Jo.* 2.34.203 and *Princ.* 4.1.3–7).

[99] *Comm. Jo.* 10.27.163. Cf. *Princ.* 4.2.1 (also citing Zech 9:10) on those "accustomed to following the letter of the prophecies regarding [the Christ], and not seeing him visibly ... destroying the chariots from Ephraim and cavalry from Jerusalem," etc. Cf. *Comm. ser. Matt.* 27. Cf. G. A. Anderson, *That I May Dwell among Them: Incarnation and Atonement in the Tabernacle Narrative* (2023), 187–88.

"scripture not being understood spiritually, but rather received only as far as the bare letter goes."[100] Understanding the ascent to Jerusalem "spiritually" thus consists first and foremost in noticing how the Gospel writer has clothed the event in prophetic imagery in such a way as to have already "translated" the prophecy. Origen is well aware that the lion's share of this prophecy wasn't fulfilled "visibly"– *but that, it seems, is the whole point.* So, he thinks, was Matthew. If one were to "think that Matthew set forth nothing beyond the historical when he wrote" this passage – if the Gospel writer, that is, wasn't already offering a "spiritual understanding" or figurative reinterpretation of this story vis-à-vis the prophetic tradition – the whole recorded event would be nonsense.[101] The objection of certain Jewish thinkers with whom Origen apparently discussed this pericope would hold. All of a sudden, Origen makes his reader see the cost of the claim: receiving the narrative "spiritually," receiving it as Matthew's own "spiritual understanding" of Jesus, becomes constitutive of the Christian proclamation, of Christianity itself.

In view of the narrative's various resistances ("impediments and impossibilities") to "bare history," what *does* the record of Jesus's ascent to Jerusalem adumbrate then? In what is now considered a groundbreaking study in the history of redaction criticism, Hans Conzelmann inadvertently provided an ideal summary of what Origen had discerned in this pericope long before: "Matthew depicts the Entry as a type of the Parousia"[102]; or, even more precisely, as Davies and Allison suggest (drawing on Conzelmann): the entry narrative "would have been understood in the first century as a *parousia*," a "foreshadowing of Jesus's eschatological entry into kingly glory."[103]

100 *Princ.* 4.2.2.

101 Cf. *Comm. Jo.* 10.26.159. Note how far Lessing's complaint about possessing only "reports" of fulfilled prophecy (rather than those "fulfilled before my eyes") misses the mark of how Origen actually understands the Gospel writers' use of prophecy to be a kind of "demonstration of spirit" (cf. "On the proof of the spirit and of power," 84–85). The kind of belief such a prophetic evocation is "capable of producing in those who attend to it" (*Cels.* 1.2) is an understanding borne out of that very authorial mediation – not as a matter of literal, visible fulfillment alone, but rather of *spiritual* understanding, which instead of "depriving" such reports of "all their force" (Lessing, ibid.) becomes the very source of it.

102 H. Conzelmann, *Die Mitte der Zeit: Studien zur Theologie des Lukas* (1954); English edition: *The Theology of St. Luke* (1982), 75 (citing Matt 23:39: "For I tell you, you will not see me again until you say, 'Blessed is he who comes in the name of the Lord,'" which Matt 21:9 anticipates, echoing Ps 117[118]:26). Cf. N. Perrin, *What Is Redaction Criticism?* 28–33.

103 W. D. Davies and D. Allison, *Matthew 19–28* (2004), 125 and 129. Receiving and developing Conzelmann also, see H. Flender, *Heil und Geschichte in der Theologie des*

Origen begins by suggesting a way of viewing the literary role of "the crowds that went before him and followed him crying out: *Hosanna to the Son of David! Blessed is he who comes in the name of the Lord! Hosanna in the highest!*"[104] "You might say," Origen suggests, "that those who 'went before' are those from the people" of Israel who followed the divine word "before the *parousia* (perhaps the righteous and the prophets), and those who 'follow' are from those who follow the word of God after the *parousia* ('those who follow him' meaning either the righteous or perhaps the apostles of Christ)."[105] In this way, Origen takes up the explicitly invoked prophetic "advent" language from Zechariah ("Behold, your king is *coming*"; likely also echoing Isaiah: "Behold, your deliverer *draws near*"[106]) and the Psalm ("Blessed is he who *comes* in the name of the Lord"[107]) and places it before the reader not only as the major theme of the entry narrative – what its figurative inflections are ultimately meant to evoke – but as an introduction to the final cadence of the Gospel as a whole.

Lukas (1965), 85; English edition: *St Luke: Theologian of Redemptive History* (1967), 91: "Thus in the earliest tradition the entry into Jerusalem includes overtones of the parousia. It was in fact 'the type of the parousia.'" See also E. Gräßer, *Das Problem der Parusieverzögerung in den synoptischen Evangelien und in der Apostelgeschichte* (1977), 24 and 27. Cf. Sanders, *Jesus and Judaism*, 308 on how the "triumphal" entry into Jerusalem was "probably deliberately managed by Jesus to symbolize the coming kingdom and his own role in it." Similarly, see J. P. Meier on the entry as symbolic action in *A Marginal Jew, Vol. 5*, 67 n. 30 (cf. Meier, *A Marginal Jew: Rethinking the Historical Jesus, Vol. 3: Companions and Competitors* [2001], 153 and 496); cf. J. Dunn on the event as "enacted parable" in *Jesus Remembered*, 642. On the Johannine development of this dynamism, see Watson, *The Fourfold Gospel*, 136: The entry "must be seen in light of the greater event to which it belongs, that of Jesus' glorification – his enthronement in heavenly glory, accomplished not only in his resurrection and ascension but also in his crucifixion. As it refers back to the prophetic text, Jesus' acclamation also points ahead to his true enthronement, of which it is a sign or parable."

104 Matt 21:9 (evoking Ps 117[118]:26). *Comm. Matt.* 16.19: "First, let us understand what it means that a large crowd followed Jesus when the disciples departed from Jericho with the savior." Cf. *Comm. Jo.* 10.157.

105 *Comm. Matt.* 16.18 (the *Vetus Interpretatio* reads *verbum dei* for ὁ λόγος here). Cf. *Comm. Jo.* 10.29.181–82.

106 Though both Matthew and John cite Zech 9:9, Matt 21:5 ("Tell the daughter of Zion, 'Behold, your king is coming to you'") subtly interweaves Isa 62:11 ("*Tell the daughter of Zion*, 'Behold, your deliverer draws near'") with Zech 9:9 ("Rejoice greatly, daughter of Zion... '*Behold, your king is coming to you*'"): an "elaborate figurative tapestry" (to steal a line from Hays, *Echoes of Scripture in the Gospels*, 108) that I believe Origen also picks up on, based on his quotation of Isa 63:1–2 immediately thereafter.

107 Ps 118:26, which appears in all four Gospels (in slightly different ways); cf. *Comm. Matt.* 16.19.

We cannot, as yet, presume to grasp the full dimensions of how Origen understands the term *parousia* ("advent" or "presence," dwelt on briefly in the closing sections of the previous chapter), or rather, what he believes Matthew understood by it. What we are able to gather, for now, is that with respect to the entry narrative,

> it is possible to see what is recorded in this passage and to understand it as referring to those who wish to live according to the word, who are willing to despise the world and all earthly things, and following Jesus and his disciples, are going out of Jericho and walking in the traces of their steps. The large crowd follows Jesus so that by walking behind him and using him as their guide they may ascend to Jerusalem.[108]

Thus, the narrative of Jesus's ascent to Jerusalem, for Origen, has been shaped to recall the whole line of all those who have left everything to follow the word of the Lord, all the righteous, the prophets, the apostles, the faithful in every age, bound together in one chorus:

> Those who precede, however, do not say one thing and those who follow another. They were all crying out together as a chorus harmoniously singing together, chanting the deliverer's human lineage in the words, "Hosanna to the son of David," his second advent in the words, 'Blessed is he who comes in the name of the Lord,' and the restoration [of all things] to the sanctuary, in the words, "Hosanna in the highest."[109]

All told, the record of the ascent to Jerusalem has been fashioned, that is, to adumbrate the mystery that Jesus will refer to as the Son of Man's exaltation to "the right hand of the power" – a mystery not unrelated, as we will see most clearly in the next chapter, to what Origen understands by Christ's *parousia* (a term frequently used in

[108] *Comm. Matt.* 16.9 (the *Vetus Interpretatio* reads "*heavenly* Jerusalem"). Cf. *Cels.* 1.2 on "those who live according to the word." See J. H. Davies, "The Purpose of the Central Section of St. Luke's Gospel" (1964), on how the whole journey ("ascent") to Jerusalem in Luke is shaped to prefigure, and somehow participate in, Jesus's ascent into heaven. On discipleship symbolism here, cf. Collins, *Mark*, 484.

[109] *Comm. Matt.* 16.18 (with ἀποκατάστασις evoking Acts 3:21 here). The language of the "sancta/sanctuary" (εἰς τὰ ἅγια) echoes Heb 9:2–3, 9:12, 9:24–25; 13:11. Note Flender's suggestion that Jesus's powerful movement directly into the Temple, as the final *telos* of this whole sequence, likewise participates in this "symbolic anticipation" of his heavenly enthronement (*Heil und Geschichte*, 87, also with reference to Hebrews in n. 20). Cf. *Comm. Matt.* 16.19 on "hosanna" as a cry for deliverance: "If you want to learn precisely what the expression" means, Origen says (because the Gospels "were frequently copied by Greeks who did not know the Hebrew language"), "listen to Aquila who translates it like this, 'Please, O Lord, save, O Lord please, help!'"

the Gospels' cultural milieu for a king's triumphant arrival).[110] The narrative of the ascent, in sum, culminates with the entry into Jerusalem (and finally into the Temple itself), which, thus figuratively bound with the mystery of Jesus's heavenly exaltation, is cast as a "type of Christ's reign in heaven," an image of "Jesus's eschatological entry into kingly glory."[111] The whole pericope bends toward the mysterious event horizon of this exaltation, a mystery no aspect of the narrative finds itself untouched by, and a mystery that somehow also involves all those faithful of every age who find themselves drawn into the same festal procession "before" and "behind" him.

As Jesus thus enters into Jerusalem "in the midst of these three acclamations," the "whole city" asks, shaken, "*Who is this*?"[112] Origen, "wanting to preserve the consistency of the figuration in the writing," recognizes a resemblance to Psalm 24 ("*Who is this*, the king of glory?") as well as "something similar" in the verses immediately following the passage from Isaiah ("Tell the daughter of Zion...") that Matthew had intermixed with Zechariah: "*Who is this* drawing near from Edom, from Bosra with crimson garments, so beautifully robed?"[113]

110 Cf. Flender, *Heil und Geschichte*, 86 (my translation): "The 'king who comes in the name of the Lord' – that is, the one now entering into Jerusalem – is the heavenly Lord, whom the community experiences as present"; and ibid., 87 n. 26: "For Luke, 'exaltation in heaven' and *parousia* are one ... The *parousia* is the manifestation on earth of the reign [Herrschaft] of Jesus in heaven." Cf. J. A. T. Robinson, *Jesus and his Coming* (1957), 136. Without reference to Origen, Flender also develops a remarkably similar sense of the coinherence and inextricability of the ideas of ascension, *parousia*, and the restoration of all things vis-à-vis Luke (see esp. *Heil und Geschichte*, 90–91 and 97). Origen would simply dispute (for reasons that will become clearer in Chapter 7), perhaps, the degree of Flender's distinction between the Matthean and Lukan visions on this matter, although even this becomes somewhat blurred as Flender's argument progresses (see ibid., 91–95).

111 Flender, *Heil und Geschichte*, 85 and Davies/Allison, *Matthew 19–28*, 129 respectively. On a similar typology in Luke, cf. Davies, "The Central Section of St. Luke's Gospel," 168. See also I. de la Potterie (citing Conzelmann and Flender), "La parabole du prétendant à la royauté (Lc 19,11–28)" (1985), esp. 629 and 633–34. The parallelism between these two scenes on the Mount of Olives (the royal entry as "préfiguration symbolique" of the heavenly enthronement), as Potterie notes, is reflected throughout the iconographic tradition, beginning at least as early as the Sarcophagus of Junius Bassus (359 CE); see T. Velmans, "Observations sur l'emplacement et l'iconographie de l'entrée à Jérusalem dans quelques églises de Svanétie (Géorgie)" (1982), esp. 476–78.

112 *Comm. Matt.* 16.19 (on Matt 21:10): τίς ἐστιν οὗτος;

113 *Comm. Matt.* 16.19: τὴν ἀκολουθίαν τῆς κατὰ τὴν γραφὴν τροπολογίας (citing Ps 23[24]:8, 10 [τίς ἐστιν οὗτος; cf. v. 3: "Who shall ascend the mountain of the Lord and who shall stand in his holy place?"] and Isa 63:1).

In a manner utterly in keeping with what he discerned to be already operative in Matthew's invocation of Zechariah (and Isaiah, simultaneously), Origen finds the Gospel writer engaging in an active translation of prophetic expectation. Just as the one who "destroys the war-bow" becomes wholly subsumed (through the Evangelist's own "abbreviation") by the figure who approaches, meekly, on a foal, so also when one beholds the entrance of the "king of glory" into his reign, into his place of triumph and exaltation, the blood that reddens his garments is – strangely – his own: he who tramples by being trampled, who crushes by being crushed.[114] The astonishment of those who say "who is this?" – prefiguring the "heavenly powers" who behold the exaltation of the Son of Man to the right hand of power – arises not merely from the bare fact of a physical resurrection,[115] but rather is stirred by seeing that his vindication and exaltation neither erases nor leaves behind the marks of his suffering, but somehow involves, indissolubly, the very vindication and exaltation of his body, raised and received into the heavenly Jerusalem, "still vested with traces of that passion."[116]

6.5 GOSPEL HARMONY?

In his *Critical History of the Principal Commentators on the New Testament*, the seventeenth-century French priest and biblical scholar

[114] Cf. *Comm. Jo.* 6.56.288–89 on John 20:17 ("do not touch me, for I have not yet ascended to the Father"; also citing Isa 63:1–3 and Ps 23[24]:8, 10): "'Who is this drawing near from Edom, from Bosra with crimson garments, so beautifully robed?' And those escorting him say to those stationed at the gates of heaven, 'Lift up your gates, and the king of glory will come in.' And they inquire further (if I may speak in this way) when they see his bloodstained right hand and his whole body filled with the works of prowess: 'Why are your garments red and your clothes like the residue of a full winepress that has been trodden down?' To which he answers, 'I have crushed them in pieces.'"

[115] See *Comm. Matt.* 16.19 on "the astonishment of the heavenly powers at the new sight of his having been borne bodily" on high. See also *Hom. Ps.* 15 2.8: "The powers are astonished [ξενίζονται] at this new story [ἐπὶ τῇ καινῇ ἱστορίᾳ], because they see flesh ascended into heaven and say, 'Who is this drawing near from Edom … with crimson garments' – they see the traces of the blood and wounds – 'so beautifully robed?'" Cf. *Hom. Judic.* 7.2 on the martyrs and all the "blessed who follow Christ in the way that he has preceded them," about whom the angels also "say that prophetic word: 'Who is this ascending from Bosra?'"

[116] *Comm. Jo.* 2.8.61 on Rev 19:13 (a vision of the ascended Lord, the "faithful and true," clad in a "robe dipped in blood and whose name is called the word of God," that is itself a striking metalepsis of Isa 63:1–2): "For perhaps, if ever we somehow come to the most exalted and highest contemplation of the word and of the truth, we shall never completely forget being introduced to him by his coming in our body."

Richard Simon concluded that Origen "establishes the spiritual sense so forcefully in many places of his *Commentary on John* that he completely destroys the truth of the historical narrative."[117] This quote has reappeared frequently in major studies on Origen throughout the last century, but (tellingly) always without Simon's own stated reason for his judgment: namely, that Origen goes to "unfortunate extremes" in his account of Gospel differences, "as if it were impossible" to harmonize "alleged contradictions" among the four Gospels simply by "sticking to the literal sense."[118]

There could hardly be a more convenient illustration of the knot of difficulties I have hoped to unwind in this chapter than this quotation. First, it shows a tendency in contemporary scholarship on Origen, and on early Christianity in general, to drive certain fundamental questions about early Christian reading practices to abstraction (that is, into matters of "history" and "spirit," "literal" vs. "allegorical" reading, etc.). But Simon's judgment actually arises from more basic literary and historiographical issues vis-à-vis the scandal of differences among the four canonical narratives of Jesus's life – and how Origen accounts for them. Second, this quote surfaces an amnesia endemic to most modern genealogies of Gospel scholarship. In a case of supreme irony, one finds Richard Simon – the putative "founder of modern biblical criticism"[119] – censuring Origen for holding a position that nearly every New Testament scholar would now consider to be self-evident: namely, that one *cannot* fully harmonize the four Gospels, not by way of purely historical or literal reading alone.

In view of this doubly misremembered history (of which Simon is only one small representative), it is especially striking to see now that Origen didn't simply exhibit an inchoate awareness of the various literary and historiographical difficulties that arise when one reads the four Gospels synoptically; he engaged these challenges in great detail and developed a sophisticated account of the Gospels' literary formation in light of them. Moreover, it is precisely through such critical analysis that Origen comes to see the Gospels as principally figurative narratives – that is, narratives

117 Simon, *Histoire critique des principaux commentateurs du Nouveau Testament*, 47.

118 Simon, *Histoire critique des principaux commentateurs du Nouveau Testament*, 47. Cf. De Lubac, *History and Spirit*, 18 and Torjesen, *Hermeneutical Procedure*, 2.

119 Baird, *History of New Testament Research*, I:17: "If any individual can be named as the founder of modern biblical criticism, that person would have to be Richard Simon." Cf. G. Gaber, "What Was Critical History? A Reading of Richard Simon's *Histoire critique du Vieux Testament*" (2018).

of those who developed their own notions of "who Jesus is" and shaped their stories of his life accordingly.

The Gospels, in this view, are consumed with presenting a vision – a *spiritual* vision, a "sense of what isn't sensory" – of *who this is*. And the mystery of this identity is precisely what constitutes the "beyond" of what Origen believes "Matthew set forth beyond the historical as he wrote his Gospel."[120] The healing of the blind thus becomes a kind of type-scene of "some remnant of Israel 'sitting beside the road,' that is beside the prophetic scriptures," engaged in "serious study of the law and the prophets."[121]

> These are the ones who say, "Have mercy on us" and, "We want our eyes to be opened." Would that we too, sensing that we are blind and do not see, *as we sit beside the very road of the scriptures and hear that Jesus is passing by*, might stop him by our request and say that we want our eyes to be opened.[122]

Whatever differences or discord one discovers among the Gospels on the level of history, of narrative, and even of their very notions of Jesus, there also remains, for those with eyes to see, a more fundamental agreement – a harmony of spirit – among the four Evangelists' visions of the "mysteries born" from that history[123]: just like the harmony one may yet discern between those who "go before" (the prophets and righteous of Israel) and those who "follow after," the apostles and all the faithful of every age who "follow Jesus, so that by walking behind him and using him as their guide, they too may ascend to Jerusalem."[124]

120 *Comm. Jo.* 10.26.159. 121 *Comm. Matt.* 16.10.

122 *Comm. Matt.* 16.11 (emphasis added). On the symbolic valences of the healing of the blind, cf. Luz, *Matthew 8–20* (2001), 551. Similarly vis-à-vis Mark, cf. Collins, *Mark*, 91, 395, 397, and 507, and J. R. Donahue and D. J. Harrington, *The Gospel of Mark* (2002), 258 and 319.

123 Cf. *Comm. ser. Matt.* 77. In a fragment from *Comm. Matt.* Book 2 (preserved in *Philoc.* 6), Origen applies "blessed are the peacemakers" (Matt 5:9) to those who strive to present the inner harmony of all the canonical writings, "whether of the old with the new, or of the Prophets with the Law, or of the Gospels with each other, or of an apostle with a Gospel, or with himself, or with the other apostles" (cf. *Comm. Matt.* 10.15). Cf. S. Morlet, *Symphonia: La concorde des textes et des doctrines dans la littérature grecque jusqu'à Origène* (2019), 289–348. See also *Comm. Matt.* 5.7 (preserved in *Philoc.* 5.6): "just as he is one whom many proclaim, so also is the Gospel recorded by many, in effect, one, and there is truly one Gospel through four."

124 *Comm. Matt.* 16.9.

7

The Sign of His Presence

The Coming of the Son of Man

"What will the sign of your presence be?"[1]

I have argued throughout this study that Origen's figurative sensibilities originate in a particular view of the literary form and formation of the Gospels. Origen, we have found, makes sense of the Gospels by receiving them as if the Evangelists were themselves figurative readers of the life of Jesus. Now, advancing this thesis one stage further, the closing sections of the previous chapter discovered Origen locating the inspiration for the Gospels' literary form in the figure of Jesus himself. That is, Origen believes the canonical records of Jesus's life indicate that he too was a "spiritual reader" of this particular epoch in the history of Israel and, ultimately, the role of his own life therein. Origen presents – and understands the Gospel writers to have presented – Jesus as a man who also "made full use of" certain symbolic gestures and figures of speech in order to "announce, in his own way, what he had seen in the spirit."[2]

As we turn to examine an archetypal expression of Jesus's figurative mode of discourse, no sequence of passages more clearly establishes Origen's view – that Jesus himself was "one who intended to teach what he perceived in his own understanding by way of figures" – than his interpretation of Jesus's prophetic Son of Man sayings.[3] In fact, this final

[1] Matt 24:3.

[2] Cf. *Comm. Jo.* 10.5.18 and 10.4.15 on the Evangelists. For other expressions of Jesus's figurative and parabolic manner of teaching, cf. *Comm. Matt.* 17.34–35 and *Hom. Isa.* 6.3.

[3] Cf. *Comm. Jo.* 10.5.18 on the Evangelists. On "parables" as a form of discourse broadly considered, see Section 2.5. Cf. *Comm. Jo.* 13.39.250 and 13.40.261.

chapter will show that one can take up the whole matrix of first principles developed in the preceding chapters on the nature of the Gospel narratives and the character of their authorship, and may, with startling immediacy, transpose them into a distillate of the nature of Jesus's own visionary character.

Having departed from the Temple and prophesied its destruction, Jesus is said to have sat down along the hillside directly across from the Temple (the Mount of Olives), where the "disciples approach him privately" to ask: "When will these things be? And what will the sign of your advent [παρουσία] be? And of the consummation of the age?"[4] Origen is well aware that the church as a whole "seems to have received a tradition (along with others about this matter) that there will be a second advent of Christ 'in glory.'" This, at least, "is clear."[5] What is less clear, however, is what was ever meant by this tradition. Origen, that is, accepts the basic datum of belief in some kind of "second advent," but then asks: what does it mean, exactly, to receive such a tradition?[6] What did the complex of associated ideas and images signify in the first place? And by what criteria ought one to interpret this tradition as it appears in the Gospels? Origen's answers to these questions (that is, his readings of the passages in question) depend, as ever, on collecting plausible literary precedents, establishing some sense of genre, and remaining persistently skeptical that the intent of every discourse was ever reducible to a plainly literalized sensibility alone.

So one finds that here, near the end of his life, Origen has never departed from the fundamental criteria developed in *On First Principles*. Now, however, the question has turned from the nature of Gospel narrative in general to the nature of Jesus's sayings: for neither, it appears, is Jesus's characteristic manner of expression "completely unmixed," there being things interwoven which were never intended to be taken as if they did, or would, happen "physically."[7] It is clear that the discourses on the "coming of the Son of Man" and "the consummation of the age" are styled as *historia*, that is, as a narrative of events "as (if) they will happen."[8] But with Jesus, no less than for the Evangelists, Origen does

[4] Matt 24:1–3. See *Comm. ser. Matt.* 32. Cf. *Princ.* 3.6 on the "consummation."
[5] *Comm. ser. Matt.* 50. Cf. *Comm. ser. Matt.* 70.
[6] On the early history of the phrase "second advent" (δεύτερα παρουσία), see G. Stanton, "The Two Parousias of Christ: Justin Martyr and Matthew" (2013).
[7] Cf. *Princ.* 4.2.9 (Section 2.2).
[8] Reapplying *Princ.* 4.3.1 (Section 2.2): ἀναγεγραμμένα μὲν ὡς γεγονότα, οὐ γεγενημένα δὲ κατὰ τὴν λέξιν.

not presume that this guarantees they were meant to be received (only) in their most superficial sense.[9] It means only that they speak "in the form of history" or in "historical images," nothing more and nothing less, and by thus interweaving "things that seem historical" even if they wouldn't happen literally, so to "disclose, in a figurative way, certain mysteries" of the coming age.[10]

7.1 LITERAL PROPHECY?

"In the first place," Origen acknowledges that there are certain aspects of the Olivet Discourse that are able to be received "as if the Lord" were simply "prophesying in it."[11] For instance, "most relate the statement" that "this generation will not pass away until all these things come about" to "the destruction of Jerusalem and think it said of that generation that lived at the time of Christ and witnessed his passion and which was not to pass on before the destruction of that city occurred."[12] "Such terrible

[9] Even if Reimarus never truly merited the title "founder of modern Gospel criticism," his conception of Christ's *parousia* as a failed prophecy, its publication by Lessing (cf. *Fragments*, §§36–46), its reinvigoration by Strauss (cf. *Life of Jesus*, §§115–16) and J. Weiss (*Die Predigt Jesu vom Reiche Gottes* [1892]), its lionization by A. Schweitzer, and contemporary revoicings now all together disallow superficial suturing of this ancient *skandalon* in early Christian thought (cf. 2 Pet 3:3–4; see also R. Bultmann, "New Testament and Mythology," 5; and Fredriksen, *When Christians Were Jews*, 99–107). Notably, Dale Allison has suggested that "what we find in John's Gospel, namely, the *spiritualization of eschatology*... is simply the continuation of a natural process that started long before" in Mark and Matthew; Allison tantalizingly concludes: "The process of reinterpretation continued with Origen..." (*Jesus of Nazareth: Millenarian Prophet* [1998], 168–69, emphasis added, with reference to H. Bietenhard, "The Millennial Hope in the Early Church" [1953], at 20–21). If Origen picks up on a "process of reinterpretation" already interior to the Gospels, the question still remains (1) *when* exactly (and to what degree), not *whether*, certain eschatological tropes become spiritualized, (2) what, as ever, one means by this word ("spiritualize"), and thus, (3) how distant Origen's own vision actually is from this process of reinterpretation intrinsic to the Gospel traditions themselves.

[10] Reapplying *Princ.* 4.3.1. On portraying something that didn't, or in this case won't, literally "happen" using a "semblance of history" (εἰκών ἱστορική) or in a "historical manner" (ἐν ἱστορίας τρόπῳ) or "in the form of history" (ἐν ἱστορίας σχήματι), see Chapter 2 (*Comm. Jo.* 10.4.17, *Cels.* 5.29, and *Cels.* 5.31, respectively). Cf. Strauss's discussion of the "scheinbar Geschichtliche" in *Life of Jesus*, §12. Cf. A. Y. Collins on sections of Daniel and Enoch as "history in an apocalyptic mode" or "history in symbolic or allegorical form," proffering a "symbolic account of history" and an "apocalyptic view of history," which she reapplies to her view of Gospel genre (*Is Mark's Gospel a Life of Jesus?* 46–66). See, similarly, C. H. Dodd on Daniel in *Parables of the Kingdom*, 70: "In what sense, then, did Jesus cite the prediction from Daniel? It is gratuitous to assume that He must have interpreted it with strict literalness" (cf. pp. 79–83).

[11] *Comm. ser. Matt.* 48.

[12] *Comm. ser. Matt.* 54 (on Matt 24:34).

things" – the siege of Jerusalem, the sacrilege of the holy place – did in fact "happen to those who were in Judea at that time," and "it is related by those who have written a Jewish history about the things that happened then that the people suffered a 'great tribulation such as had never occurred from the beginning of the world up to' the time of Christ."[13] Similarly, for Jesus's words regarding the "consummation of the age," Origen still allows a basic futural dimension for those who "want to understand" that Jesus is also speaking of a literal end of the world.[14] The discourse intermixes matters both present and future.[15]

Though Origen recognizes that certain aspects of the discourse can be said to refer to the imminent destruction of Jerusalem (within a "generation" in the simplest sense), he is less certain that the predictions of cosmic catastrophe possess a similar transparency.[16] Origen thinks it likelier that Jesus joins a long prophetic tradition of proclaiming "the Day of the Lord" accompanied by images of some violent turning of the worlds. One can find "many words like these in the scriptures," Origen

[13] See *Comm. ser. Matt.* 41 (with reference to Matt 24:14–24, but also echoing Luke 21:20–21). Cf. *Comm. ser. Matt.* 40, where he tentatively references Phlegon of Tralles' *Chronicles* (c. second century CE) on the dating of the destruction of Jerusalem (cf. *Cels.* 2.14, 2.33, and *Comm. ser. Matt.* 134). See also *Cels.* 1.47, 2.13, and *Comm. Matt.* 10.17 on (Pseudo-)Josephus's account of the destruction of Jerusalem (cf. *Hom. Luc.* 38.3; cf. S. Inowlocki, "Did Josephus Ascribe the Fall of Jerusalem to the Murder of James, Brother of Jesus?" [2011]).

[14] Cf. *Comm. ser. Matt.* 37. On those who wish to understand "then will be the end" literally (Matt 24:14), cf. *Comm. ser. Matt.* 39.

[15] See Davies/Allison, *Matthew 19–28*, 330–31 on the approach to these prophecies which "thinks of both AD 70 *and* the end of the world," not in a strictly "chronological sequence – first the destruction of the temple, then (soon) the end – but a single prophecy with two fulfillments" (citing Ephraim the Syrian, J. Meier, the "Antiochean school's notion of *theoria*, according to which the OT can prophesy two things at once," and Jewish apocalypses like 4 Ezra and 2 Baruch); in sum: "the discourse, which freely mixes experience with *topoi*, concerns the past, present, and the future." It goes without saying that Origen's position also fits into Davies/Allison's typology, along with (and preceding) Ephraim and the Antiochenes.

[16] Cf. D. Allison, *Constructing Jesus*, 32 n. 7: "Jesus was looking not for the literal 'end of the world' but instead for the restoration of a world in disrepair" (cf. Allison, *Jesus of Nazareth: Millenarian Prophet*, 154–57; cf. Meier, *A Marginal Jew, Vol.* 3, 624). Origen has frequently been accused of a (putatively) wide-ranging reading of γένεα. However, I am not convinced that he believes that the word *must* mean something more expansive than a single "generation"; rather, he simply thinks "this generation" may also stand as a figure for subsequent generations who suffer similar trials and persecutions (cf. *Comm. ser. Matt.* 54). Cf. A. Plummer, *An Exegetical Commentary on the Gospel according to St. Matthew* (1910), 338 (as cited by Davies/Allison, *Matthew 19–28*, 331 n. 20): "If the Day of Judgment is in any way included [in Matt 24:34], it is as being symbolized by the judgment on the guilty city." Cf. Flender, *Heil und Geschichte*, 105.

notes, citing Isaiah, Joel, and Zechariah – all of whom the Olivet Discourse directly invokes.[17] He acknowledges that it seems to some "that the interpretation ought to extend to this point and to investigate nothing" beyond the "simple words... *as if there is no need for interpretation.*"[18] But, he continues, even readers who receive these sayings as "literal" predictions must acknowledge that the cosmological imagery – which even in the preceding prophetic tradition is not without literary affect or challenges to simplistic historicizing[19] – also takes on a figurative dimension once recast in light of the Passion narrative:

> For just as in the dispensation of the cross when "the sun failed there was darkness over all the earth," so too when "the sign of the Son of Man" appears "in heaven" the light of the sun and moon will fail, and that of the stars also, as if consumed by the great power of that sign, at whose appearing "the tribes" that shall have remained on the earth at that time "will beat their breasts."[20]

Under the shadow of the Olivet Discourse, the Passion becomes, in this view (as Dale Allison puts it), "the end of the world in miniature."[21] The Gospel narrative itself seems to be telling the reader that the "sign of the Son of Man" *already* appeared when the "Son of Man was hung on the wood and his 'sign' shone brightly 'in heaven.' And the people from 'all tribes' who previously had not believed" his message, "then recognizing it by that 'sign' that was revealed will beat their breasts and lament for their ignorance and sin, because they did not accept the word of the Lord."[22]

In sum, Origen judges that certain portions of the discourse correspond directly to various tribulations suffered during the Jewish War, yet they apply equally well to other forms of oppression suffered by early Christian communities: for "that generation," through the (post-) apostolic age, and on into Origen's own day.[23] Similarly, sayings about

17 *Comm. ser. Matt.* 48 (citing Isa 13:9–11; Joel 2:10–11, 30–31; Zech 12:9–14).

18 *Comm. ser. Matt.* 48.

19 For instance, Origen points out that Isaiah speaks of both the darkening and extreme brightening of the sun and moon in different prophecies of the "Day of the Lord" (cf. Isa 13:10 and 30:26); which is it, Origen asks, if these are meant as astrophysical predictions and not apocalyptic tropes? (*Comm. ser. Matt.* 49, which also compares such sayings with similar tropes in the Apocalypse of John). Anyway, he continues, most everyone already knew that (cosmologically speaking) stars are a great deal larger than earth, so how could a multitude of stars falling to earth have been meant literally anyway?

20 *Comm. ser. Matt.* 48 (on Matt 24:29–30 and alluding to Luke 23:44–45; cf. Matt 27:45).

21 D. Allison, *The Historical Christ and the Theological Jesus*, 27.

22 *Comm. ser. Matt.* 48.

23 See Luz, *Matthew 21–28*, 203: "We must say that with Matthew the historical, eschatological, and church history interpretations are woven together." Cf. *Comm. ser. Matt.* 49 on how the "tribes" that "beat their breasts" can be taken not only for those

the darkening of the celestial bodies find themselves anticipated by certain events recorded to have taken place during the Passion but may ultimately – and figurally – signify a regeneration of the universe as a whole.[24] In Origen's view, nothing about the images employed by Jesus finally compels one to choose one cosmological model over another – whether, on the one hand, one believes that our world will meet its end suddenly in some cosmic conflagration, or, on the other hand, one "thinks that the destruction of the world will be by its exhaustion," as the light of the heavenly luminaries "diminishes little by little" until they fail completely.[25]

Nevertheless, Origen considers it implausible that any reader could explain the whole discourse "word for word" in this way. "Perhaps they can in some passages, but in others not at all"; with respect to certain portions of it, Origen doubts that "if sufficiently pressed, [such readers] would be able to say anything" whatsoever.[26] In other words, Origen suggests that the Olivet Discourse – like the Gospel narratives themselves – is "mixed": Jesus is recorded to have woven together sayings about things that were to happen (perhaps in multiple senses) with things that wouldn't happen in any plainly observable way.[27] What remains, then, is to "look into what the truth of these sayings might be according to those who are of the opinion that there is something deeper and subtler going on in these discourses," those, that is, who attend to how sayings "like those above correspond" to a broader "figurative tradition."[28] Among the most difficult are the sayings about (1) the Son of Man's ascent to the heavenly throne and (2) his coming on the clouds in glory.[29]

who first responded to the early preaching of the apostles, but also for the many other "tribes of the earth" who have since beat their breast at the sign of the cross. See similarly *Comm. ser. Matt.* 39 on the multiple dimensions of Matt 24:9 ("Then they will deliver you to tribulations and kill you, and you will be hated by all nations because of my name").

24 Cf. Matt 19:28 on the παλιγγενεσία. For Origen's lengthy deliberation on the historical plausibility (and figurative dimensions) of the darkening of the sun during the crucifixion, see *Comm. ser. Matt.* 134 (cf. D. Allison, "Darkness at Noon" [2005], esp. 88–90). Similarly vis-à-vis the earthquake that follows Jesus's death in Matthew (27:51), see *Comm. ser. Matt.* 139 (cf. J. Marcus, "Did Matthew Believe His Myths?" [2016], esp. 235–39).

25 *Comm. ser. Matt.* 48 (cf. *Princ.* 3.6.6). On the contradictory images of suddenness and of a long series of signs in the apocalyptic sayings, cf. Dodd, *Parables of the Kingdom*, 64.

26 *Comm. ser. Matt.* 54 (referring to Matt 24:2–33).

27 Cf. *Princ.* 4.2.9.

28 *Comm. ser. Matt.* 48: *consequentiam moralium traditionum.* The anonymous translator most frequently uses *moralis* (and related expressions) to translate τροπολογία (and cognates) and so should be translated in English accordingly (see Heine, *Matthew*, I:20 n. 96).

29 Matt 24:29–30, 25:31–32, and 26:64; cf. 19:28.

7.2 "YOU WILL SEE...": EXALTATION TO THE RIGHT HAND

Having been taken from the Mount of Olives to be tried before the Sanhedrin, Jesus is recorded to have remained silent before the High Priest Caiaphas, who finally demands: "I charge you under oath before the living God, tell us if you are the Messiah, the son of God." Jesus answers: "That's what you say. But I say to you, from now on you will see the Son of Man sitting at the right hand of power and coming on the clouds of heaven."[30] What is one to make of this saying, recorded in "a similar way by three Evangelists" at the moment of Jesus's condemnation – the saying, in fact, that seals his fate? Is it so clear what is meant by it?[31] Origen, at least, doesn't think so.

As we have witnessed in every paradigmatic passage treated in the preceding chapters, Origen first attempts to establish some sense of the genre this saying involves itself in.[32] "For those who assume that looking into" such questions is "overdoing it," Origen says, "it is necessary to gather" a number of other passages "about God (or Christ) 'sitting,' so that by interrogating the passages gathered on this subject, and by juxtaposing them with one another, it might be possible for some more substantial view to emerge" – that is, "by way of taking up a simpler precedent" first.[33] Only then will one be able to form a "touchstone" or "criterion" (βάσανος) for judging the intent of the saying at hand.

Origen begins by arguing that Jesus's answer to Caiaphas participates in a long and rich tradition of prophetic visionary discourses. Throne visions, he points out, were already a well-established idiom in the scriptures of Israel. For instance, he asks, "what sort of thing" is recorded in Kings when the prophet Michaiah (one of the four disciples of Elijah) testifies before the king of Israel: "'I saw the God of Israel seated on his throne, and all the host of heaven stood around him on his right and on his left,' etc."?[34] Or in Isaiah: "'I saw the Lord seated on a throne, high and lifted up,' etc."? Or in Daniel: "'I kept watching until thrones were set

[30] Matt 26:64.

[31] *Comm. ser. Matt.* 111: "It is worth investigating what it means for the Son of Man to 'sit at the right hand of power.'" See similarly *Comm. Matt.* 16.4 (on Matt 20:20–24, with reference to Matt 19:28 and echoing 16:28) where Origen invites readers to seek out "what is intended by this 'sitting' at 'the right' or 'left' of Jesus 'in his kingdom.'"

[32] Cf. *Comm. Matt.* 16.4 on determining "what kind of thing [οἷον] is written" in Matt 19:28.

[33] *Comm. Matt.* 16.4.

[34] *Comm. Matt.* 16.4 (citing 1 Kgs 22:19); a "parallel account," Origen notes, is recorded in slightly different terms in 2 Chron 18:18.

up, and an ancient of days sat,' etc."?[35] Furthermore, "one can find things similar [παραπλήσια] to these in Ezekiel," who sees the "likeness of a throne with the appearance of a lapis lazuli stone, and, above that, upon the likeness of the throne, a likeness in human form."[36] This visionary tradition, that is, develops a strain of thought inclusionary of a (human) figure sharing the throne of God, a dynamic further reflected in the Psalms, where it says, "The Lord said to my Lord, 'sit at my right hand until I make your enemies the footstool of your feet,'" which "reveals," Origen notes, another "sitting" – one that belongs to God and one that belongs to the deliverer at his "right hand."[37]

With these and "other similar passages that speak about God 'sitting'" in hand, the Gospels proceed to "speak, in a similar way, about Christ."[38] Origen draws attention to the fact, in short, that the vision Jesus promises before Caiaphas draws on a far more expansive visionary enthronement tradition, such that Jesus becomes identified with the second figure portrayed therein. Matthew, in particular, multiplies the enthronement prophecies in this vein.[39] Still, with specific regard to Jesus's saying before the Sanhedrin about seeing "the Son of Man seated at the right hand of power" in Matthew, Mark "records something to the same effect" and Luke "something similar."[40]

By virtue of these literary precedents and parallels, Origen suggests that readers may therefore understand Jesus's saying "just as one would what is written" in the foregoing prophetic theophany traditions.[41] The preceding visionary literature allows one to look beyond overly "facile, simplistic, and trivializing" ways of receiving the various images of the Son of Man being enthroned or seated "at the right hand of power" and to present them as having been set down to indicate something "more mysterious."[42] But the juxtaposition is only the first step; what is left is to

35 *Comm. Matt.* 16.4 (citing Isa 6:1 [cf. Acts 1:9] and Dan 7:9): The Psalmist similarly prays, "'You who sit upon the Cherubim, appear!' and again, 'God is seated on his holy throne'" (citing Ps 79[80]:1 and 46:9 [47:8 LXX]); cf. *Comm. ser. Matt.* 111.

36 *Comm. Matt.* 16.4 (citing Ezek 1:25–26).

37 *Comm. Matt.* 16.4 (citing Ps 109[110]:1); cf. *Comm. ser. Matt.* 111 and 5–8.

38 *Comm. ser. Matt.* 111.

39 *Comm. Matt.* 16.4: Origen cites as "paradigmatic examples" the "way in which" (τίνα τρόπον) Matthew records Jesus saying, "in the regeneration, when the Son of Man sits on the throne of his glory..." (Matt 19:28) and "When the Son of Man comes in his glory, and all the angels with him, then he will sit on the throne of his glory..." (Matt 25:31).

40 *Comm. Matt.* 16.4 (citing Matt 26:64, Mark 14:62, and Luke 22:69).

41 *Comm. ser. Matt.* 111. Cf. T. F. Glasson, "Theophany and Parousia" (1988).

42 *Comm. Matt.* 16.4: μυστικωτέραν.

develop a "criterion" from out of these comparisons in order to see if a "more substantial view" of what is meant by the saying emerges.[43] In other words, it was necessary "to compare [such passages] with the present saying so that we might see from a shallow and mythical assessment what it, by way of a human trope, might signify – this 'sitting' of Christ."[44]

Instead, Origen concludes, it "seems to him" that "the 'sitting of the Son of Man' signifies the inauguration of some kind of immovable reign."[45] So, first and foremost, Origen believes (to steal a line from Raymond Brown) that "'seeing' in an eschatological context can go beyond physical sight."[46] In line with the preceding prophetic tradition of throne visions evoked above, this saying signifies by way of a "concrete picture" or "historical image" the mystery of Jesus's exaltation to an everlasting reign, not "empirical chairs set up in the sky" somewhere.[47]

In other words, and with language bound even more tightly to the grammar developed in the preceding chapters, "this 'sitting' of God is *spiritual*... on a *spiritual* throne. And Christ being seated 'on the right hand of the power' is also spiritual."[48] Thus, as this book has repeatedly emphasized, what Origen means by "spiritual" here, quite simply, is that "nothing about this passage indicates a *physical* sitting – defining 'sitting' as setting one's butt down on some chair."[49] It is "laughable," Origen continues, "to think that, just because physical *language* was used for these things," the saying de facto means that "physical thrones had been manufactured for God, or for Christ, or for those 'for whom it has been

[43] *Comm. Matt.* 16.4.

[44] *Comm. ser. Matt.* 111 (cf. *Comm. Matt.* 16.7): *ex humili aestimatione et fabulosa*. Cf. *Cels.* 1.43 on "comparing *historia* with *historia*" (treated in Section 4.3; cf. Section 2.2 on the Gospels as a form of Jewish biblical narrative).

[45] *Comm. ser. Matt.* 111.

[46] Brown, *The Death of the Messiah, Vol. 1*, 499 (citing Isa 40:5, Isa 52:30, and Mic 7:10, 16), which continues: "The verb 'see' governs both the sitting and the coming of the Son of Man; one should not posit two different kinds of perception, one for the sitting and one for the coming... something has to happen to be seen, even if the seeing means the ability to appreciate the significance of what happens."

[47] See *Fr. Eph.* on Eph 1:20-21 (as noted by Heine, *Matthew*, I:237 n. 66): "One should consider these things to have been expressed by way of a concrete figure [σωματικῷ χαρακτῆρι], not that there are any empirical chairs or thrones set up in the heavens." For the language of εἰκών ἱστορική, see *Comm. Jo.* 10.4.17 on the Evangelists. Cf. *Comm. ser. Matt.* 7 on Jesus's interpretation of Ps 110 in Matt 22:41–46: "Lest you imagine some empirical 'sitting'" in human form (*humano schemate*) on two literal chairs, "understand that these things are said figuratively about the reign of God."

[48] *Comm. Matt.* 16.4.

[49] *Comm. Matt.* 16.4.

prepared to sit at Christ's right or left.'"[50] What would it even mean to receive this image with that degree of literalism? "What kind of material" would these sky-chairs be made out of, Origen playfully yet pointedly wonders?[51]

For Origen to suggest that the passage denotes a *spiritual* enthronement is, in his view, to say that the kind of vision prophesied here ("you will see...") involves a perception of something real precisely insofar as it is understood as the "same sort of thing" one finds in the preceding prophetic tradition of divine throne visions: a "seeing in the spirit," so that (invoking Origen's treatment of Jesus's baptismal vision) "anyone who examines this subject more deeply will say" that this saying evokes "a certain kind of 'divine sense,'" a sense which can be expressed in "many forms," but in this case elicits "a 'seeing' of things greater than physical matters."[52] The saying "interweaves language that would make it seem that something would be perceptible to the senses that would become clear in a purely interior way."[53]

Origen, moreover, does not engage in any hand-waving over the incontrovertible imminence of Jesus's language – since, as he points out, unlike (but not necessarily contrary to) Mark, Matthew's Gospel has "*from now* you will see," and Luke's "*from this time* the Son of Man will..."[54] How can this saying "be seen to have been fulfilled among those who heard what he said"?[55] For Origen, it is possible to see Jesus's culminating post-resurrection appearance in Matthew as a vision of "the Son of Man sitting at the right hand of the power," a scene which therefore serves to fulfill the prophecy uttered before the Sanhedrin. "His disciples saw him rising from the dead, *and in this way*, they saw him established 'at the right hand of power.'"[56] Resurrection and enthronement signify one and the same mystery of exaltation.

Now the full dimensions of Origen's reading begin to emerge: "The 'sitting of the Son of Man' signifies the inauguration [*fundatum*] of some

50 *Comm. Matt.* 16.4 (citing Matt 20:23). 51 *Comm. Matt.* 16.4.

52 Reapplying *Cels.* 1.48 (treated at length in Section 4.5).

53 Reapplying *Comm. Jo.* 10.5.18 on the Evangelists (cf. Section 3.2).

54 *Comm. ser. Matt.* 111 (citing Matt 26:64 and Luke 22:69). 55 *Comm. ser. Matt.* 111.

56 *Comm. ser. Matt.* 111 (cf. *Comm. Jo.* 10.37.245): "Perhaps it was then that *the Lord said to my Lord: 'Sit at my right hand until I make your enemies a footstool for your feet'*" (Ps 109[110]:1), suggesting that Jesus is also purposely evoking the rest of this verse ("until I make your enemies a footstool") as a covert condemnation of Caiaphas. Cf. Robinson, *Jesus and His Coming*, 51: "If this is a saying of vindication, then there can be no doubt that it refers to the only moment to which all the enthronement language applied to Jesus does refer, namely, to the moment of the Resurrection onwards."

kind of immovable reign" – a reign inaugurated, that is, when he has been exalted to the "right hand of power," he "who receives from the Father all authority as 'in heaven so also on earth.'"[57] By virtue of this allusion to Matthew 28:18, Origen further identifies the end of Matthew's Gospel – the appearance of the risen Christ as one to whom "all authority on heaven and earth has been given" – as a vision of one who is "*now* seated at the right hand of the power." Or, in the words of John Meier, "We have here the fulfillment of what the Matthean Jesus prophesied at his trial… The Son of Man, exalted by the resurrection to God's right hand, comes to his church in proleptic parousia."[58]

Furthermore, Origen's reference to Matthew 28:18 ("all authority…") includes a subtle allusion to Matthew 6:10 – or rather draws out Matthew's own subtle allusion to the Lord's Prayer in his Gospel's final scene: The raising of the Son of Man to the "right hand of power" signifies a certain irrevocable reign inaugurated when "he receives from the Father 'all authority' *as* 'in heaven so also on earth.'"[59] By adding "as" (ὡς), Origen creates an amalgam of Matthew 6:10 and 28:18 ("your kingdom come… *as in heaven, [so] also on earth*" || "all authority has been given to me *in heaven and on earth*"[60]), an amalgam that allows readers to anticipate his view of the intimate interrelation between the two halves of Jesus's oracle before Caiaphas: the vision of the Son of Man's exaltation to "the right hand of power" and the vision of his "coming on the clouds of heaven," the second of which we turn to now.[61]

57 *Comm. ser. Matt.* 111 (citing Matt 28:18).

58 J. P. Meier, *The Vision of Matthew: Christ, Church, and Morality in the First Gospel* (1979), 37–38 (cf. p. 212). See similarly Robinson, *Jesus and His Coming*, 131 (citing R. H. Lightfoot, *Locality and Doctrine in the Gospels* [1938], 84): "Matthew describes… an appearing of Jesus to the disciples which is a *Parousia* scene in all but name. It is, as Lightfoot says, a 'manifestation of the Lord as possessing after the Resurrection all the attributes expected to be found in him at the *Parousia*, that is, above all, as the Son of man." Cf. A. M. Ramsey, "What was the Ascension?" (1951); and E. Lohmeyer, "'Mir ist gegeben alle Gewalt!' Eine Exegese von Mt. 28, 16–20" (1951). On this pericope as a depiction of a "proleptic parousia," cf. C. H. Dodd, "Matthew and Paul" (1947), 294.

59 *Comm. ser. Matt.* 111 (citing Matt 28:18).

60 Matt 6:10: ὡς ἐν οὐρανῷ καὶ ἐπὶ γῆς || Matt 28:18: ἐν οὐρανῷ καὶ ἐπὶ γῆς.

61 *Comm. ser. Matt.* 111: "And he prophesied not only that they would see him 'sitting' at the right hand 'of power,' but also that they would see him 'coming' (as Matthew, at least, says) 'on the clouds of heaven'" (noting that Luke's version lacks the second half of the saying). See a similar meditation drawing together Matt 6:10, 28:18, and the "coming" of Christ in *Hom. Isa.* 1.2; cf. *Or.* 26.1–4, where Origen also notes that the phrase "as in heaven so also on earth" is uniquely Matthean (both quoted in this chapter's conclusion below). Cf. J. T. Pennington, *Heaven and Earth in the Gospel of Matthew* (2007), 205–206.

7.3 "YOU WILL SEE...": COMING ON CLOUDS

When introducing the Olivet Discourse's saying about seeing "the Son of Man coming on the clouds," Origen lays three fundamental paths before the reader: "Ought we, based on what is written in this passage, to judge" that

(Option 1): The saying means Jesus is to be borne on "physical, empirical clouds?" Does the "great power and glory" of Christian expectation look to "clouds of this sort" – literal clouds in the sky?

Or (Option 2): "Is it necessary, while preserving the simpler sense of the saying, to consider it to have been said in a figurative way too?"

Or (Option 3): "Should we not preserve the plain meaning of the saying at all but only pursue understanding it as a figure of speech?"[62]

Origen initially resists favoring any of the three options above for a priori reasons external to the text. Instead, he says, one must "carefully weigh and diligently scrutinize every passage individually," and, "having drawn out the argument for each" position, "pronounce on this basis which of them is most likely."[63]

Origen then proceeds with his exposition in much the same way as we saw vis-à-vis the baptismal vision in Chapter 4 (and throughout Part II): by "comparing *historia* with *historia*."[64] "What," he asks, "ought we to say about 'the clouds of heaven' on which 'they,' who will see him then, 'will see the Son of Man coming with much power and glory'?"[65] As the chief literary parallel, Origen cites the overshadowing of the "bright cloud" during the Transfiguration: "And just as when he was transfigured before the three disciples a 'bright cloud overshadowed them,' so also at the second *parousia*, having been transfigured even more gloriously, he will come on a multitude of 'clouds,' since he is to be seen not by three but by multitudes."[66] The comparison, of course, does not resolve any of the

[62] *Comm. ser. Matt.* 50 (on Matt 24:30). [63] *Comm. ser. Matt.* 50.

[64] Cf. *Cels.* 1.43.

[65] *Comm. ser. Matt.* 50. When attending to the parallel saying recorded in Jesus's enigmatic reply to Caiaphas, Origen performs a similar interrogation of the cloud language found in both: "But what are the clouds 'on' which he who has been firmly established 'at the right hand of power' will come, or 'with' which he will come?" (*Comm. ser. Matt.* 111; cf. Matt 24:30 and 26:64). "On" vs. "with" reflects Matthew vs. Mark's (14:62) phrasing, which in turn reflects the differences between Dan 7:13 LXX (ἐπὶ τῶν νεφελῶν) and Theodotian (μετὰ τῶν νεφελῶν).

[66] *Comm. ser. Matt.* 50 (with reference to the Greek fragment: οὕτως ἐν τῇ δευτέρᾳ παρουσίᾳ ἐνδοξότερον μεταμορφωθεὶς ἐπὶ πλειόνων ἥξει νεφελῶν). Cf. the same comparison in *Comm. ser. Matt.* 70, treated in Section 7.5.

critical questions; it is merely the first step in considering whether there is anything "subtler" being expressed by the language.[67]

The tradition of Christ's appearance "on" or "with" clouds is not unique to the Gospels. Acts, Origen notes, also narrates a similar tradition of Jesus "having been taken up, coming in clouds."[68] The Apocalypse of John, too, says "in an analogous way, 'Behold he will come with the clouds, and every eye will see him, even those who pierced him.'"[69] "Among these traditions" one may also include Paul's first letter to the Thessalonians, where the blessed are said to be "caught up in the clouds to meet the Lord in the air, and so be with the Lord always."[70] The tradition among New Testament authors (whether depicting Christ's going to God, his coming to his own, or their going to him) is both diverse and ubiquitous. But this imagery is not isolated to the Jesus tradition.

Origen also asks his readers to recall similar Mosaic, prophetic, and Wisdom traditions about some kind of sitting and/or coming with, in, or on clouds. For instance, "consider what Isaiah says in his 'vision of Egypt': 'Behold, the Lord is sitting on a light cloud and will come to Egypt.'"[71] "Likewise," Origen adds, "a cloud overshadowed the people coming out of Egypt."[72] And, finally, if "it is *Wisdom* that 'became' for the people then 'a column of cloud in the day and a flame of fire at night,'" how "does it not follow – if these things are believed – that the 'clouds of heaven'" represent that which "bears the Lord of the people, that he might abide [*sedeat*] over them?"[73] Therefore, Origen concludes, "one might say that the 'clouds' on which 'they will see the Son of Man coming'" invoke and belong to this same literary tradition, and so, in this

[67] Cf. *Comm. ser. Matt.* 48 and 70. At this point he is still only finding correspondences purely on a literary or textual level (*secundum textum*); cf. *Comm. Matt.* 16.4 (cited in Section 7.2) on the necessity of juxtaposing parallel scriptural images, so that one can then form some "criterion" (βάσανος) for establishing a "more substantial view."

[68] *Comm. ser. Matt.* 50 (citing Acts 1:9–11; Greek fragment: καθὰ καὶ ἀνελήφθη ἐρχόμενος ἐν νεφέλαις).

[69] *Comm. ser. Matt.* 50 (citing Rev 1:7).

[70] *Comm. ser. Matt.* 50 (citing 1 Thess 4:17). Cf. *Hom. Ps.* 81 1.1 on 1 Thess 4:17 as a depiction of divinization, with parallels in M. D. Litwa, *We Are Being Transformed: Deification in Paul's Soteriology* (2012), 162.

[71] *Comm. ser. Matt.* 50 (citing Isa 19:1).

[72] *Comm. ser. Matt.* 50 (cf. Exod 13:22 and 40:35). Notice it is the people who are "coming/going" here.

[73] *Comm. ser. Matt.* 50 (citing Wis 10:17); based on the Latin translation of *Comm. Matt.* 16.19, it appears *vehiculum* translates ὄχημα.

context, are rendered a figural expression of the Lord's glorious presence and dominion – even of his "spirit" and "power."[74]

Thus, Origen has applied the same approach for interpreting the saying about seeing the "Son of Man seated at the right hand of power" to the sayings about seeing his "coming on clouds." Comparing the language of these discourses to preceding scriptural traditions about the coming of the Lord (on clouds) opens up a way past more "simplistic" or "trivializing" reductions and enables one to consider the imagery of the Son of Man's "coming on clouds" as having been set down to indicate something "more mysterious."[75]

Nevertheless, in "comparing *historia* with *historia*" Origen judges that the imagery associated with the "coming of the Son of Man" finds its nearest parallels in the Transfiguration narrative, of which this advent will somehow be an intensification or universalization.[76] Having established the broader literary parallels, the Transfiguration becomes Origen's primary "touchstone" for seeing if a "more substantial view" of the coming of the Son of Man can be developed. "So that," no less than for the "sitting" of the Son of Man at the right hand of power, we may also see "from a shallow and mythical appraisal what it, by way of a human trope, might signify": this "coming" of Christ in glory.[77]

7.4 TRANSFIGURED VISION

Earlier in the *Commentary on Matthew*, prior to setting out an explanation of the Transfiguration narrative that "seems right to us," Origen

[74] *Comm. ser. Matt.* 50 (alluding to Luke 1:35): "Someone might say that the 'clouds' on which they will see the 'Son of Man coming' are the 'power of the most high' and the 'holy spirit' which "become 'clouds of heaven' for him that he may be borne by them." The cloud imagery, in short, finally denotes "spirit" and "power" (imagery, as he points out, that had already been spiritualized in the Wisdom of Solomon, though he appears to believe it need not have been utterly literalized in earlier scriptural traditions either). Cf. *Comm. Matt.* 12.42. Cf. *Comm. ser. Matt.* 111 on clouds as an "image of what is heavenly" (evoking 1 Cor 15:49). Cf. *Hom. Ps.* 77 3.2.

[75] So "Option 3" from *Comm. ser. Matt.* 50 and reapplying *Comm. Matt.* 16.4 (both cited above). Cf. G. B. Caird, *Jesus and the Jewish Nation* (1965), 22 (cf. his *New Testament Theology* [1994], 366): "Is it indeed credible that Jesus, the heir to the linguistic and theological riches of the prophets ... should ever have turned their symbols into flat and literal prose?" For a counterpoint, cf. D. Allison, "Jesus & the Victory of Apocalyptic" (1999).

[76] Cf. *Comm. ser. Matt.* 50 on Matt 24:30 (cited above) and *Comm. ser. Matt.* 70 on Matt 25:31 (cited below).

[77] Reapplying *Comm. ser. Matt.* 111.

notes that he does not disallow that something like this may have "happened" at the time, "as written."[78] But he immediately proceeds to call into question what it is, exactly, one would be saying "happened." He encourages readers, that is, to understand what was narrated here "spiritually, noticing that it is not said that 'he was transfigured' without any qualification, but that 'he was transfigured *before them*' – a crucial qualification inscribed in both Matthew and Mark."[79] The qualification "before them" renders what the disciples are recorded to have "seen" irreducibly subjective, for Origen, making it possible to read the kind of vision described in the narrative as if Jesus could have "been 'transfigured' before some but not before others at the exact same moment of time."[80]

In a manner that readily recalls his treatment of other visionary events recorded in the Gospels (Jesus's vision on the banks of the Jordan, Zechariah's vision in the Temple, etc.), Origen once again asks his readers to consider what kind of "seeing" is being depicted in the narrative. His account of the Transfiguration follows the same line of argument and remains beholden to the same visionary grammar developed in preceding chapters (involving a "certain kind of divine sense," a "sense of what isn't sensory," a "seeing in the spirit"). There are a multitude of ways to conceive of Jesus, Origen reminds us in his account of the Gospels' literary formation in the *Commentary on John*.[81] So too, the Transfiguration narrative shows how Jesus was beheld "in whatever way [people] were capable of seeing him" and did not appear to all the same way.[82] Thus, in Origen's view, the story of the Transfiguration is not – and never was –

[78] *Comm. Matt.* 12.36: γεγονέτω πάλαι καὶ ὡς πρὸς τὴν λέξιν.

[79] *Comm. Matt.* 12.37 (cf. Matt 17:2 and Mark 9:2). [80] *Comm. Matt.* 12.37.

[81] *Comm. Jo.* 10.5.21.

[82] *Comm. Matt.* 12.41 (cf. *Comm. ser. Matt.* 100). Cf. *Cels.* 2.64 (evoking Luke 9:32): "Though Jesus was one, he was a multitude with respect to the ways he was thought of [πλείονα τῇ ἐπινοίᾳ]; and to those who saw him he did not appear alike to all... Moreover, that he did not appear in the same way to those who saw him, but according to their individual capacity, will be clear to those who carefully consider why, when he was about to be transfigured on the high mountain, he did not take all the apostles, but only Peter, James, and John. For they alone had the capacity then to 'see his glory.'" See also *Hom. Gen.* 1.7, *Cels.* 4.16, *Cels.* 6.68, and *Cels.* 6.77 in particular, where Origen anticipates the objection that the Transfiguration narrative is "fiction, no different than myth," just "like the other strange stories about Jesus" in the Gospels. Rather brilliantly, the editors of the *Philocalia* splice Origen's comparison of Gospel genre to classical epic and tragedy just prior to his treatment of Jesus's baptismal vision (*Cels.* 1.42; see Section 2.4) into the middle of this section on the Transfiguration (*Cels.* 6.77) at precisely this point (*Philoc.* 15.15). Cf. A. Blaski, "The *Philocalia* of Origen: A Crude or Creative Composition?" (2019).

about some plainly empirical event (available to any stray hiker with "healthy eyesight" who happened to have been in the right place at the right time[83]), but about a particular vision of Jesus made clear to the disciples "in the spirit."

I should reemphasize: Origen allows that the Gospels preserve a memory of something that "happened."[84] He does not subject the possibility of facticity to total erasure. But his reading does raise the question of what it would even mean to receive the statement "he was transfigured before them" as something that "happened." In this case, Origen's qualification "as written" (ὡς πρὸς τὴν λέξιν) does not mean "physically" or "empirically" but only that there were those long ago (πάλαι) who had seen Jesus in such a way that they could confess "we have seen his glory."[85] Origen does not dwell further on what he means by this allowance ("*Let this have happened then*...”), and this, I suspect, is quite intentional.

The story of the Transfiguration becomes, rather, a preeminent archetype of the kind of literary tradition Origen believes the Lukan preface is also, in its own way, attempting to introduce: a tradition that belongs not only to those who had "'looked at' Jesus physically" but had also "seen his glory" – and sought to hand on the same.[86] Bultmann's interpretation of John 1:14 therefore once again offers a superb epitome of Origen's understanding of "he was transfigured before them." For Origen, the transfiguration "clearly does not occur, as some might naively wish to imagine, in a divine demonstration visible to the natural eye of the body"[87]; rather, "the notion of the vision of the glory has been

83 Cf. *Hom. Luc.* 3.1.
84 *Comm. Matt.* 12.36: γεγονέτω πάλαι καὶ ὡς πρὸς τὴν λέξιν.
85 John 1:14 (cf. Luke 9:32). Cf. Young, *Biblical Exegesis*, 78 on how the technical phrase πρὸς τὴν λέξιν means a kind of critical analysis that attends to the literary stylings or phraseology of a text, including "elucidating figures of speech" (cf. Tzamalikos, *New Fragments*, CLV n. 685). In this context, therefore, ὡς πρὸς τὴν λέξιν does not mean "literal" *if* one means by the English word only "observable by the senses" (where "light" indicates some plainly physical manifestation), although elsewhere Origen does speculate about how physical perception itself may appear to be affected in the midst of such experiences (e.g., *Cels.* 2.64; I do not consider *Fr. Luc.* 140 to be authentic). Rather, Origen's allowance that something "happened" at the time "as written" (ὡς πρὸς τὴν λέξιν) only indicates the idea that Jesus's disciples really came to such a vision of him.
86 Cf. *Comm. Matt.* 12.30 and *Hom. Luc.* 1.4; see *Philoc.* 15.19 (citing John 1:14): if we "are able to follow him when he ascends the lofty mountain, we shall say 'we have seen his glory.'" *Philoc.* 15.19 does not appear in any extant manuscripts of *Cels.*, but there are good reasons to believe it is authentic (see R. P. C. Hanson, "The Passage Marked *Unde?* in Robinson's Philocalia XV,19,84–86" [1980]; M. Harl adopts his conclusion: SC 302 p. 442). Cf. *Comm. ser. Matt.* 35.
87 Bultmann, *The Gospel of John*, 68.

historicized."[88] It is a vision, moreover, "not limited to the contemporaries" of these events, "but passed on by them to all the succeeding generations," a vision neither "spoken outside the history which is founded on the believing eye-witnesses and the tradition passed on by them" nor merely standing as "guarantee for some later generation," but one that "confront[s] every generation anew."[89]

Thus, the Transfiguration narrative also becomes a paradigmatic expression of the Gospel stories' "mixed" character, wherein the Evangelists have used "language that makes it seem that something made clear to them in a purely interior way was perceptible to the senses."[90] In this way, the literary form(ation) of the pericope becomes the very means of passage into the Gospel writer's more "mysterious aim"[91] – namely, handing on this selfsame vision to those who follow after:

> If you wish to see the transfiguration of Jesus "before" those who ascended "the high mountain privately" with him, look with me at the Jesus of the Gospels understood in a simpler way and, as someone put it, known "according to the flesh"... [92]

Note Origen's emphasis: "If *you* wish to see Jesus transfigured... look with *me*" at how Jesus is "*understood* in the Gospels." Once again, the whole question turns on how Jesus is "understood" and "known" – on what, that is, the Gospel writers (and their tradents) "perceived in their own understanding" in "accordance with the seasons of their own progress."[93] Origen's account of the form, formation, and finally interpretation of the narrative follows suit. The Gospels *do* present a vision of Jesus in a simpler sense (in a Pauline idiom, "according to the flesh"): certain facts about his life, his teaching, deeds, and suffering. But, just as we saw in Origen's treatment of the Lukan infancy narrative, the tradition they hand on is not *just* this: "...he is known, however, by those who 'ascend,' 'no longer according to the flesh,' but is spoken of as divine [θεολογούμενον] throughout the Gospels and is perceived as having been 'in the form of God' in accordance with their knowledge" of him.[94] The Transfiguration is a vision of Jesus "theologized" (θεολογούμενον).

88 Bultmann, *The Gospel of John*, 68. 89 Bultmann, *The Gospel of John*, 70.

90 Cf. *Comm. Jo.* 10.5.18.

91 *Comm. Jo.* 10.5.19. *Pace* Lessing's view of the Gospels' narrative mediation as a dissolving of, rather than a passage into, their spirit and power ("On the proof of the spirit and of power," 85).

92 *Comm. Matt.* 12.37 (alluding to 2 Cor 5:16). 93 *Comm. Jo.* 10.5.18 and 10.4.15.

94 *Comm. Matt.* 12.37 (citing 2 Cor 5:16). For more on 2 Cor 5:16, cf. *Hom. Ex.* 12.4, *Cels.* 6.68, and *Comm. Jo.* 2.3.29.

"For it is before these," those who have come to know and understand him in this way, "and among none of those 'below,' that Jesus is 'transfigured.'"[95]

One may put Origen's view even more strongly: *Jesus's transfiguration is the transformed understanding of those who beheld him.*[96] And one may discern this transfiguration of their perception of him in the very form(ation) of the Gospel narrative – so intimately, in fact, that one could say that it simply *is* the narrative of the transfiguration. For, Origen writes, the bright "garments" of Jesus precisely are the "words and letters of the Gospels."[97] That is, it is the Gospel text itself in which he appears – and *is* – transfigured, the narrative itself that offers us the vision of the transfigured Christ. "The things that are made clear about Jesus to the apostles" or that are "made known about Jesus *by* the apostles" (Origen's text, fittingly, can be translated either way here) simply "*are* his 'garments' which become 'white' to those who ascend" with him.[98]

This transfigured understanding is, for Origen, so indivisible from the narrative of the Transfiguration itself that one can simply identify them: the narrative both signifies and *is* this transformed perception. "Understanding the Law and the Prophets as one with the teaching of Jesus" is what it means to have "seen Moses and Elijah 'in glory,'" to have "seen them with Jesus."[99] So just as the appearance of "Moses" and "Elijah" is a figure for the Law and the Prophets "sharing a common discourse with Jesus (for this is what is meant by the words 'speaking with him')," the Transfiguration narrative both signifies and is what the Gospels as a whole both signify and are: a transfigured vision of Jesus.[100]

Is there, then, a "literal" sense of the Transfiguration for Origen? It is difficult to say.[101] One can say that such a vision "happened long ago,"

[95] *Comm. Matt.* 12.37.

[96] See Section 3.2: the formation of the Gospels *is* the formation of the Evangelists. Cf. *Hom. Ps.* 15 2.8; cf. *Comm. Jo.* 32.27.338–39.

[97] *Comm. Matt.* 12.38. [98] *Comm. Matt.* 12.38.

[99] *Comm. Matt.* 12.38 (cf. Luke 9:31).

[100] So *Comm. Matt.* 12.37: "If you wish to see the transfiguration of Jesus... look with me at" how he is "spoken of as divine [θεολογούμενον] throughout the whole of the Gospels" (cf. *Philoc.* 15.19). See *Comm. Matt.* 12.38: "Whenever he is understood and perceived thus – as the son of God, transformed so that 'his face' is 'as the sun and his garments are white as the light' – immediately there may appear to the one who sees Jesus in this way Moses (the Law) and Elijah (not as a single prophet but as all the prophets by synecdoche) sharing a common discourse [κοινολογούμενοι] with Jesus, for this is what is meant by the words 'speaking with him.'" Cf. *Comm. Rom.* 1.10.3 and *Hom. Lev.* 6.2.5.

[101] His argument rather drives the reader to ask: What would a literal sense of the Transfiguration even mean? (If, that is, what one means by "literal" is only something

but to receive the narrative "as written," for Origen, is to receive it as presenting the "transfiguration" of the disciples' own understanding of Jesus.[102] Therefore what the narrative offers is a particular spiritual vision or spiritual understanding of who Jesus is, made available to readers under the very form of the narrative. To discern how Jesus is "theologized" (θεολογοῦμαι: to be understood as, spoken of, acknowledged as divine) throughout the Gospels is to share in each Evangelist's own vision of the transfigured Lord; it is, at least in part, to "see his glory" (cf. Luke 9:32). *This* is what, for Origen, the Transfiguration narrative intimates: Jesus "understood as divine" – a consummate instance of what Origen ultimately means by a spiritual vision or divine "sense." It depicts something "seen in the spirit," a vision of glory "portrayed historically," and narrates what the disciples were said to have "perceived in their own understanding" in "figures" and "concrete images."[103] To see the light of his transfigured face, "shining as the sun," is to have learned to see him as "the sun of righteousness."[104]

As we have said all along, Origen doesn't perform a spiritual reading *on* the Transfiguration so much as he thinks the Transfiguration is already a spiritual "reading" – really "reception" – of Jesus already handed on under the very form of the narrative. The Transfiguration narrative itself is a "translation of the perceptible Gospel into the spiritual," such that the whole point of the Gospels is both to (re)present and to *be* this very vision – not just to preserve some memory of some fact experienced by others long ago (*pace* Lessing), but for the very narrative to become this vision for the reader, for *you*. "Whenever, therefore, you see someone not only thoroughly understanding the divine identity of Jesus but also

that "physically" happened – an observable, sensory, empirical event.) Is there a "literal sense" to any vision or apparition in Jewish or Christian prophetic or mystical traditions? Not all of scripture, as he says in *On First Principles* (4.3.5; cf. 4.2.5), has a "material" or "physical" referent, though all of it does have a spiritual referent.

102 Cf. *Comm. Matt.* 12.36. Rather astonishingly, in *Comm. Matt.* 12.41 Origen confirms that the preceding sections of the commentary covered above were *not* his more elaborate figurative reading of the passage, but an "interrogation" of these matters "as described" (ὡς πρὸς τὸ ῥητὸν).

103 Cf. *Comm. Jo.* 1.3.20, 10.4.15, 10.4.17, and 10.5.18; cf. *Fr. Eph.* on Eph 1:20–21.

104 See *Comm. Matt.* 12.37 (citing Mal 4:2). Furthermore, according to two possible fragments, the story does not depict a glory exclusively appropriated to Jesus alone, but "describes in a shadow what will come to pass *for them*" in the age to come (Tzamalikos, *New Fragments*, 248); through the transfiguration they see "the icon of the coming splendor that will be" for all the saints (ibid., 240). Jesus's life becomes a "shadow" or "image" of the coming age (cf. *Hom. Jes. Nav.* 8.4 and *Dial.* 27–28, often citing Lam 4:20 and/or Heb 10:1).

clarifying every text in the Gospels, do not hesitate to say that for such a person 'the garments' of Jesus have become 'white as the light.'"[105]

7.5 THE CONSUMMATION OF THE AGE

Like the enigmatic saying before the Sanhedrin, the portion of the Olivet Discourse devoted to the Son of Man's judgment of the nations similarly binds his enthronement with a certain "coming in glory": "'But when the Son of Man *shall come in his glory* and all the angels with him, then *he will sit on the throne of his glory*, and all the nations will be gathered before him,' etc."[106] As we have seen so often before, Origen proceeds to judge that the parable's literary qualities, its imagery and visionary mode of discourse, hardly bear reduction to (what he considers) an unreflective literalism. For instance, there is the question of whether the text can only be indicating that the "coming of the savior 'in glory'" will be in some particular "place"? Is it all that certain that this is what Jesus is recorded to have meant, or should one "look into an alternate explanation"? "For where," he asks, "would that place be that might receive in one glance 'all' the angels coming with Christ and 'all the nations' gathered there?"[107] And is this all that the Evangelist had in view when speaking of the "throne of his glory"? A prediction that Jesus would literally mount a "physical judge's bench" someday in the future at some (as yet undisclosed and rather unimaginable) location? Or does all this call for "a

105 *Comm. Matt.* 12.38: οὐ μόνον τὴν περὶ Ἰησοῦ θεολογίαν ἀκριβοῦντα, ἀλλὰ καὶ τὴν λέξιν τῶν εὐαγγελίων πᾶσαν σαφηνίζοντα. This understanding, for Origen, is nevertheless not a matter of mere literary "embellishment." For that which has "shown 'his garments' 'glistening' to those who have ascended" – "representing in these written expressions (which many look down on) the 'glistening' of what was understood [τῶν νοημάτων]" – is none other than the very word of God; "it is then that Jesus's clothing, according to Luke, becomes 'white' and 'flashes like lightning'" (*Comm. Matt.* 12.39, citing Luke 9:29).

106 *Comm. ser. Matt.* 70 (citing Matt 25:31–32). In a way also reminiscent of his initial approach to the oracle before Caiaphas about seeing the coming of the Son of Man, Origen once again acknowledges the fundamental datum of Christian belief: "Certainly the whole church believes there will be a second and glorious advent of Christ, when the son of God, 'who was taken up in glory,' will return here 'in the same way' with 'glory' in his splendor and beauty" (*Comm. ser. Matt.* 70; citing 1 Tim 3:16 and evoking Acts 1:11; cf. *Comm. ser. Matt.* 50). "These things are *said*," Origen notes; "*however*," he goes on, it is not at all unambiguous how this *credendum* about the "coming of Christ in glory" ought to be interpreted (*Comm. ser. Matt.* 70: *tamen quibusdam videtur de differentia earum, quae crediderunt, haec esse dicta*).

107 *Comm. ser. Matt.* 70. Cf. *Princ.* 4.3.1 on the impossibility of taking the story about Jesus being led up to a high mountain to see "the kingdoms of all the world" literally (cf. n. 56 in Chapter 4).

subtler interpretation," for any who wish to "understand all these things" a little more "reasonably"?[108]

For Origen, rather, the Matthean vision of the *parousia* involves a kind of universalizing of the mystery depicted in the Transfiguration narrative: *Then* he will be just as he was "when he was transfigured on the mountain before the three disciples who ascended with him, so that thenceforth he might appear not to three or a few others, but to 'all the nations gathered before him.'"[109] "I think, then, that the time of Christ's 'advent' will be when there is so great a manifestation of Christ and of his divinity that no one... will be ignorant of Christ 'as he is.'"[110]

When one integrates Origen's reading of the prophecy before Caiaphas with his interpretation of the Transfiguration, therefore, the whole logic of his understanding of Matthew's vision of the Son of Man's "coming in glory" begins to emerge: this "coming" or "appearance" indicates the manifestation of his universal and abiding reign, a mystery the Judgment of the Nations discourse signifies by the "throne of his glory." And this universally unfolding revelation "is what 'all the nations will be gathered before him' means"[111]: "'all nations' will be 'gathered' and stand 'before him' when what has taken place will have become clear to all – good and bad, faithful and unfaithful – *before the eyes of their mind.*"[112]

The Judgment of the Nations discourse thus imbues the vision that Jesus promises before the Sanhedrin with a universal dimension. Its riddling language expresses the consummation of what was set in motion when "all authority in heaven and on earth" was handed over to the risen

[108] *Comm. ser. Matt.* 70.

[109] *Comm. ser. Matt.* 70 (alluding to Matt 25:32). Cf. *Comm. ser. Matt.* 50 (cited above): "just as when he was transfigured... a bright cloud overshadowed them, so also at the second *parousia*, having been transfigured even more gloriously, he will come on a multitude of clouds." Cf. *Philoc.* 15.19, which binds the transfiguration and ascension together: "those who are able to follow after the footsteps of Jesus as he ascends and is transfigured from the sight of earth shall behold his transfiguration in every passage." See similarly *Comm. Matt.* 12.43 (citing Matt 17:9 and 16:20), which interrelates the transfiguration, resurrection, and seeing him "as the Christ": Jesus exhorts the disciples to *tell no one of the vision until the Son of Man has arisen from the dead* "since his glorification in the resurrection was to be akin [συγγενές] to his glorification in the transfiguration... Now the command, 'Tell no one the vision,' is similar to... when 'he commanded the disciples that they tell no one that he was the Christ.'" Note the resonances of the logic here with Origen's presentation of the kind of vision Luke ultimately looks to hand on in his narrative (see Chapter 5).

[110] *Comm. ser. Matt.* 70 (evoking 1 John 3:2). On the transfiguration as a prefiguring or prolepsis of the *parousia*, cf. G. H. Boobyer, *St. Mark and the Transfiguration Story* (1942) and A. M. Ramsey, *The Glory of God and the Transfiguration of Christ* (1949).

[111] *Comm. ser. Matt.* 70. [112] *Comm. ser. Matt.* 70.

Christ (signified by the imagery of the Son of Man being "seated" at the "right hand of power"): when, that is, his reign will reach to the ends of the earth, such that "all nations will" come to be "gathered before him," yes, but not "'before him' in a spatial sense, just as we do not hear in a spatial sense that the righteous will say to him what they will say."[113] Inasmuch as Origen identifies the symbolic language of the Son of Man "sitting" at the "right hand of power" as an image of what the risen and glorified Christ already possesses (Matthew 28:16–20), then the "consummation of the age" will be when *all* nations "come to know him 'as he is,'" such that "they will stand before 'the throne of his glory,' *that is,* before his kingdom and the authority of his dominion."[114]

The position Origen develops on the Matthean vision of the coming of the Son of Man therefore anticipates C. H. Dodd's pithy conclusion that "the coming of the Son of Man is the coming of the Kingdom of God."[115] But the subtleties of his own view call for just a bit more scrutiny. As Origen looks ahead to the rest of the Judgment of the Nations discourse, the Matthean vision of the Son of Man's appearance "in glory" – the unfolding of his universal dominion "on earth as it is in heaven" – is not made to dwell in pure abstraction. That is, for Origen, Matthew's Gospel finally discourages readers from looking for "signs of his *parousia*" anywhere other than in the communal "you" to which the exalted Christ promises his abiding presence (Matthew 28:20).[116]

Origen believes the Judgment of the Nations discourse itself intimates these ecclesial dimensions to the exalted Lord's *parousia*, as he turns to the vision the saying as a whole is finally ordered to: the Son of Man's total identification with the "least of these" – the hungry, thirsty, stranger, naked, weak, and imprisoned – and all those who draw near to them.[117]

113 *Comm. ser. Matt.* 70.

114 *Comm. ser. Matt.* 70 (on Matt 24:26–27, evoking 1 John 3:2; note the telling *hoc est*). "All nations" language appears in both Matt 25:32 and 28:19.

115 Dodd, *Parables of the Kingdom*, 86–87. Cf. T. Kazen, "The Coming of the Son of Man Revisited" (2007), and Kazen, "Son of Man as Kingdom Imagery: Jesus Between Corporate Symbol and Individual Redeemer Figure" (2007). Cf. C. Evans, "Daniel in the New Testament: Visions of God's Kingdom" (2001). Cf. *Fr. Matt.* 38.

116 Cf. M. Bockmuehl, "Being Emmanuel: Matthew's Ever-Present Jesus?" (2022). Cf. Hays, *Echoes of Scripture in the Gospels*, 183–85.

117 Matt 25:34–46. Cf. *Comm. ser. Matt.* 47 (quoted in this chapter's conclusion below). On the ecclesial dimensions of Matthew's vision of the *parousia*, see J. P. Meier, *Matthew* (1980), 369–70, and Meier, *The Vision of Matthew*, 215 n. 270 and 263–64. Cf. Robinson, *Jesus and his Coming*, 184-85. Cf. C. H. Dodd, "Matthew and Paul," 296.

Origen thus invites his readers to understand those "at the right hand" as those who "have turned more fully to righteousness, which is ever 'at the right hand' of God."[118] Those who keep the commandments have already drawn "near" to God's word, and they, in the end, "are called that they may be made even nearer when they hear, '*Come*, blessed of my Father.'"[119] Only then will "'the king say to those on his right hand' – inviting them to himself – 'Come,' so that, whatever may have been lacking in them, when they shall have been more completely united with Christ, they may follow, hearing 'Come,' and do so."[120]

Thus the mystery expressed by the "coming of the Son of Man" in Matthew, Origen suggests, is the same mystery expressed by this invitation to "come" ever more fully into communion with (the reign of) the exalted Christ – into a communion marked by the kind of righteousness that "says out of love, 'Who is weak, and I am not weak?'"[121] For when one of those with whom Christ identifies himself, one of his "members" in a Pauline idiom, "has been put in prison, [Christ] himself is not free of prison, he who says of the righteous, '*I am with him* in affliction,' that is, *I share* in his affliction. For just as he who is mine is in affliction *with me*, so too am I in affliction *with him*.'"[122] As the soul is to the body, so will the presence of the exalted Son of Man be to his own.[123] Whether such

118 *Comm. ser. Matt.* 70 (cf. Isa 41:10 on the "right hand of righteousness"); thus, he goes on, one "stands 'at the right hand' to the degree that one's actions are worthy" of this "right hand" of righteousness.

119 *Comm. ser. Matt.* 72.

120 *Comm. ser. Matt.* 70, with all language of "coming" and "going" here belonging to the saying's intrinsically parabolic idiom. On spatial language of "coming/going" in the Gospels more broadly, see *Or.* 23.1–5. Cf. Robinson, *Jesus and his Coming*, 51 and 185. Cf. *Cels.* 5.12.

121 *Comm. ser. Matt.* 73 (alluding to Col 1:13 and 2 Cor 11:29): "For if Paul, out of love, may say" this, "cannot the 'son of God's love,' the savior, say even more fittingly than Paul (and every person adorned with love), 'Who is weak, and I am not weak? Who is made to stumble, and I do not burn?' For this reason, he says, '*I* was weak and in prison, and you did not visit me.'" Cf. *Comm. Rom.* 6.9.12. In a more Johannine key, see *Comm. Cant.* pr.2 on how the Lord "comes" to one who "abides" in love. Cf. D. Allison, *The Historical Christ and the Theological Jesus*, 28 on how 1 Cor 11–13 "surely reflects the continuing influence of [Jesus's] spirit of self-sacrificial love. Jesus wrote nothing to the Corinthians, but without him 1 Corinthians 13 would not have been written."

122 *Comm. ser. Matt.* 73 (alluding to Ps 90[91]:15: μετ' αὐτοῦ εἰμι ἐν θλίψει).

123 *Comm. ser. Matt.* 73: "Just as the soul inhabiting the body hungers for bodily food because it is joined to its body, although it does not hunger insofar as its own spiritual substance is concerned, so also the savior suffers what his body, the church, suffers." The Pauline vision (1 Cor 12:27: "You are the body of Christ, and each members of it"), for Origen, therefore becomes an especially fitting analogue for unfolding Matthew's ecclesial vision. Cf. *Hom. Lev.* 7.2.1–13, *Hom. Ps.* 15 1.3, and *Or.* 11.2. Cf. Dodd, "Matthew and Paul," 296.

are said to come to him or he to them, whether one speaks of the coming of the Son of Man, of the kingdom on earth, or of the blessed to God, all belong to a vast complex of images variously expressing the mystery of this reign "prepared from the foundation of the world" and to be realized "unto the consummation of the age."[124]

7.6 EVEN NOW AND ALWAYS

With the end of this study in view, Origen's defense of those who believe there may be something "deeper and subtler" at play in these enigmatic sayings has ushered us up to the very summit of his account of what the Gospels are and how to read them. And we find there, simultaneously, the riches of Origen's own spirit as well, in what is, to my mind, the purest expression of both the breadth of his capacities vis-à-vis the critical challenges of the *Gospels* and the depth of his vision of the Christian *Gospel*, each incomplete and unimaginable without the other, ringing in a total, indivisible unity.

What kind of vision, after all, sees Jesus of Nazareth in the "I" of "I was hungry, and you gave me food" (etc.) if not a consummately spiritual one? To whom does this vision belong other than to "certain people who see in the spirit," those to whom Christ "becomes manifest through that manner of presence by which he draws near to them"?[125] *This* is what Matthew "sees in the spirit": the person who "has performed a good deed of whatever kind for the sake of God gives food and drink to Christ who is hungry and thirsty."[126] What is this but a "sense of what isn't sensory," a "divine sense" of the highest order?

Thus, the principles underlying Origen's account of the Gospels' literary formation become the principles underlying his vision of the Gospel itself: there are those who had come to see the life of Jesus "in the spirit," as his "words" and "the presence by which he drew near to them" became progressively more manifest.[127] And "*each one in his own way related what he saw in the spirit* about [Christ] and his words, as well as the ways he becomes manifest to the holy."[128] And "to *those who understand in this way*, we say that... this 'great glory' that appears in the second advent of the word even now becomes visible."[129]

[124] Matt 25:34 and 28:20.
[125] Reapplying *Comm. Jo.* 10.4.15: παρουσίαν, ἣν πάρεστιν αὐτοῖς.
[126] *Comm. ser. Matt.* 72.
[127] Cf. *Comm. Jo.* 10.4.15 (cf. Section 3.2).
[128] Cf. *Comm. Jo.* 10.4.15.
[129] *Comm. ser. Matt.* 50.

In answer then to the disciples' twofold question, "What will the sign of your *parousia* be? And of the consummation of the age?" (Matthew 24:3), Origen discerns a twofold answer: 1.) "Behold, I am with you always..." 2.) "...unto the consummation of the age" (Matthew 28:20). The signs of his ongoing presence are one thing, its consummation "in glory" another, when his "authority in heaven and on earth" is realized before all everywhere.[130] In other words, the apocalyptic images woven into these sayings finally express the consummate advent and realization of this mysterious reign, when the dominion of him who is "with us" is made gloriously manifest and present to all.[131]

Thus in the "parable of the fig tree" Origen sees the flowering of the whole Matthean vision: "For just as a fig tree in wintertime still has the power of life in itself, though hidden and not fully manifest, but afterward, when winter is past, the power of life shall have begun to show itself more clearly, as from its own natural vigor its branches are made tender and 'bring forth leaves'"; and "just as a tree has leaves and fruit in potency, and first there is a bud, then little by little it proceeds until, finally, it produces them in fact," so too the unfolding of this present age.[132] It is like the movement from winter to spring, when seeds buried

[130] See *Hom. Isa.* 1.2 (cf. 1.5), where Origen speaks of Christ's "coming" in terms of the "whole earth [being] filled with his glory" (Isa 6:3), a mystery fulfilled only when the "will of the Father" is accomplished on "earth as it is in heaven" (Matt 6:10) – when, that is, all things are subjected to the reign of him who received "all authority in heaven and on earth" (Matt 28:18). Origen allows that the "consummation of the age" may suggest a literal end of the world as it is presently known – a true "regeneration" or "restoration" of all things, a "new heaven" and a "new earth" – though he does not think the (apocalyptic) imagery forswears an "end" unfolding in accordance with the full freedom of history (cf. *Comm. ser. Matt.* 48 on Matt 24:29–30, treated in the first section of this chapter). Yet he also believes the logic of these discourses begins to relativize the question, since the suffering of any finality – even one's own death – will be for that person a "consummation of the age" (*Comm. ser. Matt.* 59).

[131] Cf. *Or.* 26.4: "At the 'consummation of the age' that which is 'in heaven' will be established also 'on earth' by imitating what the savior received through the 'authority' given" him. Cf. Davies/Allison, *Matthew 19–28*, 358–59 (on Matt 24:30): The coming of the Son of Man "takes place neither in desert nor inner room but is rather universally witnessed [...] When the Son of man finally appears, all will recognize what the church even now confesses: that he has all authority in heaven and earth."

[132] *Comm. ser. Matt.* 53 (on Matt 24:32–35). On this broader vernal imagery in the tradition, Origen cites the *Shepherd of Hermas* (Herm. Sim. 3): "'the present age is winter for the just,' who appear like their neighbors in nature – that is, like other dried up trees – but at the appropriate season they appear with their fruits" (cf. *Comm. Rom.* 5.9.6). Cf. J. H. Newman, *Sermons on the Subjects of the Day* 21 ("The Invisible Presence of Christ"): "a great and wide-spreading kingdom came into existence all at once, like spring after winter, from within."

deep in the heart of the earth strike root, and tender shoots begin to break through the surface – the sign and presence of what is to come. There remains, then, the mystery of a people in whom the "regeneration" and "restoration of all things" has already begun: the first flowers of the coming age. "Let us not, therefore, give heed to those who say, 'Behold, here is the Christ,' but do not show him" in those to whom he has promised his presence: that is, "in the church... in whose totality is the total advent of the Son of Man, who says to all people everywhere: 'Behold, I am with you all the days of your life, unto the consummation of the age.'"[133]

[133] *Comm. ser. Matt.* 47 (citing Matt 28:20 and alluding to Matt 24:23).

Conclusion

The Eternal Gospel

"Now is the Son of Man glorified..."[1]

And so we discover, standing here at the headwaters of the entire history of Gospel reading, a figure fully conscious of the manifold "scandals" that are intrinsic to critical examination of the Gospels; a figure who develops, in light of these very difficulties, a thoroughgoing account of the nature, formation, and purpose of their narratives; a figure, finally, for whom the diverse impediments and impossibilities interior to these texts form the bedrock of his vision of the Christian Gospel itself – a vision now woven indelibly into the interpretive, theological, and spiritual heritage of the whole Christian tradition.[2]

The primordial subject of the Evangelists' narratives, as noted from the beginning, is the life of Jesus: "his deeds, sufferings, and words."[3] We have also seen how, for Origen, the term *historia* identifies the literary form of Gospels, as each of the Evangelists narrates the life of Jesus "in the form of history."[4] But this is only to say that the Gospel writers *portray* everything historically, even if this means they sometimes narrate some spiritual vision, interior perception, or theological understanding through pictorial imagery.[5]

[1] John 13:31.

[2] The "second teacher of the churches after the apostle[s]" (Didymus the Blind, via Jerome's preface to his translation of Origen's *Homilies on Ezekiel*; cf. Rufinus, *Apol. Hier.* 2.13, as well as his preface to *Princ.*). See J. A. McGuckin, *Origen of Alexandria: Master Theologian of the Early Church* (2022).

[3] *Comm. Jo.* 1.3.20.

[4] Cf. *Cels.* 5.31: ἐν ἱστορίας σχήματι.

[5] Cf. *Comm. Jo.* 10.4.17: εἰκὼν ἱστορική.

In any case, Origen believes a great deal of what is narrated happened in some form or another (though often with certain details adjusted), even as one finds many other things consistently intermingled that didn't or couldn't happen. Through all, he locates the development of these constitutive characteristics of Gospel narrative in the freedom the Evangelists felt to "make full use" of the Jesus tradition according to how they had come to conceive of this life – a freedom reflected in the individuation of their narratives, which differ according to how "each in his own way" related what he had "seen in the spirit," according to each of their "mysterious aims," and according to what had become manifest to them through the progress of their own understanding, in such a way that one might call the Evangelists themselves figurative readers of the life of Jesus.

Origen does not consider any of these basic principles to be speculative. He presents this view of the Evangelists as authors and the nature of their narratives as a demonstrable historiographical and literary fact. No "sensible person," no one who hasn't "entirely lost their edge," would doubt that "the Gospels are full" of passages that were "recorded as if they happened but that didn't *literally* take place," along with "countless" other occasions where "stories of things that happened as described are interwoven with others that didn't occur."[6] A "critical reader will observe" all this, Origen concludes, and be "convinced" of it.[7] The *onus* falls rather upon readers with a literalism so inflexible that they end up eschewing the Evangelists' own form of writing, the very spirit in which they wrote.

Origen's sense that the Evangelists were themselves "spiritual readers" of Jesus's life extends, moreover, to his sense of the figure of Jesus himself. That is to say, Origen believes that Jesus, throughout his public ministry, construed his own words and deeds symbolically. The Gospels, then, are themselves a "shadow" of the "mysteries set forth by Christ's words and the things which his deeds wrapt in riddles."[8] The impediments to simple

6 *Princ.* 4.3.1: συνυφαίνεσθαι ταῖς κατὰ τὸ ῥητὸν γεγενημέναις ἱστορίαις ἕτερα μὴ συμβεβηκότα.

7 *Princ.* 4.3.1.

8 *Comm. Jo.* 1.7.39–40 (citing Heb 10:1 and Rev 14:6): "Just as there is a 'law' which contains a 'shadow of the good things to come' … so also the Gospel, which is thought to be understood by all who approach it, teaches a shadow of the mysteries of Christ. And that which John calls an 'eternal Gospel,' which might fittingly be called 'spiritual,' clearly presents both the mysteries set forth by his words and the things of which his acts were enigmatic figures." Cf. S. W. J. Keough, "The Eternal Gospel: Origen's Eschatological Exegesis" (2008). Curiously, following Origen the motif of the "eternal Gospel" does not

and obvious understanding found within the four Gospels originate in the impediments Jesus's own life presented for simple and obvious understanding. By all accounts, there was little that was "plain" about the way Jesus habitually spoke and acted. Jesus's own characteristic manner of teaching in the Gospels appears to Origen to have been intrinsically figurative. So it is not simply the Evangelists who present Jesus's life as a "sign of the coming age" for Origen; rather, Jesus understood his own life as a kind of sign, both embodying the trials and terrors of his own age and inaugurating the age of the coming kingdom: "The Son of Man will be a sign for this generation."[9]

Thus Origen conceives of Jesus himself as first among "those who see in the spirit." What the Evangelists came to see grew out of what they perceived Jesus (and those nearest him) to have seen. Their spiritual vision arises out of his, with his own prophetic spirit ultimately responsible for the spirit of each Evangelist's narrative, forming a unity not simply in spite of, but productive of their diversity of expression. For Origen, it was Jesus himself who first "intended to teach what he had perceived in his own understanding by way of figures." It was he who first, for the sake of some "mysterious aim," made "full use of many of the things he said and did" throughout his public ministry in order to "signify something."[10] And thus, by interweaving "stories of things that happened as described" with others that wouldn't "*literally* take place" in his teaching, he set out to "disclose, in a figurative way, certain mysteries" of the age to come.[11] The Evangelists then grew to associate the mystery of this divine kingdom so intimately with Jesus himself – his deeds, sufferings, and words – that his whole life became the very "image of the coming good things."[12] The

possess much of a *Nachleben* prior to its explosive appropriation by the followers of Joachim of Fiore (c. 1135–1202), whence it reemerges forcefully in none other than Lessing's *The Education of the Human Race* (1777; published in the midst of the *Fragmentenstreit* and in the same year as "On the proof of the spirit and power"), and finally leaves its indelible mark on some of the most significant figures in the next two centuries of European thought (including Ernest Renan); see W. Gould and M. Reeves, *Joachim of Fiore and the Myth of the Eternal Evangel in the Nineteenth and Twentieth Centuries* (2001).

9 See Luke 11:30. Cf. *Comm. Matt.* 12.3: "You should inquire into what that which is called a 'sign' in the New Testament is a sign *of* [σημεῖον τίνος], whether it be indicative of something in the age to come or in later generations after the sign occurred."

10 Cf. *Comm. Jo.* 10.5.18–19 and *Cels.* 2.69.

11 *Princ.* 4.3.1 reapplied.

12 Cf. Heb 10:1. See *Hom. Isa.* 6.3: "For what happened in his bodily life was an image and type of what is to come." Cf. D. Allison, *The Historical Christ and the Theological Jesus*, 117: "his life incarnates the eschatological pattern." Cf. *Comm. Cant.* 3.12. See also

life of Jesus itself becomes the *sacramentum evangelii*, the "mystery of the Gospel."[13]

Yet for all this, the many impediments to a purely literalized sense of the life of Jesus intrinsic to the form of the Gospel narratives become, in Origen's view, passages to an even higher vision of these stories, of the life they narrate, and perhaps, finally, of the history of a whole people enfolded therein – a higher vision, I should add, of even their lowliest aspects. For, on the one hand, Jesus's prophetic saying before Caiaphas about seeing the Son of Man exalted "from now on" refers to the brief interval until "his disciples saw him rising from the dead, and in this way, saw him established 'at the right hand of power.'"[14] Yet on the other hand, for Origen, the vision of the exalted Christ at the end of Matthew also casts its light back onto the "now" of the trial itself.[15] For lest one be tempted to think that being "seated at the right hand of power" means being above the "disgrace of spitting," Matthew's evocations of Isaiah's servant seem to suggest "that he who was spit on and struck is about one who was full of glory."[16] Therefore, it was precisely so that "his face might be glorified" that "Christ did not turn his face away 'from the shame of spit.'"[17]

Thus for Origen, in the final analysis, the Matthean and Johannine visions of the glory of the Son of Man begin to converge.[18] In a manner directly analogous to the saying before the high priest in Matthew ("*from now* you will see the Son of Man sitting at the right hand of power…"), John, once the events of the passion are inexorably set in motion, has Jesus declare, "*now* has the Son of Man been glorified," such that he identifies – or rather, in consummately Johannine language, *signifies* – his own form of death by the language of being "exalted" (literally: "lifted

Princ. 4.3.13 (citing Heb 10:1 and Rev 14:6). On the indeterminacy of μέλλειν, cf. *Comm. Rom.* 5.1.38–41.

13 See *Hom. Luc.* 21.1. Cf. J. C. Cavadini, "The Church as the Sacrament of Creation: A Reading of Origen's *Commentary on the Song of Songs*" (2015). Cf. J. W. Bowker, "Prophetic Action and Sacramental Form" (1964).

14 *Comm. ser. Matt.* 111.

15 *Comm. ser. Matt.* 112.

16 *Comm. ser. Matt.* 113 (on Matt 26:67–68, also citing Deut 25:7–9 on the "extreme insult" of spitting and Isa 50:6: "I have offered my back to the whips and my cheeks to slaps; I have not turned my face away from the shame of spit"). Cf. Isa 52:13 LXX on the exaltation and glorification of the servant.

17 *Comm. ser. Matt.* 113. Cf. *Hom. Jer.* 19.12.3.

18 Cf. J. P. Meier, "Salvation-History in Matthew: In Search of a Starting Point" (1975). Cf. J. A. T. Robinson, "The Parable of the Sheep and the Goats" (1956), esp. 237. Cf. D. Allison, *The End of the Ages Has Come: An Early Interpretation of the Passion and Resurrection of Jesus* (1985), 59.

up").[19] For "the glory that resulted from his death" was not the glory of the "word" or "wisdom" or "truth" (or "any of the other divine characteristics that were said to belong to Jesus" which, of course, "by nature do not die"), but "was the glory of that human being, the one who was the 'Son of Man.'"[20] Thus the exceedingly high exaltation or "lifting up" of "the Son of Man that took place when he glorified God in his own death consisted in this: that he was no longer anything other than this word, but identical with it."[21] This kind of vision, in other words, is what the Gospels were formed to inspire: that all those who approach these writings might also, "even now," learn to behold in the crucified Jesus not only the glorified Son of Man, but the very word of God, resounding throughout the whole of this present age, and that they too might "follow him until they may say to Christ, 'My soul has clung to you.'"[22]

[19] Cf. *Comm. Jo.* 32.25.318–20 (on John 13:31-32, here citing John 12:32–33: "'When I am lifted up from the earth, I will draw all people to myself.' He said this to signify by what death he was to die"; cf. John 21:19). Cf. J. Frey, *The Glory of the Crucified One: Christology and Theology in the Gospel of John* (2018), 237–58. Origen notes how the language of "glory" here is drawn primarily from Jewish traditions of divine epiphany (also reflected in the Lukan Transfiguration narrative, as he points out), especially those "in the Tabernacle and Temple at their completion" and "in Moses's face after he had conversed with God" (*Comm. Jo.* 32.27.338, citing Exod 24:39 and 40:34–35, and 1 Kgs 8:10–11).

[20] *Comm. Jo.* 32.25.322. Cf. *Cels.* 1.66 (possibly evoking Acts 2:22), where Origen responds to Celsus's question about why Jesus bleeds like any other human being and not with "Ichor, such as flows in the veins of the blessed gods" (*Iliad* 5.340; cf. *Cels.* 2.36 and Hunter, "Homer in Origen, *Against Celsus*," 235): "he wanted to teach, as a human being attested by God, that there was something even more divine in the visible human being."

[21] *Comm. Jo.* 32.25.325. Cf. *Comm. Jo.* 1.32.231–33.

[22] *Comm. Jo.* 32.32.400 (citing Ps 62[63]:9). In striking, and ultimately absolute, contrast to Strauss, as his "Concluding Dissertation" on the "dogmatic import of the life of Jesus" makes evident (*Life of Jesus*, §§144–52, esp. §151). Origen might agree, in his own way, that the Gospel tradition ultimately brings into view the "idea of humanity as one with God," but the overarching witness of his writings simply does not allow one to conclude that therefore, for him, "the object of faith is completely changed": that it is now "a spiritual and divine idea" *instead* of "a sensible, empirical fact," such that "when the mind has thus gone beyond the sensible history, and entered into the domain of the absolute, the *former ceases to be essential*" (§151, emphasis added). Rather, for Origen, one could say that "the spiritual and divine idea" shows itself most radiantly, and becomes most intensely present, in the lowliest of the "sensible, empirical facts" – in this literal spit and blood, and in "the lines of his gentle face" (cf. *Hom. Lev.* 16.7.3). Origen therefore sees no reason to conclude that "the Idea" is not "wont to lavish all its fulness on one exemplar" (*Life of Jesus*, §151), precisely because, for him, this "lavish fulness" is at no point more transparent than in his "death, even death on a cross" (*Comm. Jo.* 32.25.323–24, citing Phil 2:6–9). Again, Origen might agree that the Gospel

No "spiritual understanding" of Jesus's life – his deeds, sufferings, and words – ascends to anything higher than this Johannine vision, which is itself, for Origen, but the consummate flowering of the whole preceding Mosaic and prophetic traditions – of a vision that belonged, mysteriously, to all those possessed by the word of the Lord in every age, whose "firstfruits," Origen says, is the four Gospels, and the "firstfruits of the firstfruits," John.[23] For even if the divine word has perhaps appeared in "differing glories" through all ages "in accordance with what each soul has shown itself capable of perceiving," to "the person who has been perfected and has come, so far as is possible in oneself, to the 'consummation of the age,' the word appears in such a way that the one who sees him says: 'We have seen his glory...'"[24]

In this way, one may discover a "demonstration" of the Gospels' "spirit and power" (evoking Lessing's dispute with *Against Celsus*) in the light that plays on the very surface of their narratives and in the depths of their form. Even if his greatness "shone forth only afterward, when his enemies seemed to have extinguished it," Jesus's life nevertheless "became, over the course of what was historically narrated, a kind of universal event that illuminated the whole world," and "after this visible dwelling, he dwells with us again."[25] For

> "The sound of his teaching has gone out into every land, and his words to the ends of the earth." Our Lord Jesus has been poured forth into all the world, because he is God's power. And he is with us now, in a manner similar to how the apostle

tradition is ordered to the hope for a divine humanity, but one comes away with a very different sense, finally, of what "divine" even means.

23 *Comm. Jo.* 1.2.14 and 1.4.22–23. Cf. *Comm. Jo.* 6.4.17–24. See A. Blaski, "Jews, Christians, and the Conditions of Christological Interpretation in Origen's Work" (2019).

24 *Comm. ser. Matt.* 35 (citing Matt 28:20 and John 1:14). The heart of Origen's approach thus finally withstands, at every turn, Strauss's archetypal contrast between the "unrestrained arbitrariness" of the allegorical view and the way the mythical view "searches out the ideas which are embodied in the narrative" (*Life of Jesus*, §12). Which is not to say that there doesn't remain plenty in Origen's Gospel commentaries that many might now find exegetically artificial or objectionable. (Cannot one say the same of Strauss, or any reader in any age, who has dared to write about the Gospels at length? Cf. the extant remains of *Comm. Jo.* Book 5.) The point, rather, is to have shown that Strauss – or any number of other claimants to the dubious title "founder of modern Gospel criticism" – was not the first to suggest, let alone argue at length, that the Gospels consist of narratives "which may be considered not [only] as the expression of a fact, but [also] as the product of an idea of his earliest followers," or that the Gospels present an idea of Jesus "invested with imagery" (Strauss, *Life of Jesus*, §§14–15).

25 *Hom. Jer.* 9.1.1: καὶ μετὰ τὴν ἐπιδημίαν αὐτοῦ ταύτην τὴν βλεπομένην πάλιν ἡμῖν ἐπιδημεῖ.

says: "When you are gathered and my spirit is with you in the power of the Lord Jesus..." For the power of the saving Lord is also with those who are in Britain... and with those who are in Mauretania, and with everyone under the sun who has believed in his name.[26]

Just as, for Origen, the mystery of John the Baptist (*sacramentum Ioannis*) "fills the world even to this day," so all the more is the *sacramentum Iesu*, his spirit and power, and thus his very presence, filling the world "even now."[27]

The Gospels, in other words, "show themselves, to those who approach their writing more attentively, to be a sign of something as well"[28]: namely, this second mode of Christ's presence (δεύτερα παρουσία). Accordingly, the Gospel narratives themselves – in their form, formation, and purpose – become "demonstrations" of this very spirit and power, a spiritual presence of the risen Lord that is precisely as such a real presence. For, Origen suggests,

Traces of that sacred spirit that appeared in the form of a dove are still preserved among Christians... Even if Celsus would ridicule what I am about to say, nevertheless, it must be said that many have come to Christianity in spite of themselves, so to speak, some spirit having turned their mind suddenly from hating the word [of the Gospel] to dying for it after some vision became manifest to them, whether while awake or in a dream. We have inquired into [ἱστορήσαμεν] many instances like this. But if we were to commit them to writing, even if we ourselves happened to have been present and had seen these things for ourselves, we would bring upon ourselves widespread mockery from unbelievers, who would think that we were making these things up ourselves [πλάσσειν], just like those whom they assume have fabricated [ἀναπεπλακέναι] the same stories.[29]

Such testimony may not conform to the canons of empirical or dialectical "demonstration," but it nevertheless retains a kind of persuasive power "proper to the word."[30] For, like the Gospels themselves, "what is true and what false" about such stories is not finally "judged from visible signs and portents but by the account" (λόγος) one makes of them.[31] Rather, it

[26] *Hom. Luc.* 6.9 (citing Ps 19:4 [18:5 LXX] and 1 Cor 5:4; cf. Rom 10:18). Cf. *Hom. Luc.* 7.6–7. See also *Comm. ser. Matt.* 65.

[27] Cf. *Hom. Luc.* 4.6 (reapplied). Cf. *Hom. Jer.* 1.12.2 (on Jer 1:5: "I have appointed you a prophet to the nations"; also citing Ps 44:3 [45:2 LXX]): Jesus "is also a prophet 'appointed to the nations,' and he received from God 'grace poured upon his lips,' so that not only when he was present in a physical way [παρῆν τῷ σώματι], but also now, when he is present in power and in the spirit [πάρεστι δυνάμει καὶ τῷ πνεύματι], he prophesies to 'all the nations.'"

[28] Cf. *Cels.* 2.69. [29] *Cels.* 1.46. Cf. *Comm. Jo.* 20.35.315. [30] Cf. *Cels.* 1.2.

[31] See *Hom. Luc.* 1.3.

is a persuasiveness that manifests itself in a way not unlike what the two disciples on the road to Emmaus are recorded to have experienced: "Did not our hearts burn within us while he talked to us on the road, while he opened to us the scriptures?"[32]

Origen's first principles of "what a Gospel is" may then also be viewed from the inside out. That is, as soon as one comes to terms with his historiographically and literarily sensitive criteria for how to read and understand the Gospel narratives, one may realize that the Gospels have simultaneously formed his vision of what history itself is: by presenting this life to us "in the form of history" and "in figures" they reveal that history is itself a "sign of something"; they adjust details and interweave things that didn't or couldn't literally happen in order to show that the world itself has a more "mysterious aim"; they cultivate a spiritual understanding of this life because the ground of this life is the spirit; and they behold his "deeds, sufferings, and words" in such a way that somehow the very wisdom of God

> can be believed to have been within the compass of that man who appeared in Judea; yes, and that the wisdom of God entered into a woman's womb, to be born a little child, with cries like those of any wailing infant; then, after, that he was troubled in the hour of death, as it is related... and that, in the end, he was led to that death people consider to be the most shameful of all – even if on the third day he rose again. When, then, we see in him some things so human that they appear to differ in no way from the common frailty of mortals, and some things so divine that they are appropriate to nothing other than the primordial and inexpressible nature of deity, the narrowness of human understanding is bewildered, and struck with amazement at so great a wonder, and knows not which way to turn, what to hold to, or whither to betake itself. If it thinks of God, it sees a mortal; if it thinks of a human being, it perceives one returning from the dead with spoils after vanquishing the kingdom of death.[33]

As with the Gospels, so too with Jesus; as with Jesus, so too with the Gospels. Origen sees in their narratives "some things that differ in no way from the common frailty" of human history and "some things so divine" that the "narrowness of human understanding is bewildered" and "knows not which way to turn" or "what to hold to" when it sees things both so human and so divine "in one and the same" story.[34] Thus, for Origen, when one finally reaches into the "depths of the evangelical mind" and discerns "the naked truth of the figures therein," one discovers

[32] See *Comm. Jo.* 1.8.49–50 (citing 1 Cor 2:4 and Luke 24:32). [33] *Princ.* 2.6.2.
[34] *Princ.* 2.6.2 reapplied.

a "spiritual Gospel," yes, but one breaks through the "shell" of these narratives only to find history anew, even one's very own, transfigured and "taken up into the Gospel" – the eternal Gospel – whose sacrament is the glorified Son of Man.[35]

As stated from the beginning, the function or purpose of any "Gospel," in the end, is to relate tidings of joy to its hearers: it either "contains the presence [παρουσίαν] of something good" or "announces that an expected good is present."[36] In other words, following Origen, perhaps one could say that the first kind of "Gospel" (a word "*containing* the presence of something good") is like hearing a beloved say, "I am here"; whereas the second kind (a word "*announcing* that a hoped-for good is present") is like hearing a dear friend say, "your beloved is here."

The end of the Christian Gospel, in particular, then, is to confer what the Evangelists had themselves "seen in the spirit," to make it available to every generation anew, and so to "present the advent of Christ, prepare for his *parousia*, and produce it in the souls of those who are willing to receive the word of God, who 'stands at the door and knocks.'"[37] The Gospels "gladden – for good reason!" Origen continues, as each one "teaches about the saving advent of Christ Jesus"; yet "it is also clear to everyone who believes that each Gospel is a discourse that teaches about the dwelling of the good Father in the Son in all those willing to receive him."[38] In other words, the Gospels, somehow, both "*announce* the presence of something good" and "*contain* the presence of something good." In them, simultaneously, one may hear the friends of the Bridegroom saying, "he comes," and the Bridegroom himself saying, even now and always, "I am here."

[35] Cf. *Comm. Jo.* 1.8.46 and 1.11.68. Cf. J. C. Cavadini, "From Letter to Spirit: The Multiple Senses of Scripture" (2019), esp. 137–38.

[36] *Comm. Jo.* 1.5.27 (cf. *Comm. Jo.* 10.4.15: τὴν παρουσίαν, ἣν πάρεστιν αὐτοῖς. . .).

[37] *Comm. Jo.* 1.4.26 (evoking Rev 3:20). [38] *Comm. Jo.* 1.5.28.

Bibliography

ORIGEN'S GOSPEL COMMENTARIES

Origen. *Commentaire sure l'Évangile selon Matthieu, Tome I (Livres X et XI)*. Edited and translated by Robert Girod. SC 162. Paris: Éditions du Cerf, 1970.

Commentaire sur Saint Jean, Tome I (Livres I-V). Edited and translated by Cécile Blanc. SC 120 bis. Paris: Éditions du Cerf, 1996.

Commentaire sur Saint Jean, Tome II (Livres VI et X). Edited and translated by Cécile Blanc. SC 157. Paris: Éditions du Cerf, 1970.

Commentaire sur Saint Jean, Tome III (Livre XIII). Edited and translated by Cécile Blanc. SC 222. Paris: Éditions du Cerf, 2006.

Commentaire sur Saint Jean, Tome IV (Livres XIX et XX). Edited and translated by Cécile Blanc. SC 290. Paris: Éditions du Cerf, 1982.

Commentaire sur Saint Jean, Tome V (Livres XXVIII et XXXII). Edited and translated by Cécile Blanc. SC 385. Paris: Éditions du Cerf, 1992.

Commentarius in Matthaeum I. Edited by Erich Klostermann and Ernst Benz. Origenes Werke 10. GCS 40. Leipzig: J. C. Hinrichs, 1935.

Commentarius in Matthaeum II. Edited by Erich Klostermann and Ernst Benz. Origenes Werke 11. GCS 38. Leipzig: J. C. Hinrichs, 1933.

Commentarius in Matthaeum III, 1. Edited by Erich Klostermann and Ernst Benz. Origenes Werke 12. GCS 41.1. Leipzig: J. C. Hinrichs, 1941.

Commentarius in Matthaeum III, 2. Edited by Erich Klostermann, Ludwig Früchtel, and Ursula Treu. 2nd ed. GCS 41.2. Berlin: AkademieVerlag, 1968.

Commentary on the Gospel According to John, Books 1–10. Translated by Ronald E. Heine. FC 80. Washington, DC: Catholic University of America Press, 1989.

Commentary on the Gospel According to John, Books 13–32. Translated by Ronald E. Heine. FC 89. Washington, DC: Catholic University of America Press, 1993.

Commentary on the Gospel according to St. Matthew. Translated by Ronald E. Heine. Oxford Early Christian Texts. Oxford, UK: Oxford University Press. 2018.

"Commentary on the Gospel of Matthew." In *The Gospel of Peter, The Diatessaron of Tatian, The Apocalypse of Peter, the Vision of Paul, The Apocalypses of the Virgin and Sedrach, The Testament of Abraham, The Acts of Xanthippe and Polyxena, The Narrative of Zosimus, The Apology of Aristides, The Epistles of Clement (Complete Text), Origen's Commentary on John, Books 1-10, and Commentary on Matthew, Books 1, 2, and 10–14*. Edited by Allan Menzies and translated by John Patrick. 4th ed. Ante-Nicene Fathers 9. Peabody, MA: Hendrickson Publishers, 1994. Pp. 411–512.

Homélies sur S. Luc. Translated by Henri Crouzel, François Fournier, and Pierre Périchon. SC 87. Paris: Éditions du Cerf, 1962.

Homiliae in Lucam. Edited by M. Rauer. 2nd ed. Origenes Werke 9. GCS 49. Berlin: Akademie-Verlag, 1959.

Homilies on Luke. Translated by Joseph T. Lienhard. FC 94. Washington, DC: Catholic University of America Press, 1996.

Der Kommentar zum Evangelium nach Mattäus. Translated by Hermann J. Vogt. Bibliothek der griechischen Literatur 18, 30, 38. Stuttgart: Anton Hiersemann, 1983, 1990, 1993.

New Fragments from the Commentary on Matthew, Codices Sabaiticus 232 & Holy Cross 104, Jerusalem. Edited by P. Tzamalikos. Leiden: Ferdinand Schöningh, 2020.

OTHER WORKS OF ORIGEN

Origen. *An Exhortation to Martyrdom, Prayer, First Principles: Book IV, Prologue to the Commentary on the Song of Songs, Homily XXVII on Numbers*. Translated by Rowan A. Greer. Mahwah, NJ: Paulist Press, 1979.

Commentarium in Canticum Canticorum. In Origenes Werke 8, edited by W. A. Baehrens, 61–241. GCS 33. Leipzig: Teubner, 1925.

Commentary on the Epistle to the Romans, Books 1-5. Translated by Thomas P. Scheck. FC 103. Washington, DC: Catholic University of America Press, 2001.

Commentary on the Epistle to the Romans, Books 6-10. Translated by Thomas P. Scheck. FC 104. Washington, DC: Catholic University of America Press, 2002.

Contra Celsum. Translated by Henry Chadwick. New York: Cambridge University Press, 1953.

Contre Celse, Tome I (Livres I et II). Edited and translated by Marcel Borret. SC 132. Paris: Éditions du Cerf, 1967.

Contre Celse, Tome II (Livres III et IV). Edited and translated by Marcel Borret. SC 136. Paris: Éditions du Cerf, 1968.

Contre Celse, Tome III (Livres V et VI). Edited and translated by Marcel Borret. SC 147. Paris: Éditions du Cerf, 1969.

Contre Celse, Tome IV (Livres VII et VIII). Edited and translated by Marcel Borret. SC 150. Paris: Éditions du Cerf, 1969.

Contre Celse, Tome V (Introduction générale, Tables et Index). Edited by Marcel Borret. SC 227. Paris: Éditions du Cerf, 1976.

Die Neuen Psalmenhomilien: Eine Kritische Edition Des Codex Monacensis Graecus 314. In GCS 19. Edited by Lorenzo Perrone. Berlin: De Gruyter, 2015.

De oratione. In GCS 3. Edited by Paul Koetschau. Leipzig: J. C. Hinrichs, 1925. Pp. 297–403.

Entretien d'Origène avec Héraclide. Translated by Jean Scherer. SC 67. Paris: Éditions du Cerf, 1960.

Fragmenta ex Libro de Proverbiis Salomonis. In *Patrologiae Cursus Completus (Series Graeca)*. Edited by J.-P. Migne, vol. 13, cols. 17–34. Paris: Migne, 1857.

Homélies sur Ézéchiel. Edited and translated by Marcel Borret. SC 352. Paris: Éditions du Cerf, 1989.

Homélies sur Jérémie, Tome I (Homélies I-XI). Translated by Pierre Husson and Pierre Nautin. Edited by Pierre Nautin. SC 232. Paris: Éditions du Cerf, 1976.

Homélies sur Jérémie, Tome II (Homélies XII-XX et Homélies latines). Translated by Pierre Husson and Pierre Nautin. Edited by Pierre Nautin. SC 238. Paris: Éditions du Cerf, 1977.

Homélies sur Josué. Translated by Annie Jaubert. SC 71. Paris: Éditions du Cerf, 1960.

Homélies sur l'Exode. Translated by Marcel Borret. SC 321. Paris: Éditions du Cerf, 1985.

Homélies sur la Genèse. Translated by Louis Doutreleau. SC 7 bis. Paris: Éditions du Cerf, 1996.

Homélies sur le Lévitique, Tome I (Homélies I–VII). Translated by Marcel Borret. SC 286. Paris: Éditions du Cerf, 1981.

Homélies sur le Lévitique, Tome II (Homélies VIII–XVI). Translated by Marcel Borret. SC 287. Paris: Éditions du Cerf, 1981.

Homélies sur les Juges. Translated by Pierre Messié, Louis Neyrand, and Marcel Borret. SC 389. Paris: Éditions du Cerf, 1993.

Homiliae in Isaiam. In GCS 33. Edited by W. A. Baehrens. Leipzig: Teubner, 1925. Pp. 242–289.

Homilies 1-14 on Ezekiel. Translated by Thomas P. Scheck. Ancient Christian Writers 62. New York, NY: The Newman Press, 2010.

Homilies on Genesis and Exodus. Translated by Ronald E. Heine. FC 71. Washington, DC: Catholic University of America Press, 1982.

Homilies on Isaiah. Translated by Elizabeth A. Dively Lauro. FC 142. Washington, DC: Catholic University of America Press. 2021.

Homilies on Jeremiah; Homily on 1 Kings 28. Translated by John Clark Smith. FC 97. Washington, DC: Catholic University of America Press, 1998.

Homilies on Joshua. Translated by Barbara J. Bruce. Edited by Cynthia White. FC 105. Catholic University of America Press, 2002.

Homilies on Judges. Translated by Elizabeth A. Dively Lauro. FC 119. Washington, DC: Catholic University of America Press, 2010.

Homilies on Leviticus. Translated by Gary Wayne Barkley. FC 83. Washington, DC: Catholic University of America Press, 1990.

Homilies on the Psalms: Codex Monacensis Graecus 314. Translated by Joseph W. Trigg. FC 141. Washington, DC: Catholic University of America Press, 2020.

On First Principles. Translated by G. W. Butterworth. Gloucester, MA: Peter Smith, 1973.

On First Principles. Edited and Translated by John Behr. Oxford Early Christian Texts. Oxford, UK: Oxford University Press. 2017.

Origenis Fragmenta in Ezechielem. Edited by Angelo Mai. *In Patrologiae Cursus Completus (Series Graeca)*. Edited by J.-P. Migne, vol. 17, col. 288. Paris: Migne, 1857.

Philocalie, 1–20: sur les écritures. Translated by Marguerite Harl. SC 302. Paris: Éditions du Cerf, 1983.

The Song of Songs: Commentary and Homilies. Translated by R. P. Lawson. Ancient Christian Writers 26. New York, NY: Newman Press, 1957.

St. Jerome: Commentary on Isaiah. Including St. Jerome's Translation of Origen's Homilies 1–9 on Isaiah. Translated by Thomas P. Scheck. Ancient Christian Writers 68. New York, NY: Newman Press. 2015.

Traité Des Principes, Tome I (Livres I et II): Introduction, Texte Critique de La Version de Rufin, Traduction. Edited and translated by Henri Crouzel and Manlio Simonetti. SC 252. Paris: Éditions du Cerf, 1978.

Traité Des Principes, Tome II (Livres I et II): Commentaire et Fragments. Edited and translated by Henri Crouzel and Manlio Simonetti. SC 253. Paris: Éditions du Cerf, 1978.

Traité Des Principes, Tome III (Livres III et IV): Introduction, Texte Critique de La Philocalie et de La Version de Rufin, Traduction. Edited and translated by Henri Crouzel and Manlio Simonetti. SC 268. Paris: Éditions du Cerf, 1980.

Traité Des Principes, Tome IV (Livres III et IV): Commentaire et Fragments. Edited and translated by Henri Crouzel and Manlio Simonetti. SC 269. Paris: Éditions du Cerf, 1980.

Traité Des Principes, Tome V: Compléments et Index. Edited and translated by Henri Crouzel and Manlio Simonetti. SC 312. Paris: Éditions du Cerf, 1984.

Treatise on the Passover and Dialogue of Origen with Heraclides and His Fellow Bishops on the Father, the Son, and the Soul. Translated by Robert J. Daly. Ancient Christian Writers 54. New York: Paulist Press, 1992.

OTHER

Aelius Theon. "Exercises." In *Progymnasmata: Greek Textbooks of Prose Composition and Rhetortic*. Translated with introductions and notes by George A. Kennedy. Atlanta, GA: SBL Press, 2003. Pp. 1-72.

Alexander, Loveday. *The Preface to Luke's Gospel: Literary Convention and Social Context in Luke 1.1–4 and Acts 1.1*. Cambridge, UK: Cambridge University Press, 1993.

Allison, Dale. *Constructing Jesus: Memory, Imagination, and History*. Grand Rapids, MI: Baker Academic, 2010.

"Darkness at Noon." In *Studies in Matthew*. Edited by Dale Allison. Grand Rapids, MI: Baker Academic, 2005. Pp. 79–105.

Encountering Mystery: Religious Experience in a Secular Age. Grand Rapids, MI: Eerdmans, 2022.

The End of the Ages Has Come: An Early Interpretation of the Passion and Resurrection of Jesus. Philadelphia, PA: Fortress Press, 1985.

"Jesus & the Victory of Apocalyptic." In *Jesus and the Restoration of Israel: A Critical Assessment of N. T. Wright's Jesus and the Victory of God*. Edited by Carey C. Newman. Downers Grove, IL: InterVarsity Press, 1999. Pp. 127–41.

Jesus of Nazareth: Millenarian Prophet. Minneapolis, MN: Fortress Press, 1991.

The Historical Christ and the Theological Jesus. Grand Rapids, MI: Eerdmans, 2009.

The Resurrection of Jesus: Apologetics, Polemics, History. London: Bloomsbury T&T Clark, 2021.

Ambrose of Milan. *Commentary on the Gospel according to Saint Luke*. Translated by Íde M. Ní Riain. Dublin: Halycon Press, 2001.

Anderson, Gary A. *That I May Dwell Among Them: Incarnation and Atonement in the Tabernacle Narrative*. Grand Rapids, MI: Eerdmans, 2023.

Anderson, Paul N., Felix Just, SJ, and Tom Thatcher. *John, Jesus, and History*. vols. 1–3. Atlanta, GA: SBL Press, 2007, 2009, 2016.

Angelus Silesius. *Cherubinischer Wandersmann oder Geistreiche Sinn- und Schlussreime*. Edited by Ludwig Aurbacher. Munich: Seidel, 1827.

Asirvatham, Sulochana R. "Historiography." In *The Oxford Handbook of the Second Sophistic*. Edited by Daniel S. Richter and William A. Johnson. Oxford, UK: Oxford University Press, 2017. Pp. 477–91.

Auerbach, Erich. "Figura." In idem, *Scenes from the Drama of European Literature*. Theory and History of Literature 9. Minneapolis, MN: University of Minnesota Press, 1984. Pp. 11–76.

Ayres, Lewis. "Irenaeus vs. the Valentinians: Toward a Rethinking of Patristic Exegetical Origins." *Journal of Early Christian Studies* 23.2 (2015), 153–87.

Baird, William. *History of New Testament Research. Vol. 1: From Deism to Tübingen*. Minneapolis, MN: Fortress Press, 1992.

Baltzer, K. *Deutero-Isaiah: A Commentary*. Hermeneia. Minneapolis, MN: Fortress Press, 2001.

Bauckham, Richard. *Jesus and the Eyewitnesses: The Gospels as Eyewitness Testimony*. Grand Rapids, MI: Eerdmans, 2006.

Becker, Eve-Marie. *The Birth of Christian History: Memory and Time from Mark to Luke-Acts*. Anchor Yale Bible Reference Library. New Haven, CT: Yale University Press, 2017.

Behr, John. *The Case Against Diodore and Theodore: Texts and their Contexts*. Oxford Early Christian Texts. Oxford, UK: Oxford University Press, 2011

John the Theologian and His Paschal Gospel: A Prologue to Theology. Oxford, UK: Oxford University Press, 2019.

Beiser, F. C. *David Friedrich Strauß, Father of Unbelief: An Intellectual Biography*. Oxford, UK: Oxford University Press, 2020.

Berchman, Robert M. "In the Shadow of Origen: Porphyry and the Patristic Origins of New Testament Criticism." In *Origeniana Sexta: Origène et la Bible/Origen and the Bible*. Edited by Gilles Dorival and Alain le Boulluec. Leuven: Leuven University Press, 1995. Pp. 657–73.

Bergjan, Silke-Petra. "Celsus the Epicurean? The Interpretation of an Argument in Origen, *Contra Celsum*." *Harvard Theological Review* 94.2 (2001), 181–206.

Berglund, Carl Johan. "Interpreting Readers: The Role of Greco-Roman Education in Early Interpretation of New Testament Writings." In *Scriptural Interpretation at the Interface between Education and Religion: In Memory of Hans Conzelmann*. Edited by Florian Wilk. Leiden: Brill, 2018. Pp. 204–47.

Origen's References to Heracleon: A Quotation-Analytical Study of the Earliest Known Commentary on the Gospel of John. Wissenschaftliche Untersuchungen zum Neuen Testament 450. Tübingen: Mohr Siebeck, 2020.

"Origen's Vacillating Stances toward his 'Valentinian' Colleague Heracleon." *Vigiliae Christianae* 71 (2017), 541–69.

"Understanding Origen: The Genre(s) of the Gospels in Light of Ancient Greek Philology and Modern Genre Theory." *Scrinium* 12.1 (2016), 181–214.

Bermejo Rubio, Fernando. "The Fiction of the 'Three Quests': An Argument for Dismantling a Dubious Historiographical Paradigm." *Journal for the Study of the Historical Jesus* 7 (2009), 217–23.

Betz, Otto. "Die Vision des Paulus im Tempel von Jerusalem: Apg 22,17-21 als Beitrag zur Deutung des Damaskuserlebnisses." In *Verborum Veritas: Festschrift Gustav Stiihlin*. Edited by O. Boecher and K. Haacker. Wuppertal: Brockhaus, 1970. Pp. 113–23.

Bietenhard, Hans. "The Millennial Hope in the Early Church." *Scottish Journal of Theology* 6 (1953), 12–30.

Blaski, Andrew. "Jews, Christians, and the Conditions of Christological Interpretation in Origen's Work." In *Origeniana Duodecima: "Origen's Legacy in the Holy Land – A Tale of Three Cities: Jerusalem, Caesarea and Bethlehem."* Bibliotheca Ephemeridum Theologicarum Lovaniensium 302. Edited by B. Bitton-Ashkelony, O. Irshai, A. Kofsky, and H. Newman. Leuven: Peeters, 2019. Pp. 505–18.

"The *Philocalia* of Origen: A Crude or Creative Composition?" *Vigiliae Christianae* 73.2 (2019), 174–89.

Bloch, René. "Philo's Struggle with Jewish Myth." In *Philo of Alexandria and Greek Myth: Narratives, Allegories, and Arguments*. Edited by F. Alessa and L. De Luca. Leiden: Brill, 2019. Pp. 107–26.

Bockmuehl, Markus. "Being Emmanuel: Matthew's Ever-Present Jesus?" *New Testament Studies* 68.1 (2022), 1–12.

"The Making of Gospel Commentaries." In *The Written Gospel*. Edited by Markus Bockmuehl and Donald A. Hagner. Cambridge, UK: Cambridge University Press, 2005. Pp. 274–95.

Seeing the Word: Refocusing New Testament Study. Grand Rapids, MI: Baker Academic, 2006.

Boobyer, G. H. *St. Mark and the Transfiguration Story*. New York, NY: T&T Clark, 1942.

Borg, Marcus. "David Friedrich Strauss: Miracle and Myth." *The Fourth R* 4.3 (1991).

Jesus, A New Vision: Spirit, Culture, and the Life of Discipleship. San Francisco, CA: HarperCollins, 1987.

Bornkamm, Günther. "The Stilling of the Storm in Matthew." In *Tradition and Interpretation in Matthew*. Edited by G. Bornkamm, G. Barth, and H. J. Held. London, UK: SCM Press. 1963. Pp. 52–57.

Bovon, F. *Luke 1: A Commentary on the Gospel of Luke 1:1-9:50*. Hermeneia. Minneapolis, MN: Fortress Press, 2002.

Bowker, J. W. "Prophetic Action and Sacramental Form," *Studia Evangelica* 2.3 (1964), 129–37.

Boxall, Ian. *Discovering Matthew: Content, Interpretation, Reception*. Grand Rapids, MI: Eerdmans, 2015.

"Origen's Commentary on Matthew and the Reception of Matthew's Gospel." *In The Gospel of Matthew: Studies on Its Composition, Theology, and Early Reception*. Edited by Joseph Verheyden, Jens Schröter, and David C. Sim. Tübingen: Mohr Siebeck, 2022. Pp. 321–40.

Boyarin, Daniel. "Philo, Origen, and the Rabbis on Divine Speech and Interpretation." In *The World of Early Egyptian Christianity: Language, Literature, and Social Context, Essays in Honor of David W. Johnson*. Edited by James E. Goehring and Janet A. Timbie. Washington, DC: Catholic University of America Press, 2007.

Intertextuality and the Reading of Midrash. Bloomington, IN: Indiana University Press, 1990.

Bravo, Benedetto. "*Critice* in the Sixteenth and Seventeenth Centuries and the Rise of the Notion of Historical Criticism." In *History of Scholarship: A Selection of Papers from the Seminar on the History of Scholarship Held Annually at the Warburg Institute*. Edited by C. R. Ligota and J.-L. Quantin. Oxford, UK: Oxford University Press, 2006. Pp. 135–95.

Breuss, Josef. "Das 'Leben Jesu' von David Friedrich Strauss und die Hegelsche Philosophie." *Freiburger Zeitschrift fur Philosophie und Theologie* 19 (1972), 389–409.

Brey, Steven P. "Origen's Commentary on John: Seeing All of Creation as Gospel." PhD Dissertation. University of Notre Dame, 2003.

Brown, Raymond E. *The Birth of the Messiah: A Commentary on the Infancy Narratives in the Gospels of Matthew and Luke*. The Anchor Yale Bible Reference Library. New Haven, CT: Yale University Press, 1999.

The Death of the Messiah: From Gethsemane to the Grave; A Commentary on the Passion Narratives of the Four Gospels. 2 Vols. New York: Doubleday, 1994.

"Jesus and Elisha." *Perspectives* 12 (1971), 85–104.

Bulgakov, Sergius. *Relics and Miracles: Two Theological Essays*. Translated by Boris Jakim. Grand Rapids, MI: Eerdmans, 2011.

Bultmann, Rudolph. *The Gospel of John: A Commentary*. Philadelphia, PA: The Westminster Press, 1971.

Jesus Christ and Mythology. New York, NY: Charles Scribner's Sons, 1958.
"New Testament and Mythology." In *Kerygma and Myth: A Theological Debate*. Edited by Hans W. Bartsch. New York, NY: Harper and Row, 1961. Pp. 1–16.
Burridge, Richard. *What Are the Gospels? A Comparison with Graeco-Roman Biography*. Waco, TX: Baylor University Press, 2018.
Butler, Shane. *The Matter of the Page: Essays in Search of Ancient and Medieval Authors*. Madison, WI: The University of Wisconsin Press, 2011.
Byrskog, Samuel. "From Memory to Memoirs: Tracing the Background of a Literary Genre." In *The Making of Christianity: Conflicts, Contacts, and Constructions: Essays in Honor of Bengt Holmberg*. Edited by M. Zetterholm and S. Byrskog. Coniectanea Biblica New Testament Series 47. Winona Lake, IN: Eisenbrauns, 2012. Pp. 1–21.
Caird, G. B. *Jesus and the Jewish Nation*. The Ethel M. Wood Lecture delivered before the University of London on 9 March 1965. London: The Athlone Press, 1965.
New Testament Theology. Edited by L. D. Hurst. Oxford, UK: Clarendon Press, 1994.
Calhoun, Robert M., David P. Moessner, and Tobias Nicklas, eds. *Modern and Ancient Literary Criticism of the Gospels: Continuing the Debate on Gospel Genre(s)*. Wissenschaftliche Untersuchungen zum Neuen Testament 451. Tübingen: Mohr Siebeck, 2020.
Carleton Paget, James N. "The Jew of Celsus and *adversus Judaeos* Literature." *Zeitschrift für antikes Christentum* 21.2 (2017), 201–42.
Cavadini, John C. "The Church as the Sacrament of Creation: A Reading of Origen's *Commentary on the Song of Songs*." *Communio* 42.1 (2005), 89–118.
"From Letter to Spirit: The Multiple Senses of Scripture." In *The Oxford Handbook of Early Christian Interpretation*. Edited by Paul M. Blowers and Peter W. Martens. Oxford, UK: Oxford University Press, 2019. Pp. 126–48.
Childs, Brevard. *The New Testament as Canon: An Introduction*. London: SCM Press, 1984.
Cirafesi, Wally V. and Gregory Peter Fewster. "Justin's ἀπομνημονεύματα and Ancient Greco-Roman Memoirs." *Early Christianity* 7 (2016), 186–212.
Cole, Timothy J. "Paul as Jesus: Luke's Use of Recursion in Luke-Acts." PhD Dissertation. University of Chester, 2021
Collingwood, Robin G. *The Idea of History*. Oxford, UK: Clarendon Press, 1946.
Collins, Adela Yarbro. "Historical Jesus: Then and Now." *Reflections: A Magazine of Theological and Ethical Inquiry from Yale Divinity School* (Spring 2008), 9–13.
Is Mark's Gospel a Life of Jesus? Milwaukee, WI: Marquette University Press, 1990.
Mark: A Commentary. Hermeneia. Minneapolis, MN: Fortress Press, 2006.
"Genre and the Gospels." *The Journal of Religion* 75.2 (1995), 239–46.
Collins, J. N. "Re-thinking 'Eyewitnesses' in the Light of 'Servants of the Word' (Luke 1:2)." *The Expository Times* 121.9 (2010), 447–52.

Conzelmann, Hans. *Die Mitte der Zeit: Studien zur Theologie des Lukas*. Beitrage Zur Historischen Theologie. Tübingen: Mohr Siebeck, 1954. English translation: Geoffrey Buswell. *The Theology of St. Luke*. Philadelphia, PA: Fortress Press, 1982.

Cranfield, C. E. B. "The Baptism of our Lord – A Study of St. Mark I.9-11," *Scottish Journal of Theology* 8.1 (1955), 53–63.

Crawford, Matthew R. "Ammonius of Alexandria, Eusebius of Caesarea and the Origins of Gospels Scholarship." *New Testament Studies* 61 (2015), 1–29.

Crouzel, Henri. *Origen*. Translated by A. S. Worrall. Edinburgh: T&T Clark, 1989.

Cullmann, Oscar. "Die Pluralität der Evangelien als theologisches Problem im Altertum." *Theologische Zeitschrift* 1 (1945), 23–42. English translation: "The Plurality of the Gospels as a Theological Problem in Antiquity: A Study in the History of Dogma." In idem, *The Early Church: Studies in Early Christian History and Theology*. Edited by A. J. B. Higgins. Philadelphia, PA: The Westminster Press, 1956. Pp. 37–54.

Daley, SJ, Brian E. "Origen's *De principiis*: A Guide to the 'Principles' of Christian Scriptural Interpretation." In *Nova Et Vetera: Patristic Studies in Honor of Thomas Patrick Halton*. Edited by John Petruccione. Washington, DC: Catholic University of America Press, 1998. Pp. 3–21

Daniélou, Jean. *Origen*. Translated by Walter Mitchell. New York: Sheed and Ward, 1955.

Davies, J. H. "The Purpose of the Central Section of St. Luke's Gospel." *Studia Evangelica* 2 (1964), 164–69.

Davies, W. D. and Dale Allison. *Matthew 1-7: Volume 1*. International Critical Commentary. New York, NY: T&T Clark, 1998.

Matthew 19-28: Volume 3. International Critical Commentary. New York, NY: T&T Clark, 2004.

Dawson, J. David. *Christian Figural Reading and the Fashioning of Identity*. Berkeley, CA: University of California Press, 2001.

"Plato's Soul and the Body of the Text in Philo and Origen." In *Interpretation and Allegory: Antiquity to the Modern Period*. Edited by J. Whitman. Boston/Leiden: Brill Academic, 2003. Pp. 89–107

DeCock, Miriam. *Interpreting the Gospel of John in Antioch and Alexandria*. Writings from the Greco-Roman World Supplement Series 17. Atlanta, GA: SBL Press. 2020.

De Faye, Eugène. *Origène: sa vie, son œuvre, sa pensée*. 3 vols. Paris: Éditions Ernest Leroux, 1923–1928. Translated by Fred Rothwell. *Origen and His Work*. London: George Allen and Unwin Ltd., 1926.

De la Potterie, Ignace. "La parabole du prétendant à la royauté (Lc 19,11–28)." In *À cause de l'évangile: Études sur les Synoptiques et les Actes offertes au P. Jacques Dupont, O.S.B. à l'occasion de son 70e anniversaire*. Paris: Cerf, 1985. Pp. 613–41.

De Long, Kindalee Pfremmer. "Angels and Visions in Luke-Acts." In *The Jewish Apocalyptic Tradition and the Shaping of New Testament Thought*. Edited by Benjamin E. Reynolds and Loren T. Stuckenbruck. Minneapolis, MN: Fortress Press, 2017. Pp. 79–107.

De Lubac, Henri. *History and Spirit: The Understanding of Scripture According to Origen*. Translated by Anne Englund Nash. San Francisco: Ignatius Press, 2007.

Deis, F. Lentzen. *Die Taufe Jesu nach den Synoptikern; literarkritische und gattungsgeschichtliche Untersuchungen*. Frankfurt am Main: J. Knecht, 1970.

Denniston, J. D. *The Greek Particles*. Oxford, UK: Clarendon Press, 1954.

Dimant, Devorah. "Not Exile in the Desert but Exile in Spirit: The Pesher of Isa 40:3 in the *Rule of the Community* and the History of the Scrolls." In eadem, *History, Ideology and Bible Interpretation in the Dead Sea Scrolls: Collected Studies*. Forschungen zum Alten Testament 90. Tübingen: Mohr Siebeck, 2014. Pp. 255–64.

Diodore of Tarsus. *Commentary on Psalms 1-51*. Translated by Robert C. Hill. Atlanta, GA: SBL Press, 2005.

"Commentary on the Psalms, Prologue." In *Biblical Interpretation in the Early Church*. Edited and translated by Karlfried Froehlich. Philadelphia, PA: Fortress Press, 1984. Pp. 82–86.

Dively Lauro, Elizabeth Ann. *The Soul and Spirit of Scripture within Origen's Exegesis*. Atlanta, GA: SBL Press, 2005.

Dodd, C. H. *The Interpretation of the Fourth Gospel*. Cambridge, UK: Cambridge University Press, 1953.

"Matthew and Paul." *The Expository Times* 58.11 (1947), 293–98.

The Parables of the Kingdom. Glasgow: Collins Sons & Co, 1978.

Donahue, SJ, J. R. and D. J. Harrington, SJ. *The Gospel of Mark*. Sacra Pagina Series 2. Collegeville, MN: The Liturgical Press, 2002.

Dunn, James D. G. *Christianity in the Making, Vol. 1: Jesus Remembered*. Grand Rapids, MI: Eerdmans, 2003.

Jesus and the Spirit: A Study of the Religious and Charismatic Experience of Jesus and the First Christians as Reflected in the New Testament. Grand Rapids, MI: Eerdmans, 1975.

Ecklebarger, Kermit A. "Authorial Intention as a Guiding Principle in Origen's Matthew Commentary." PhD Dissertation. University of Chicago, 1987.

Evans, Craig. "Daniel in the New Testament: Visions of God's Kingdom." In *The Book of Daniel: Composition and Reception*, vol 2. Edited by J. Collins and P. Flint. Leiden: Brill, 2001. Pp. 490–527.

Fitzmyer, Joseph A. *The Gospel According to Luke I-IX: Introduction, Translation, and Notes*. Anchor Bible 28. New Haven, CT: Doubleday, 1982.

Flender, Helmut. *Heil und Geschichte in der Theologie des Lukas*. Munich: Chr. Kaiser Verlag, 1965. Translated by R. H. and I. Fuller. *St Luke: Theologian of Redemptive History*. Philadelphia, PA: Fortress Press, 1967.

Fortunatianus of Aquileia. *Commentarii in Evangelia*. Corpus Scriptorum Ecclesiasticorum Latinorum 103. Edited by L. J. Dorfbauer. Berlin: De Gruyter, 2017. *Commentary on the Gospels*. Translated with Introduction by H. A. G. Houghton. Berlin: De Gruyter, 2017.

Fredriksen, Paula. *When Christians Were Jews: The First Generation*. New Haven, CT: Yale University Press, 2018.

Gaber, Goran. "What Was Critical History? A Reading of Richard Simon's *Histoire critique du Vieux Testament.*" *History and Theory* 57.2 (2018), 218–33.

Gathercole, Simon. *The Gospel and the Gospels: Christian Proclamation and Early Jesus Books.* Grand Rapids, MI: Eerdmans, 2022.

Glasson, T. Francis. "Theophany and Parousia." *New Testament Studies* 34 (1988), 259–70.

Gögler, Rolf. *Zur Theologie des Biblischen Wortes bei Origenes.* Düsseldorf: Patmos, 1963.

Gould, Warwick and Marjorie Reeves. *Joachim of Fiore and the Myth of the Eternal Evangel in the Nineteenth and Twentieth Centuries.* Revised Edition. Oxford, UK: Oxford University Press, 2001.

Gräßer, E. *Das Problem der Parusieverzögerung in den synoptischen Evangelien und in der Apostelgeschichte* Berlin-New York: De Gruyter, 1977.

Grant, Robert M. *The Earliest Lives of Jesus.* Eugene, OR: Wipf and Stock, 1961.

Heresy and Criticism: The Search for Authenticity in Early Christian Literature. Louisville, KY: Westminster John Knox Press, 1993.

Grube, D.-M. "The Lessing/Schumann Controversy. Lessing's Stance on Contingency Compared to Kant's Stance." In *Religions Challenged by Contingency: Theological and Philosophical Approaches to the Problem of Contingency.* Edited by D.-M. Grube and P. Jonkers. Leiden: Brill, 2008. Pp. 89–118.

Halperin, David J. "Origen, Ezekiel's Merkabah, and the Ascension of Moses." *Church History* 50.3 (1981), 261–75.

Hamilton, C. S. and J. Willitts, eds. *Writing the Gospels: A Dialogue with Francis Watson.* London: Bloomsbury T&T Clark, 2019.

Hanson, R. P. C. *Allegory and Event: A Study of the Sources and Significance of Origen's Interpretation of Scripture.* Richmond, VA: John Knox Press, 1959.

"The Passage Marked *Unde?* in Robinson's Philocalia XV, 19,84–86." In *Origeniana Secunda: second colloque international des etudes origéniennes.* Edited by Henri Crouzel and Antonio Quacquarelli. Rome: Edizioni dell'Ateneo, 1980. Pp. 293–304.

Harrill, J. Albert. "'Exegetical Torture' in Early Christian Biblical Interpretation: The Case of Origen of Alexandria." *Biblical Interpretation* 25 (2017), 39–57.

Harris, Horton. *David Friedrich Strauss and His Theology.* Cambridge, UK: Cambridge University Press, 1973.

Harris, Ruth. *Lourdes: Body and Spirit in the Secular Age.* New York, NY: Penguin, 1999.

Hays, Richard B. *Echoes of Scripture in the Gospels.* Waco, TX: Baylor University Press, 2017.

Echoes of Scripture in the Letters of Paul. New Haven, CT: Yale University Press, 1989.

Heath, Jane. "The Beginnings of a Christian Doctrine of the Spiritual Senses before Origen." In *The Intellectual World of Late Antique Christianity: Reshaping Classical Traditions.* Edited by Lewis Ayres, Michael W. Champion and Matthew R. Crawford. Cambridge, UK: Cambridge University Press, 2023. Pp. 21–46.

Heine, Ronald E. "Epinoiai." In *The Westminster Handbook to Origen*. Edited by John A. McGuckin. Louisville, KY: Westminster John Knox Press, 2004. Pp. 93–95.

"The Introduction to Origen's Commentary on John Compared with the Introductions to the Ancient Philosophical Commentaries on Aristotle." In *Origeniana Sexta: Origène et la Bible/Origen and the Bible*. Edited by Gilles Dorival and Alain le Boulluec. Leuven: Leuven University Press, 1995. Pp. 3–12.

"Origen's Gospel Commentaries." In *The Oxford Handbook of Origen*. Edited by R. E. Heine and Karen J. Torjesen. Oxford, UK: Oxford University Press, 2022. Pp. 211–28.

"The Prologues of Origen's Pauline Commentaries and the *Schemata Isagogica* of Ancient Commentary Literature." In *Studia Patristica* 36. Edited by M. F. Wiles and E. J. Yarnold. Leuven: Peeters, 2001. Pp. 421–39.

Helms, Randel. *Gospel Fictions*. Amherst, NY: Prometheus Books, 1988.

Heraclitus. *Heraclitus: Homeric Problems*. Edited and Translated by Donald A. Russell and David Konstan. Atlanta, GA: SBL Press, 2005.

Hilary of Poitiers. *Sur Matthieu I-II*. Edited by Jean Doignon. SC 254 and 258. Paris: Cerf, 1978. Translated by D. H. Williams, *St. Hilary of Poitiers: Commentary on Matthew*. FC 125. Washington, DC: Catholic University of America Press, 2012.

Hollander, John. *The Figure of Echo: A Mode of Allusion in Milton and After*. Berkeley: University of California Press, 1981.

Hooker, Morna D. *The Signs of a Prophet: The Prophetic Actions of Jesus*. Harrisburg, PA: Trinity Press International, 1997.

Houghton, H. A. G. *The Latin New Testament: A Guide to its Early History, Texts, and Manuscripts*. Oxford, UK: Oxford University Press, 2016.

Houghton, H. A. G. and D. C. Parker, eds. *Codex Zacynthius: Catena, Palimpsest, Lectionary*. Piscataway, NJ: Gorgias Press, 2020.

Houghton, H. A. G., Panagiotis Manafis, and A. C. Myshrall, eds. *The Palimpsest Catena of Codex Zacynthius: Text and Translation*. Piscataway, NJ: Gorgias Press, 2020.

Hunter, Richard. "Homer in Origen, *Against Celsus*." In *Celsus in his World: Philosophy, Polemic and Religion in the Second Century*. Edited by James Carleton Paget and Simon Gathercole. Cambridge, UK: Cambridge University Press, 2021. Pp. 215–48.

Hutt, Curtis. "'Be Ye Approved Money Changers!' Reexamining the Social Contexts of the Saying and Its Interpretation." *Journal of Biblical Literature* 131.3 (2012), 589–609.

Ierodiakonou, Katerina. "The Notion of Enargeia in Hellenistic Philosophy." In *Episteme, etc.: Essays in Honor of Jonathan Barnes*. Edited by B. Morison and K. Ierodiakonou. Oxford, UK: Oxford University Press, 2011. Pp. 60–73.

Inowlocki, Sabrina. "Did Josephus Ascribe the Fall of Jerusalem to the Murder of James, Brother of Jesus?" *Revue des Études Juives* 170.1 (2011), 21–49.

Justin Martyr. *Justin, Philosopher and Martyr: Apologies*. Edited by D. Minns and P. Parvis. Oxford Early Christian Texts. Oxford, UK: Oxford University Press, 2009.

Käsemann, E. "Die Anfänge christlicher Theologie." *Zeitschrift für Theologie und Kirche* 57 (1960), 162–85. English translation: "The Beginnings of Christian Theology." In *New Testament Questions of Today*. Translated by W. J. Montague. London: SCM Press, 1969. Pp. 82–107.

Kazen, Thomas. "The Coming Son of Man Revisited." *Journal for the Study of the Historical Jesus* 5.2 (2007), 157–76.

"Son of Man as Kingdom Imagery: Jesus Between Corporate Symbol and Individual Redeemer Figure." In *Jesus from Judaism to Christianity: Continuum Approaches to the Historical Jesus*. Edited by T. Holmén. London: T&T Clark, 2007. Pp. 87–108.

Keith, Chris. *The Gospels as Manuscript: An Early History of the Jesus Tradition as Material Artifact*. Oxford, UK: Oxford University Press, 2020.

"Social Memory Theory and Gospels Research: The First Decade (Part One)." *Early Christianity* 6.3 (2015), 354–76.

"Social Memory Theory and Gospels Research: The First Decade (Part Two)." *Early Christianity* 6.4 (2015), 517–42.

Kelhoffer, J. "'How Soon a Book' Revisited: ΕΥΑΓΓΕΛΙΟΝ as a Reference to 'Gospel' Materials in the First Half of the Second Century." *Zeitschrift für die neutestamentliche Wissenschaft* 95 (2004), 1–34.

Keough, Shawn W. J. "The Eternal Gospel: Origen's Eschatological Exegesis." In *The Reception and Interpretation of the Bible in Late Antiquity: Proceedings of the Montréal Colloquium in Honour of Charles Kannengiesser, 11–13 October 2006*. Edited by Lorenzo DiTommaso and Lucian Turescu. Leiden/Boston: Brill, 2008. Pp 193–226.

Kirk, J. R. Daniel. "Conceptualising Fulfilment in Matthew." *Tyndale Bulletin* 59.1 (2008), 77–98.

Knohl, Israel. *The Messiah Confrontation: Pharisees versus Sadducees and the Death of Jesus*. Philadelphia, PA: The Jewish Publication Society, 2022.

Kolbet, Paul R. "Rethinking the Rationales for Origen's Use of Allegory." *Studia Patristica* 56 (2013), 41–49.

Köpf, Ulrich. "Ferdinand Christian Baur and David Friedrich Strauss." In *Ferdinand Christian Baur and the History of Early Christianity*. Edited by M. Bauspiess, C. Landmesser, and D. Lincicum. Oxford, UK: Oxford University Press, 2017. Pp. 3–44.

Kozitza, Evangeline M. "Aesthetic Piety and the Infant Christ: Seeing and Hearing in Infancy Traditions from the New Testament to Origen." DPhil Thesis. University of Oxford, 2020.

Lamberton, Robert. *Homer the Theologian: Neoplatonist Allegorical Reading and the Growth of the Epic Tradition*. Berkeley, CA: University of California Press, 1986.

Lee, Dorothy. "The Gospel of John and the Five Senses." *Journal of Biblical Literature* 129.1 (2010), 115–27.

Lessing, Gotthold Ephraim. "Über den Beweis des Geistes und der Kraft." In *Philosophische und Theologische Schriften II, Gesammelte Werke* Vol. 8. Edited by P. Rilla. Berlin: Aufbau, 1968. Pp. 9–16.

Lessing: Philosophical and Theological Writings. Trans. H. B. Nesbit. Cambridge, UK: Cambridge University Press, 2005.

Lightfoot, R. H. *Locality and Doctrine in the Gospels*. New York, NY: Harper, 1938.

Litwa, M. David. *How the Gospels Became History: Jesus and Mediterranean Myths*. New Haven, CT: Yale University Press, 2019.

We Are Being Transformed: Deification in Paul's Soteriology. Berlin: De Gruyter, 2012.

Lohmeyer, Ernst. "'Mir ist gegeben alle Gewalt!' Eine Exegese von Mt. 28, 16–20." In *In Memoriam Ernst Lohmeyer*. Edited by W. Schmauch. Stuttgart: Evangelischer Verlagswerk, 1951. Pp. 22–49.

Lonergan, SJ, Bernard. "Cognitional Structure." In *Collected Works of Bernard Lonergan, Vol. 4: Collection*. Edited by Frederick E. Crowe and Robert M. Doran. Toronto: University of Toronto Press, 1988. Pp. 205–21.

Luijendijk, AnneMarie. "Reading the *Gospel of Thomas* in the Third Century: Three Oxyrhynchus Papyri and Origen's *Homilies*." In *Reading New Testament Papyri in Context*. Edited by Claire Clivaz and Jean Zumstein. Leuven: Peeters, 2011. Pp. 241–67.

Luz, Ulrich. *Matthew 8–20*. Hermeneia. Minneapolis, MN: Fortress Press, 2001.

Matthew 21–28. Hermeneia. Minneapolis, MN: Fortress Press, 2005.

Marcus, Joel. "Did Matthew Believe His Myths?" In *An Early Reader of Mark and Q*. Edited by Joseph Verheyden and Gilbert Van Belle. Leuven: Peeters, 2016. Pp. 217–49.

Martens, Peter W. "Origen Against History? Reconsidering the Critique of Allegory," *Modern Theology* 28 (2012), 635–56.

Origen and Scripture: The Contours of the Exegetical Life. Oxford, UK: Oxford University Press, 2012.

"Revisiting the Allegory/Typology Distinction: The Case of Origen." *Journal of Early Christian Studies* 16 (2008), 283–317.

Marxsen, Willi. *Mark the Evangelist: Studies on the Redaction History of the Gospel*. Nashville, TN: Abingdon Press, 1969.

McCown, C. C. *The Search for the Real Jesus: A Century of Historical Study*. New York, NY: Charles Scribner's Sons, 1940.

McGinn, Bernard. "Mystical Consciousness: A Modest Proposal." *Spiritus* 8.1 (2008), 44–63.

McGuckin, John Anthony. "Changing Forms of Jesus." In *Origeniana Quarta: Die Referate des 4. Internationalen Origeneskongresses (Innsbruck, 2–6 September 1985)*. Edited by Lothar Lies. Innsbruck: Tyrolia, 1987. Pp. 215–22.

"Origen's Eschatology." In *The Oxford Handbook of Origen*. Edited by R. E. Heine and Karen J. Torjesen. Oxford, UK: Oxford University Press, 2022. Pp. 410–26.

"Origen as Literary Critic in the Alexandrian Tradition." In *Origeniana Octava: Origen and the Alexandrian Tradition*. Edited by L. Perrone. Vol. 1. Bibliotheca Ephemeridum Theologicarum Lovaniensium 164. Leuven: Leuven University Press, 2003. Pp. 121–35.

Origen of Alexandria: Master Theologian of the Early Church. Lanham, MD. Lexington Books, 2022.

"Structural Design and Apologetic Intent in Origen's Commentary on John." In *Origeniana Sexta: Origène et la Bible / Origen and the Bible, Actes du Colloquium Origenianum Sextum Chantilly, 30 août - 3 septembre 1993*. Edited by G. Dorival and A. Le Boulluec. Leuven: Peeters, 1995. Pp. 441–57.

The Transfiguration of Christ in Scripture and Tradition. Lewiston, NY: Edwin Mellen Press, 1986.

The Westminster Handbook to Origen. Louisville: Westminster John Knox Press, 2004.

McInroy, Mark J. "Origen of Alexandria." In *The Spiritual Senses: Perceiving God in Western Christianity*. Edited by Paul L. Gavrilyuk and Sarah Coakley. Cambridge, UK: Cambridge University Press, 2012. Pp. 20–35.

McKnight, Scot. "Jesus and Prophetic Actions." *Bulletin for Biblical Research* 10 (2000), 197–232.

Meier, John P. *A Marginal Jew. Rethinking the Historical Jesus. Volume One: The Roots of the Problem and the Person*. Anchor Bible Reference Library. New York, NY: Doubleday, 1991.

A Marginal Jew. Rethinking the Historical Jesus. Volume Two: Mentor, Message and Miracles. Anchor Bible Reference Library. New York, NY: Doubleday, 1994.

A Marginal Jew: Rethinking the Historical Jesus. Volume Three: Companions and Competitors. Anchor Bible Reference Library. New York, NY: Doubleday, 2001.

A Marginal Jew: Rethinking the Historical Jesus, Vol. 5: Probing the Authenticity of the Parables. Anchor Yale Bible Reference Library. New Haven, CT: Yale University Press, 2016.

Matthew. New Testament Message 3. Collegeville, MN: The Liturgical Press, 1980.

"Salvation-History in Matthew: In Search of a Starting Point." *Catholic Biblical Quarterly* 37.2 (1975), 203–15.

The Vision of Matthew: Christ, Church, and Morality in the First Gospel. New York, NY: Crossroad, 1979.

Merkel, Helmut. *Die Pluralität der Evangelien als theologisches und exegetisches Problem in der Alten Kirche*. Bern: Peter Lang, 1978.

Die Widersprüche zwischen den Evangelien: Ihre polemische und apologetische Behandlung in der Alten Kirche bis zu Augustin. Tübingen: Mohr Siebeck, 1971.

Meyer, Ben F. *The Aims of Jesus*. Eugene, OR: Wipf and Stock, 2002.

Michalson, Jr., G. E. *Lessing's "Ugly Ditch": A Study of Theology and History*. University Park, PA: Penn State University Press, 1985.

Mitchell, Margaret M. "Gospel Optics." In *Writing the Gospels: A Dialogue with Francis Watson*. Edited by C. S. Hamilton and J. Willitts. London: Bloomsbury T&T Clark, 2019. 184–205

"Patristic Rhetoric on Allegory: Origen and Eustathius Put 1 Kingdoms 28 on Trial." In *The "Belly-Myther" of Endor: Interpretations of 1 Kingdoms 28 in the Early Church*. Translated by Rowan A. Greer and Margaret M. Mitchell. Atlanta, GA: SBL Press, 2007. Pp. lxxxv–cxxiii.

Paul, the Corinthians and the Birth of Christian Hermeneutics. Cambridge, UK: Cambridge University Press, 2010.

Moessner, David P. "Luke as Tradent and Hermeneut: 'As one who has a thoroughly informed familiarity with all the events from the top' (παρηκολουθηκότι ἄνωθεν πᾶσιν ἀκριβῶς, Luke 1:3)." *Novum Testamentum* 58 (2016), 259–300.

Morlet, Sébastien. *Symphonia: La concorde des textes et des doctrines dans la littérature grecque jusqu'à Origène*. Paris: Les Belles Lettres, 2019.

Moyise, Stephen. "The Wilderness Quotation in Mark 1:2-3." In *Wilderness: Essays in Honour of Frances Young*. Edited by R. S. Sugirtharajah. London & New York: T&T Clark, 2005. Pp. 78–87.

Mulder, Frederik S. "Gospel Contradictions, Harmonizations, and Historical Truth: Francis Watson and Origen's Comprehensive Paradigm Shift." In *Writing the Gospels: A Dialogue with Francis Watson*. Edited by C. S. Hamilton and J. Willitts. London: Bloomsbury T&T Clark, 2019. Pp. 166–83.

Müller, Mogens. "Were the Gospel Authors Really 'Simple Christians Without Literary Gift' (Albert Schweitzer)?: Arguments for the Quest for the Sources Behind the Gospels." In *Gospel Interpretation and the Q-hypothesis*. Edited by Mogens Müller and Heike Omerzu. New York, NY: T&T Clark, 2018. Pp. 79–96.

Neil, Bronwen. "Dream-visions, Prophecy and Contemplation in Origen's *Contra Celsum*." In *Praying and Contemplating*. Edited by E. Pachoumi and M. Edwards. Tübingen: Mohr Siebeck, 2018. Pp. 123–37.

Neuschäfer, Bernhard. *Origenes als Philologe*. 2 vols. Basel: Friedrich Reinhardt, 1987.

Newman, John Henry. *Sermons on the Subjects of the Day*. London: Longmans, Green, and Co., 1902.

Niehoff, Maren R. "Homer between Celsus, Origen and the Jews of Late Antique *Palaestina*." In *Text and Intertext in Greek Epic and Drama: Essays in Honor of Margalit Finkelberg*. Edited by Jonathan J. Price and Rachel Zelnick-Abramovitz. New York, NY: Routledge, 2021. Pp. 185–209.

Jewish Exegesis and Homeric Scholarship in Alexandria. Cambridge, UK: Cambridge University Press, 2011.

Novenson, Matthew. *The Grammar of Messianism: An Ancient Jewish Political Idiom and Its Users*. Oxford, UK: Oxford University Press, 2017.

Novick, Tzvi. "Biblicized Narrative: On Tobit and Genesis 22." *Journal of Biblical Literature* 126.4 (2007), 755–64.

Nünlist, René. *The Ancient Critic at Work: Terms and Concepts of Literary Criticism in Greek Scholia*. Cambridge, UK: Cambridge University Press, 2009.

Outler, Albert C. "Origen and the Regulae Fidei." *Church History* 8.3 (1939), 212–21.

Pennington, Jonathan T. *Heaven and Earth in the Gospel of Matthew*. Leiden: Brill, 2007.

Perrin, Norman. *What Is Redaction Criticism?* Philadelphia, PA: Fortress Press, 1969.

Philo. *On the Decalogue. On the Special Laws, Books 1-3*. Translated by F. H. Colson. LCL 320. Cambridge, MA: Harvard University Press, 1937.

On the Cherubim. The Sacrifices of Abel and Cain. The Worse Attacks the Better. On the Posterity and Exile of Cain. On the Giants. Translated by F. H. Colson and G. H. Whitaker. LCL 227. Cambridge, MA: Harvard University Press, 1929.

Pierce, Madison, Andrew Byers, and Simon Gathercole, eds. *Gospel Reading and Reception in Early Christian Literature*. Cambridge, UK: Cambridge University Press, 2022.

Plümacher, E. "TEPATEIA: Fiktion und Wunder in der hellenistisch-römischen Geschichtsschreibung und in der Apostelgeschichte." *Zeitschrift für die neutestamentliche Wissenschaft* 89 (1998), 66–90.

Plummer, A. *An Exegetical Commentary on the Gospel according to St. Matthew*. New York, NY: Charles Scribner's Sons, 1910.

Poirier, John C. "Seeing What Is There in Spite of Ourselves: George Tyrrell, John Dominic Crossan, and Robert Frost on Faces in Deep Wells." *Journal for the Study of the Historical Jesus* 4.2 (2006), 127–38.

Ramelli, Ilaria L. E. "John the Evangelist's Work: An Overlooked *Redaktionsgeschichtliche* Theory from the Patristic Age." In *The Origins of John's Gospel*. Edited by Stanley E. Porter and Hughson T. Ong. Leiden: Brill, 2016. Pp. 30–52.

"Origen and the Stoic Allegorical Tradition: Continuity and Innovation." *Invigilata Lucernis* 28 (2006), 195–225.

"Prophecy in Origen: Between Scripture and Philosophy." *Journal of Early Christian History* 7.2 (2017), 17–39.

Ramsey, A. M. *The Glory of God and the Transfiguration of Christ*. London: Longman, Green and Co., 1949.

"What Was the Ascension?" *Studiorum Novi Testamenti Societas* Bulletin II (1951), 43–50.

Reed, Annette Yoshiko. "Εὐαγγέλιον: Orality, Textuality, and the Christian Truth in Irenaeus' *Adversus Haereses*." *Vigliae Christianae* 56 (2002), 11–46.

Reynolds, Benjamin E. and Loren T. Stuckenbruck, eds. *The Jewish Apocalyptic Tradition and the Shaping of New Testament Thought*. Minneapolis, MN: Fortress Press, 2017.

Robinson, John A. T. *Jesus and His Coming*. Nashville, TN: Abingdon Press, 1957.

"The Parable of the Sheep and the Goats." *New Testament Studies* 2.4 (1956), 225–37.

Rowland, Christopher. *The Open Heaven: A Study of Apocalyptic in Judaism and Early Christianity*. London: SPCK, 1982.

"Visionary Experience in Ancient Judaism and Christianity." In *Paradise Now: Essays on Early Jewish and Christian Mysticism*. Edited by April DeConick. Atlanta, GA: SBL Press, 2006. Pp. 41-56.

Rowland, Christopher and Christopher R. A. Morray-Jones, eds. *The Mystery of God: Early Jewish Mysticism and the New Testament*. Leiden: Brill, 2009.

Rufinus of Aquileia. "Apology against Jerome." In *Theodoret, Jerome, Gennadius, & Rufinus: Historical Writings, Etc.* Edited by P. Schaff and H. Wace and translated by W. H. Fremantle. Nicene and Post-Nicene Fathers Series 2 Vol. 3. Peabody, MA: Hendrickson Publishers, 1994. Pp. 434–82.

Runia, David T. *Philo in Early Christian Literature: A Survey.* Minneapolis: Fortress Press, 1993.

Russell, D. A. *Criticism in Antiquity.* Berkeley, CA: University of California Press, 1981.

Sanders, E. P. *The Historical Figure of Jesus.* New York, NY: Penguin Press, 1993.

Jesus and Judaism. London: SCM Press, 1985.

Schumann, J. D. *Über die Evidenz der Beweise für die Wahrheit der christlichen Religion.* Hannover: Schmidt, 1778.

Schäublin, C. "Homerum ex Homero." *Museum Helveticum* 34.4 (1977), 221–27.

Scheck, Thomas P., trans. *St. Pamphilus: Apology for Origen, with the Letter of Rufinus on the Falsification of the Books of Origen.* FC 120. Washington, DC: Catholic University of America Press, 2010.

Schwáb, Zoltán. "The Value of a Curious Translation: Revisiting Proverbs 2:5." *Journal of Biblical Literature* 133.4 (2014), 739–49.

Schweitzer, Albert. *Von Reimarus zu Wrede: eine Geschichte der Leben-Jesu-Forschung.* Tübingen: Mohr Siebeck, 1906. English translation (of the 2nd ed., 1913): *The Quest of the Historical Jesus.* Edited by John Bowden. Minneapolis, MN: Fortress Press, 2001.

Sextus Empiricus. *Against Professors.* Translated by R. G. Bury. LCL 382. Cambridge, MA: Harvard University Press, 1949.

Simon, Richard. *Histoire critique des principaux commentateurs du Nouveau Testament, depuis le commencement du Christianisme jusques à nôtre tems.* Rotterdam, 1693.

Smyth, Herbert W. *A Greek Grammar for Colleges.* Cambridge, MA: Harvard University Press, 1956.

Stanton, Graham. "The Two Parousias of Christ: Justin Martyr and Matthew." In *Studies in Matthew and Early Christianity.* Edited by Markus Bockmuehl and David Lincicum. Tübingen: Mohr Siebeck, 2013. Pp. 339–49.

Sterling, Gregory E. "The Body as Metaphor: The Structure of a Human and the Meaning of Scripture." *Novum Testamentum* 61 (2019), 26–39.

Strabo. *Geography, Volume. I: Books 1-2.* Translated by Horace L. Jones. LCL 49. Cambridge, MA: Harvard University Press, 1917.

Strauss, David. F. *Das Leben Jesu kritisch bearbeitet.* Tübingen: C. F. Osiander, 1835. English translation: George Eliot. *The Life of Jesus Critically Examined.* London, UK: Chapman Bros, 1846. Edited with an introduction by Peter C. Hodgson. Minneapolis, MN: Fortress Press, 1972.

Streitschriften zur Vertheidigung meiner Schrift über das Leben Jesu und zur Charakteristik der gegenwärtigen Theologie. Drittes Heft: Die evangelische Kirchenzeitung, die Jahrbücher für wissenschaftliche Kritik, und die theologischen Studien und Kritiken in ihrer Stellung zu meiner Kritik des Lebens Jesu. Tübingen: C. F. Osiander, 1837. English translation (partial): Marylin

C. Massey. *In Defense of My "Life of Jesus" against the Hegelians.* Hamden, CT: Archon Books, 1983.

Studer, Basil. "Der Begriff der Geschichte im Schrifttum des Origenes von Alexandrien." In *Origeniana Octava: Origen and the Alexandrian Tradition.* Edited by L. Perrone. Vol. 1. Bibliotheca Ephemeridum Theologicarum Lovaniensium 164. Leuven: Leuven University Press, 2003. Pp. 757–77.

Strutwolf, Holger. "Kelsos und Origenes: Die Anfänge der Schriftkritik." In *Heilige Schriften in der Kritik. XVII. Europäischer Kongress für Theologie (5.–8. September 2021 in Zürich).* Edited by Konrad Schmid. Leipzig: Evangelische Verlagsanstalt, 2022. Pp. 333–50.

Talbert, C. H, ed. *Reimarus: Fragments.* London, UK: SCM Press, 1970.

Thatcher, T. "Why John Wrote a Gospel: Memory and History in an Early Christian Community." In *Memory, Tradition, and Text: Uses of the Past in Early Christianity.* Edited by A. Kirk and T. Thatcher. Atlanta, GA: SBL Press, 2005. Pp. 79–97.

Theissen, Gerd and Annette Merz. *The Historical Jesus: A Comprehensive Guide.* Minneapolis, MN: Fortress Press, 1998.

Theodore of Mopsuestia. *Commentary on the Gospel of John.* Ancient Christian Texts. Translation with an introduction and notes by Marco Conti. Downers Grove, IL: InterVarsity Press Academic, 2010.

The Commentaries on the Minor Epistles of Paul. Translated by Rowan A. Greer. Atlanta, GA: SBL Press, 2010.

"Traité contre les allégoristes." In *Théodore de Mopsueste. Fragments syriaques du Commentaire des Psaumes (Psaume 118 et Psaumes 138-148).* Edited by L. Van Rompay. Leuven: Peeters, 1982. Pp. 1–13. English translation: Frederick McLeod. *Theodore of Mopsuestia.* Early Church Fathers. New York, NY: Routledge, 2009. Pp. 75–79.

Therrien, Mark E. *Cross and Creation: A Theological Introduction to Origen of Alexandria.* Washington, DC: Catholic University of America Press, 2022.

Torjesen, Karen Jo. *Hermeneutical Procedure and Theological Method in Origen's Exegesis.* Patristic Texts and Studies 28. Berlin: De Gruyter, 1985.

"'Body,' 'Soul,' and 'Spirit,' in Origen's Theory of Exegesis." *Anglican Theological Review* 67.1 (1985), 17–30.

Trapnell, William H. *Thomas Woolston: Madman and Deist?* Bristol, UK: Thoemmes Press, 1994.

Trzaskoma, Stephen M. "Mythography." In *The Oxford Handbook of the Second Sophistic.* Edited by Daniel S. Richter and William A. Johnson. Oxford, UK: Oxford University Press, 2017. Pp. 463–75.

Turner, Denys. "Allegory in Christian Late Antiquity." In *The Cambridge Companion to Allegory.* Edited by Rita Copeland and Peter Struck. Cambridge, UK: Cambridge University Press, 2010. Pp. 71–82.

Tyrrell, George. *Christianity at the Crossroads.* London: George Allen & Unwin, 1909.

Tzamalikos, Panayiotis. *Origen: Philosophy of History and Eschatology.* Boston: Brill, 2007.

Van den Hoek, Annewies. "Clement and Origen as Sources on 'Noncanonical' Scriptural Traditions during the Late Second and Earlier Third Centuries." In *Origeniana Sexta: Origène et la Bible / Origen and the Bible, Actes du Colloquium Origenianum Sextum Chantilly, 30 août - 3 septembre 1993*. Edited by G. Dorival and A. Le Boulluec. Leuven: Peeters, 1995. Pp. 93–113.

"The Concept of σῶμα τῶν γραφῶν in Alexandrian Theology." In *Studia Patristica 19: Papers presented to the Tenth International Conference on Patristic Studies held in Oxford 1987. Historia, Theologica, Gnostica, Biblica et Apocrypha*. Edited by E.A. Livingstone. Leuven: Peeters, 1989. Pp. 250–54.

"Philo and Origen: A Descriptive Catalogue of their Relationship." *Studia Philonica Annual* 12 (2000), 44–121.

Velmans, Tania. "Observations sur l'emplacement et l'iconographie de l'entrée à Jérusalem dans quelques églises de Svanétie (Géorgie)." In *Rayonnement grec: hommages à Charles Delvoye*. Edited by L. Hadermann-Misguich, G. Raepsaet, and G. Cambier. Bruxelles: Editions de l'Université de Bruxelles, 1982. Pp. 471–81.

Vines, Michael E. *The Problem of Markan Genre: The Gospel of Mark and the Jewish Novel*. Leiden: Brill, 2002.

Vogt, Hermann Josef. *Origenes als Exeget*. Edited by Wilhelm Geerlings. Munich: Ferdinand Schöningh, 1999.

Von Balthasar, Hans Urs, ed. *Origen: Spirit and Fire: A Thematic Anthology of His Writings*. Translated by Robert J. Daly. Washington, DC: Catholic University of America Press, 1984.

Vos, J. S. "Das Agraphon 'Seid Kundige Geldwechsler!' bei Origenes." In *Sayings of Jesus: Canonical Canonical and Non-Canonical. Essays in Honour of Tjitze Baarda*. Edited by William L. Petersen, Johan S. Vos, and Henk J. de Jonge. Supplements to Novum Testamentum 89. Leiden: Brill, 1997. Pp. 277–302.

Walker, Jeffrey. *Rhetoric and Poetics in Antiquity*. Oxford, UK: Oxford University Press, 2000.

Walsh, Robyn F. *The Origins of Early Christian Literature: Contextualizing the New Testament within Greco-Roman Literary Culture*. Cambridge, UK: Cambridge University Press, 2021.

Watson, Francis. *The Fourfold Gospel: A Theological Reading of the New Testament Portraits of Jesus*. Grand Rapids, MI: Baker Academic, 2016.

Gospel Writing: A Canonical Perspective. Grand Rapids, MI: Eerdmans, 2013.

"Toward a Literal Reading of the Gospels." In *The Gospels for All Christians: Rethinking the Gospel Audiences*. Edited by Richard Bauckham. Grand Rapids, MI: Eerdmans, 1998. Pp. 195–218.

What Is a Gospel? Grand Rapids, MI: Eerdmans, 2022.

Weiss, Johannes. *Die Predigt Jesu Gottes*. Göttingen: Vandenhoeck, 1892. Translated, edited, and with an introduction by Richard Hyde Hiers and David Larrimore Holland. *Jesus' Proclamation of the Kingdom of God*. Minneapolis, MN: Fortress Press, 1971.

Wiles, Maurice F. "Origen as Biblical Scholar." In *The Cambridge History of the Bible, Vol. 1: From the Beginnings to Jerome*. Edited by P. R. Ackroyd and C. F. Evans. Cambridge, UK: Cambridge University Press, 1970. Pp. 454–89.

Witherington III, Ben. *The Christology of Jesus*. Minneapolis, MN: Fortress Press, 1990.

Jesus the Seer: The Progress of Prophecy. Minneapolis, MN: Fortress Press, 2014.

Woolston, Thomas. *Defence of His Discourses, Parts I and II*. London, 1729–1730.

Six Discourses on the Miracles of our Saviour. London, 1727–1729.

Wrede, William. *Das Messiasgeheimnis in den Evangelien: zugleich ein Beitrag zum Verständnis des Markusevangeliums*. Göttingen: Vandenhoeck & Ruprecht, 1901.

Wucherpfennig, Ansgar. *Heracleon Philologus: Gnostische Johannesexegese im zweiten Jahrhundert*. Wissenschaftliche Untersuchungen zum Neuen Testament 142. Tübingen: Mohr Siebeck, 2002.

Young, Frances M. *Biblical Exegesis and the Formation of Christian Culture*. New York, NY: Cambridge University Press, 1997.

"John and the Synoptics: An Historical Problem or a Theological Opportunity?" In *Ways of Reading Scripture: Collected Papers*. Tübingen. Mohr Siebeck, 2018. Pp. 171–81.

Zimmermann, Ruben. "Imagery in John: Opening Up Paths into the Tangled Thicket of John's Figurative World." In *Imagery in the Gospel of John: Terms, Forms, Themes, and Theology of Johannine Figurative Language*. Edited by J. Frey, J. G. Van der Watt, R. Zimmermann, and G. Kern. Tübingen: Mohr Siebeck, 2006. Pp. 1–43.

Scripture Index

General Index

For EU product safety concerns, contact us at Calle de José Abascal, 56–1°, 28003 Madrid, Spain or eugpsr@cambridge.org.

www.ingramcontent.com/pod-product-compliance
Ingram Content Group UK Ltd.
Pitfield, Milton Keynes, MK11 3LW, UK
UKHW011002081025
463730UK00005B/22

* 9 7 8 1 0 0 9 4 6 5 6 0 1 *